*Board of Governors
of the John Carter Brown
Library*

JOSÉ AMOR Y VÁZQUEZ

JOHN BOCKSTOCE

T. KIMBALL BROOKER

J. CARTER BROWN

VINCENT J. BUONANNO

MARY MAPLES DUNN

GEORGE D. EDWARDS, JR.

VARTAN GREGORIAN, *Chairman*

ARTEMIS A. W. JOUKOWSKY

FREDERICK LIPPITT

JOSÉ E. MINDLIN

EUSTASIO RODRIGUEZ ALVAREZ

CLINTON I. SMULLYAN, JR.

FRANK S. STREETER

MERRILY TAYLOR

CHARLES C. TILLINGHAST, JR.

LADISLAUS VON HOFFMANN

WILLIAM B. WARREN

CHARLES H. WATTS, II

Sponsors and Patrons

Sponsors

THE DRUE HEINZ FOUNDATION
THE DUNVEGAN FOUNDATION

Honorary Patron

LORD PERTH OF PERTHSHIRE

Patrons Committee

MRS. STANLEY D. SCOTT
MR. TIMOTHY C. FORBES, *Co-chairmen*

THE HONORABLE J. SINCLAIR ARMSTRONG
MR. GEORGE D. EDWARDS, JR.
MRS. ROBERT H. I. GODDARD
DR. ALEXANDER C. MCLEOD
MRS. PETER SAINT GERMAIN
MR. J. THOMAS TOUCHTON

THE HONORABLE J. SINCLAIR ARMSTRONG
MRS. VINCENT ASTOR
MR. LYMAN G. BLOOMINGDALE
DR. JOHN AND LADY ROMAYNE BOCKSTOCE
MR. AND MRS. DOUGLAS W. BROWN
MR. J. CARTER BROWN
MRS. JOSEPH CARSON
MR. MAURICE L. CLEMENCE
MRS. FRANCES MASSEY DULANEY
DR. MARY MAPLES DUNN
MR. AND MRS. GEORGE D. EDWARDS, JR.
MR. LINCOLN EKSTROM
MRS. RUTH B. EKSTROM
MR. WILLIAM FERN
MR. TIMOTHY C. FORBES
MR. HELMUT N. FRIEDLAENDER
MR. R. B. GLYNN
MR. AND MRS. ROBERT H. I. GODDARD
MRS. DRUE HEINZ

MR. AND MRS. REINALDO HERRERA
HROSWITHA SOCIETY
MR. AND MRS. JAY I. KISLAK
MR. SIDNEY LAPIDUS
MR. MAGNUS LINKLATER
MR. GEORGE S. LOWRY
MR. N. DOUGLAS MACLEOD
DR. ALEXANDER C. MCLEOD
MR. AND MRS. ROBERT L. MCNEIL, JR.
THE HONORABLE J. WILLIAM MIDDENDORF, II
MR. RICHARD W. MONCRIEF
MR. GEORGE PARKER
MR. WILLIAM S. REESE
MR. AND MRS. DAVID F. REMINGTON
MR. ROBERT A. ROBINSON
MR. MORDECAI K. ROSENFELD
THE ROYAL BANK OF SCOTLAND
MR. CHARLES M. ROYCE
MRS. JANE GREGORY RUBIN
MR. AND MRS. PETER SAINT GERMAIN
MR. AND MRS. STANLEY DEFOREST SCOTT
DR. AND MRS. THOMAS SCULCO
MR. AND MRS. ROBERT B. SHEA
MR. AND MRS. CLINTON I. SMULLYAN, JR.
MR. AND MRS. FRANK S. STREETER
MRS. JAMES M. STUART
MR. CHARLES TANENBAUM
MR. AND MRS. GUSTAVO A. TAVARES
MR. AND MRS. J. THOMAS TOUCHTON
MR. THOMAS M. VALENZUELA
MRS. JAMES H. VAN ALEN
MRS. ALEXANDER O. VIETOR
MR. AND MRS. WILLIAM B. WARREN
MR. AND MRS. CHARLES H. WATTS, II

SCOTLAND
AND THE AMERICAS

SCOTLA

Catalogue of an exhibition at the

JOHN CARTER BROWN LIBRARY
Providence, Rhode Island

and the

FORBES MAGAZINE GALLERIES
New York, New York

ND AND THE AMERICAS

AMERICAS

1600 TO 1800

With an Introduction by
MICHAEL FRY

and Contributions by
DAVID ARMITAGE · ROBERT KENT DONOVAN · ROBIN FABEL
MICHAEL FRY · DAVID HANCOCK · NED C. LANDSMAN
BRUCE LENMAN · JAMES MCLACHLAN

Bibliographical Supplement by
BURTON VAN NAME EDWARDS

John Carter Brown Library · Providence, Rhode Island · 1995

"Scotland and the Americas, 1600 to 1800: Rare Books, Maps, and Prints from the Collection of the John Carter Brown Library," was on display at the John Carter Brown Library from May 13 to October 30, 1994, and at the Forbes Magazine Galleries in New York City from September 30 to November 25, 1995.

FRONTISPIECE

Robert Burns's collected *Poems, Chiefly in the Scottish Dialect* was first published in Kilmarnock, Scotland, in 1786, in a relatively small edition. Less than a year later, in April 1787, an Edinburgh edition of 3,000 appeared, and by July 1787 copies were already advertised for sale in the United States. But such was the interest in, and demand for, the work of the celebrated Ploughman Poet that English exports alone would not do, and no less than two American editions appeared in 1788, the first in Philadelphia, shown here, and the second in New York.

The rapid spread of Burns's fame to America is but one more indication of the ubiquitous interconnections between Scotland and America. Scottish men-of-letters, in Scottish periodicals that were read in America, praised Burns; hundreds of Scottish emigrants also carried the word; Scottish booksellers and printers in this country, themselves recent immigrants, ensured that copies of Burns's *Poems* could be bought here within months after the work was first printed.

Copyright 1995
The John Carter Brown Library.

This work may not be reproduced in part or whole, in any form or medium, for any purpose, without prior permission in writing from the copyright owner.

Correspondence should be directed to:

The John Carter Brown Library
Box 1894
Providence, Rhode Island 02912

ISBN 0-916617-48-3

The John Carter Brown Library is an independently funded and administered center for advanced research in history and the humanities at Brown University.

Contents

List of Illustrations x

Preface by Norman Fiering xiii

Introduction by Michael Fry xvii

CHAPTER ONE:
The Darien Venture, by David Armitage 3

CHAPTER TWO:
Immigration and Settlement, by Ned C. Landsman 15

CHAPTER THREE:
Trade, by David Hancock 27

CHAPTER FOUR:
Scots in Georgia and the British Floridas, by Robin Fabel . . . 39

CHAPTER FIVE:
Religion in the Affairs of Scotland and America,
by Robert Kent Donovan and Michael Fry 53

CHAPTER SIX:
Education, by James McLachlan 65

CHAPTER SEVEN:
Colonial Warfare and Imperial Identity, by Bruce Lenman . . . 77

CHAPTER EIGHT:
Scotland and the American Revolution, by Michael Fry 89

About the Authors 99

Appendix: by Burton Van Name Edwards 101
    Bibliographical Supplement 110
    Additional Resources 124

List of Illustrations

FRONTISPIECE
Robert Burns, *Poems, Chiefly in the Scottish Dialect* (Philadelphia, 1788)

FIG. 1
A Draft of the Golden & Adjacent Islands with Parts of the Isthmus of Darien and *A New Map of the Isthmus of Darien in America*, 1699.

FIG. 2
An Act of Parliament, for Encourageing the Scots Affrican and Indian Company, 1695.

FIG. 3
A Letter, Giving a Description of the Isthmus of Darian, [1699].

FIG. 4
A New Map of the Isthumus of Darian, [1699]

FIG. 5
Caledonia Triumphans, 1699.

FIG. 6
A Defence of the Scots Settlement at Darien, 1699.

FIG. 7
Scotland's Lament for Their Misfortunes, 1700.

FIG. 8
Sir William Alexander, Earl of Stirling.

FIG. 9
An Encouragement to Colonies, 1624.

FIG. 10
A Map of "New Scotlande" in *An Encouragement to Colonies*, 1624

FIG. 11
A Mapp of New Jersey, 1677.

FIG. 12
The Model of the Government of the Province of East-New-Jersey, 1685.

FIG. 13
Rules of the St. Andrew's Club, at Charlestown in South-Carolina, 1762.

FIG. 14
Certificate of membership in the St. Andrew's Club of Charleston, 1768.

FIG. 15
Informations Concerning the Province of North Carolina, 1773.

FIG. 16
A Map of the Caribbee Islands and Guayana from *Candid and Impartial Considerations on the Nature of the Sugar Trade*, 1763.

FIG. 17
The Present State of the Tobacco-Plantations in America, 1708.

FIG. 18
Candid and Impartial Considerations on the Nature of the Sugar Trade, 1763.

FIG. 19
Information to Emigrants, 1773.

FIG. 20
An Inquiry into the Nature and Causes of the Wealth of Nations, 1776.

FIG. 21a and 21b
A cargo of slaves as transported from Africa to the West Indies.

FIG. 22
The Creek Chief McIntosh in tartan fabric.

FIG. 23a and 23b
A Map of South Carolina and a Part of Georgia, 1780.

FIG. 24
A Draught of West Florida, 1766.

FIG. 25
View of Savannah, 1734.

FIG. 26
A Concise Natural History of East and West Florida, 1775.

FIG. 27
A True and Historical Narrative of the Colony of Georgia, [1741].

FIG. 28
The Case of the Inhabitants of East-Florida, 1784.

FIG. 29
Apology for the True Christian Divinity, 1729

FIG. 30
Apologie oder Vertheidigungs-Schrift der wahren christlichen Gottesgelahrheit, 1776.

FIG. 31
Proposals Concerning the Propagating of Christian Knowledge, [1707]

FIG. 32
A Sermon Delivered at the South Church, 1746.

FIG. 33
Distinguishing Marks of a Work of the Spirit of God, 1742.

FIG. 34
Short Narrative of the Extraordinary Work at Cambuslang, 1742.

FIG. 35
A General Idea of the College of Mirania, 1753.

FIG. 36
Address to the Inhabitants of Jamaica, 1772.

FIG. 37
Short Introduction to Moral Philosophy, 1788.

FIG. 38
Elements of Logic, 1792.

FIG. 39
A New Plan of the Harbour, City, & Forts of Cartagena, [1741].

FIG. 40
The Spanish Empire in America, 1747.

FIG. 41
Spartan Lessons; or, The Praise of Valour, 1759.

FIG. 42
An Account of the Spanish Settlements in America, 1762.

FIG. 43
A Review of the Bloody Tribunal, 1770.

FIG. 44
The History of America, 1777.

FIG. 45
The Life of David Hume, 1778.

FIG. 46
Shall I Go to War with My American Brethren?, 1776.

FIG. 47
The Scotch Butchery, 1775.

FIG. 48
The Rights of Great Britain Asserted, 1776.

FIG. 49
The Interest of Great-Britain with Regard to Her American Colonies, 1782.

Preface

AMONG THE GENERAL benefits of the study of history is the attention it draws necessarily to the importance of precision and specificity in all discourse. Dig into almost any subject in the past, and it will surely turn out that the way things happened was more complex than one had assumed at the beginning. This exhibition on "Scotland and the Americas, 1600 to 1800" is in good part the result of such a concern for proper differentiation.

In the twentieth century, Scotland remains a culturally distinctive geographical place, but in most respects it is merged into Great Britain or the United Kingdom. The study of the relations between Scotland and the United States today would consist mostly of the evocation of sentimental ties based upon genealogy and a recognition of the Scottish cultural heritage in music and song, in recreation, and in literature.

In the eighteenth century, however, Scotland and the Scottish people were a separately recognizable force in commerce, education, Calvinist religion, philosophy, science, and political administration. In the seventeenth century, Scotland even harbored imperial ambitions—not unlike those of the Netherlands and Portugal, equally small, talented, and ambitious countries—which led to the Darien venture in the area of present-day Panama. So influential and ubiquitous were Scots in American affairs in this period that it is a phenomenon that truly cries out for special treatment.

This exhibition claims no originality on the subject of Scotland and the Americas, with the one exception of the pluralizing of America in the title. In the course of the past forty years or so, there has been excellent scholarly scrutiny of a wide range of interconnections between Scotland and British America (see, as an outstanding recent example, Richard B. Sher and Jeffrey R. Smitten, eds., *Scotland and America in the Age of Enlightenment* [Princeton, 1990], and the many suggestions for further reading at the end of each chapter in this catalogue). What this book does aim to do, however, is to forge a link between, on the one hand, scholars, who delve into primary sources and are in constant touch with one another about the state of the field, and on the other, general audiences, who it may be said would tend to have little or no awareness of the extraordinary significance of Scotland in particular in the story of the colonial Americas.

By its inclusion, also, of the history of the Darien venture, this catalogue and the exhibition attempt to correct the common illusion that the mainland British colonies were somehow perceived in the eighteenth century, before let's say the 1790s, as a country with the special destiny of becoming the great democratic republic of the United States. For most of the eighteenth century, the importance for mankind of the mainland British colonies was yet to be revealed. No person viewing the Atlantic world of the eighteenth century could, however, overlook the enormous Spanish presence in that world, not to speak of the French in the Caribbean and on the mainland. The territorial picture was far from fixed, in other words, and the estimation of the desirability of land or trade connections here or there, or of matters of political importance, was nothing like what it became by the second quarter of the nineteenth century, when the future of the Americas began to assume definition closer to that of our own day. Only with this corrected perception is it possible to understand what the Scots were doing in Panama, which may seem today to have been a rather exotic choice for the establishment of an entrepôt, or why the most famous work of the great Scottish historian William Robertson, *The History of America* (1777), is principally about Spanish America.

This catalogue has another purpose more specific to the John Carter Brown Library itself. Nearly always when the Library mounts an exhibition, one of our goals is to inform scholars of the range of our holdings in a particular subject area. The corresponding catalogue of the exhibition serves as a permanent guide to a segment of the collection and, to some degree, as a stimulus to research. When historians are shown outcroppings of valuable ore, they are induced to begin mining. As is true of the Library's holdings of the printed works of virtually all European countries that had any connection with, or interest in, the Western Hemisphere—whether German, French, Portuguese, Italian, Dutch, Spanish, whatever—the John Carter Brown Library's collection of materials related to Scottish involvement with the Americas is extensive, and in some special areas unmatched.

In order to serve this scholarly end more effectively, the catalogue includes a special component. In addition to the narrative information in each chapter covering about 56 contemporary titles in all, the book contains an appendix that lists another 91 primary sources related to the subject of Scotland and the Americas that may be found at the John Carter Brown Library.

This list, initially compiled by Professor Kent Donovan of Kansas State University, and expanded and developed by Dr. Burton Van Name Edwards on the John Carter Brown Library staff, is arbitrary in the sense that hundreds of other titles could just as well have been listed rather than these titles in particular. But the existing list succeeds very well in revealing the potential of the John Carter Brown Library for research on the theme of the exhibition.

The preparation of this appended list of Additional Resources in good bibliographical style, and the formal Bibliographical Supplement to the catalogue, which provides full and complete cataloguing data on each of the books that are featured in the exhibition, is the work of Dr. Edwards, who has approached this project with genuine enthusiasm.

Professor Donovan was the original inspiration behind the exhibition and the catalogue, and we wish to acknowledge here his fundamental contribution to both. His work was extended and amplified by Michael Fry, to whom the Library is much indebted for an introduction to this book and for general editorial support.

The John Carter Brown Library's "Scotland and the Americas" project began in 1992, with the initial planning for the 1994 annual meeting of the Eighteenth-Century Scottish Studies Society. It was the aim of the Society's leadership to hold this meeting on the Brown University campus, with the John Carter Brown Library as host, and to focus in particular on America. The annual meeting of ECSSS held here June 8 to 12, 1994, was in fact a full scale, four-day conference on the theme, with the presentation of about forty scholarly papers. The experience of this conference, for which Professor Ned Landsman was the able program chairman, was naturally enriching to the development of the exhibition and this catalogue. It is anticipated that in addition to this exhibition catalogue a collection of selected essays from the conference will be published next year by ECSSS.

Finally, the Library wishes to express its profound gratitude to those friends of the John Carter Brown Library and of Scotland who through their contributions have helped to alleviate the cost of this project, from its inception with the 1994 ECSSS conference to the 1995 exhibition at the Forbes Magazine Galleries. A list of sponsors and patrons of the project appears on p. iv, facing the half title page.

NORMAN FIERING
Director and Librarian

Introduction

When Americans think of Scotland today, they probably think first of colorful traditions, chiefs and clans, kilts and tartans, dancing and bagpipes, the things they are likely to see at any Highland Games in the United States. These actually form only a small part of our national life, and historically not a very authentic part: most are the products of Victorian romanticism. While enjoyable enough, they have unfortunately tended to obscure more serious aspects of Scottish history, and the deeper connections between our small country and the great continents of the New World. To appreciate these, we must step back in time, to the centuries before anyone thought of inventing synthetic heritages, when America was still being formed, and when Scotland's genuine traditions vigorously flourished. I had a chance to do that myself as a visiting scholar at the John Carter Brown Library in 1993-4, working in this field of early Scottish-American relations. I was astonished and delighted to discover the richness of the library's holdings. I trust that the sample offered in the present exhibition and catalogue will help to enlighten in the same way a much wider public.

They tell us first that Scotland was not, as is commonly supposed, an eternal victim in European history, a scene of unceasing oppressions from which her people took refuge in America. In the age of discoveries Scots were a fairly typical nation of the Old World, which like others eagerly sought out the opportunities opening up to them. In fact they stood among those in the forefront of European colonization in North America, as is shown by two of the essays which follow, a case study by Robin Fabel and a general survey by Ned Landsman.

In 1620, as the Pilgrim Fathers set sail for Massachusetts, a Scottish expedition went to Newfoundland. Soon afterwards, another planted a short-lived settlement on the territory known ever since as Nova Scotia. More permanent colonies followed in New Jersey, the Carolinas, and elsewhere. Still, there were never enough Scots to make up more than a minor part of the stock of population in America. Till the mid-eighteenth century they numbered only just over a million (there are only five million of us even today). Mass emigration had started from some regions, notably the Highlands, but on nothing like the scale of the main movements after 1800. There was great prejudice against emigration, among the country's rulers, who wanted to conserve its economic and military resources, and among the people themselves, who shared with modern Scots a deep attachment to their homeland. Millions of Americans claim Scottish descent, and we in Scotland are flattered that they do, but cool historical analysis suggests the claims may be exaggerated.

Landsman finally stresses that their contribution came not so much through numerical strength as through cultural influence. Some of the settlers intended, and a few managed, to preserve the way of life they brought with them. Even so, in the long run it was bound to be lost, because the social structures of the New World were inevitably more fluid than those of the Old World. A Scottish social structure, deeply rooted in history, strongly bonded by family and clan, or by allegiance to civil and religious authority, could not survive in this environment, quite apart from the fact that before long the independent United States would found a new polity on entirely different principles. Yet these immigrants did leave their mark in other ways.

Lack of numbers was, after all, no bar to an enterprising spirit. In fact Scotland's most important American contacts came through trade rather than colonization. Though she was small and poor, that did not by itself preclude oceanic ventures, any more than they had been precluded by the originally similar circumstances of the Dutch and Portuguese. Scots had long been seafarers, because incessant warfare with England always obliged them to travel abroad by ship. Soon Scottish merchants were familiar figures in the growing colonies along the eastern Atlantic seaboard, so much so that the English tried to ban them. That pointed up the difficulties of Scotland's situation after the Union of the Crowns with England in 1603. She became increasingly subordinated to her larger neighbor, since she could not conduct any independent foreign policy or defend by her own arms her interests overseas, this in an era of intensifying competition among the European powers. Nothing illustrated the predicament so well as the attempt to establish a Scottish trading station at Darien, on the isthmus of Panama, in 1698. It was a disastrous failure, as David Armitage's essay recounts, and brought these independent ventures to an end. Indeed it played a large part in bringing Scottish independence to an end, for the Union of Parliaments shortly followed in 1707.

That Union removed all barriers to Scots in the colonies. They came now, whether as traders or settlers, possessed of the full rights of British citizens. They showed themselves well able to exploit these rights, most famously in the tobacco trade, but in much else besides. This activity has attracted increasing attention from modern scholars. David Hancock's essay points out, however, that there are still intriguing questions to be answered about its effects on both sides of the Atlantic. We still do not know enough of how the rising prosperity prompted the evolution of the modern Scottish economy, or indeed of how the commercial innovations pioneered by Scots in America altered the course of colonial development in ways that may well have brought significant political changes in their wake.

As the Scots' presence in America grew, the Presbyterian nexus of religion and education proved to be of special importance. The Scottish Reformation of 1560 restored the individual's relationship to God as the central pillar of faith. It depended on his understanding of Scripture. That in turn required a learned ministry and a literate population. One result was to produce a national church notable for its tendency towards dispute and schism. Calvinists were quick, when in disagreement with one another or with the civil authorities, to wander off and work out a solution for themselves. This was, of course, true in both England and Scotland: it was precisely the motivation of the Pilgrim Fathers. But in Scotland the impulse was certainly stronger and, transferred across the ocean, contributed to the remarkable diversity of American religion. Kent Donovan's essay shows us this development at work.

Just as significant was the importance attached by Presbyterians to education, as James McLachlan sets out. In pursuit of her religious commitments, Scotland stood among the foremost nations in Europe in trying to erect a system of universal schooling, a system for the masses rather than for an elite. Its first aim was to teach them to read the Bible, but a literate population grew eager for secular knowledge, and thus amenable to social and economic innovation. In the process, higher education also became more widely diffused in Scotland than in most other countries. Her universities expanded the curriculum to cover not only those subjects necessary for the ministry of the Kirk, but also natural science, medicine, rhetoric and, crucially, moral philosophy. This last provided the framework for the others and enabled the pupil to conceive of them in terms of their first principles. Because Scotland had a surplus of graduates, many were able to come to America, where their influence was felt in formulating the college ideal, of a broad education for broad masses of the people.

The study of moral philosophy gave rise to a number of new disciplines, falling within the range of what we call today the social sciences: indeed this is the most permanent legacy of the Scottish Enlightenment. If there was a unifying concept it was that of conjectural history, by which society was held to develop by stages towards commercial civilization, with moral, intellectual, and religious attainments to match.

America presented fascinating material for such study because it was advancing so quickly. Though recently settled, it had already reached a stage not so far behind Europe. Most Scottish thinkers who applied their minds to the matter therefore agreed that constraints on the colonies applied at an earlier stage were by the end of the eighteenth century superfluous, and ought to be lifted. "A system of perfect liberty," as Adam Smith summed up his prescriptions in *The Wealth of Nations*, would make sure that the colonies continued to flourish. Yet this was not, to most other Scots at least, the same as advocating the political independence of America.

The new freedom and individualism bred by the Enlightenment were never unbridled, nor did its leading thinkers mean them to be. The progress of society, the dissolution of old bonds and the formation of new ones, made it to the Scottish mind all the more desirable to confirm, uphold, even entrench certain essential institutions. Bruce Lenman's essay outlines the Scottish conception of the British Empire which emerged triumphantly, covering most of North America, from the Treaty of Paris in 1763. It was to be ruled from the metropolis, to which the settlers would remain subject. The conception was thus a conservative one. Not that it ignored the problem of provincial identity within an imperial community: indeed this problem continued to preoccupy Scots right to the recent end of the British Empire. Provincial identity was something on which they and the Americans had a fruitful exchange of ideas, but it had not got far before the provincial Englishmen in Virginia and Massachusetts rose up to destroy this first British Empire. Perhaps because they had enjoyed the exchange, Scots were remarkably hostile to the American Revolution, horrified at its defiance of the state and the law, as I explain in my own article below. They predicted, wrongly, that it would take the Americans back to the anarchy which they had found on arrival in their continent, and which they had to rise above if they were to progress through the historical stages awaiting them. It could not have been foreseen in 1776 that they were, working from the first principles which Scots had helped to teach them, to erect a new system of the state and the law entrenched in a constitution which has proved its worth down to the present day.

SCOTLAND
AND THE AMERICAS

CHAPTER ONE: *The Darien Venture*

DAVID ARMITAGE

THE SCOTTISH ATTEMPT to plant a colony and trading-post on the isthmus of Panama in 1698–1700 marked a pivotal moment in the relationship between Scotland and the Americas. The scope and ambition of the Darien venture made it the most spectacular of all the Scottish attempts to establish an independent settlement in the Americas, in comparison with those in Nova Scotia, Cape Breton Island, East New Jersey, or South Carolina. On the other hand, in the light of Scotland's involvement in the eighteenth-century British Empire, the venture has looked more like a desperate attempt to escape the brutal economic logic that determined that Scotland should never be able to succeed as an independent colonial power, with its own exclusive trade and settlements. Such assessments only partly capture the historical importance of the venture, which should instead be seen as part of a larger movement towards economic modernization in Britain after the Glorious Revolution.

The attempt to modernize was all the more necessary for Scotland because of its unequal constitutional relationship with England. This inequality crippled Scotland economically, and it also made the country vulnerable in the harshly competitive world of the late seventeenth century. As many observers noted at the time, trade had become an inescapable motive for international rivalry, and just as defense had become dependent on economic strength, so that strength in turn relied on trade. The Navigation Acts narrowed the possible range of Scottish commerce, while Scotsmen were drafted into King William's armies to fight in his European wars in the interests of Anglo-Dutch trade. The bad harvests, poverty, and trade slump which afflicted Scotland in the 'seven lean years' of the 1690s made these grievances more evident and acute. The only solution which was available to an independent Scotland would be its own trade outside the bounds of the English empire. The Darien venture seemed to provide just such a solution for Scotland. The full course of the venture's development, from its instigation in 1695 to its dissolution in the Union of 1707 can be traced in materials from the John Carter Brown Library. The Library holds the world's most extensive collection of materials relating to the venture and the company which promoted it, and it includes many unique and ephemeral items.

The proposal to plant a trading entrepôt at Darien in present-day Panama was the brainchild of the Dumfriesshire projector, William Paterson. Though Paterson is perhaps best known as the intellectual godfather of the

FIG. 1
A Draft of the Golden & Adjacent Islands with Parts of the Isthmus of Darien and *A New Map of the Isthmus of Darien in America*, London, 1699 (23¾ × 19¼"). These maps conveyed up-to-the minute, eye-witness news about the site of the new Scottish colony at Darien, as gathered by one Capt. Jenefer. In the map on the top, one can see Scottish flags planted on Golden Island and at New Edinburgh. The bottom map emphasizes the strategic advantages of the Darien location, with access to both the North Sea (i.e., the Atlantic) and the South Sea (i.e., the Pacific).

Bank of England, he considered the Panamanian plan to be the preeminent project of his life. The strategic importance of the isthmus of Panama had been evident since the sixteenth century, but Paterson seems to have been the first to propose an entrepôt on the site through which goods from both eastern and western hemispheres could be exchanged between the Atlantic and Pacific Oceans. (Fig. 1). From the mid-1680s, Paterson hawked his plan among the principalities of Germany, and in 1687 he was advertising it in the coffeehouses of Amsterdam. But the great opportunity for which he had been waiting came in 1695, with the foundation of the Company of Scotland Trading to Africa and the Indies under the terms of an Act of the Scottish Parliament. The Company was founded by a group of Anglo-Scottish merchants who sought a means to circumvent the English East India Company's monopoly of colonial trade. The Scottish Parliament empowered them to make treaties and plant colonies, and to have exclusive trade with the Americas for thirty-one years. It was to draw investment from both England and Scotland, and Paterson was among the first ten directors named in the Act.

The Company of Scotland Trading to Africa and the Indies is best known for its promotion of the Darien settlement but, as its title stated, its vision extended much more widely. A West Indian plantation was not its original intention, and the only profitable piece of business it undertook before its dissolution in 1707 was a cargo of African goods. Nevertheless, Paterson persuaded the other

FIG. 2
An Act of Parliament, for Encourageing the Scots Affrican and Indian Company, [Edinburgh(?), 1695]. The earliest known version of the act that created Scotland's first joint-stock trading company and made possible the Darien venture. (Cat. no. 1).

directors of the Company that its most potentially profitable venture would be the foundation of a free port in Darien which could channel colonial goods to Scotland, and from which the Scots could cream off profitable excise duties, free from the legal restrictions of the Navigation Acts which effectively protected the English colonies from foreign (and this included Scottish) traders. Yet even before the Company had adopted any specific plan, a remarkable wave of enthusiasm to subscribe swept across Scotland in the spring of 1696, leaving the Company with promised capital of £400,000. The East India Company's opposition had prevented any English investment in the Company, so that the prospect of such a huge sum—calculated to be equivalent to a sixth or a quarter of Scotland's total floating capital—was all the more remarkable. That prospect, and the great hopes that were invested along with the money, also meant that the disappointment of failure was to be all the more painful when it came.

The plans for a colony were unclear, and the risks enormous. Yet the potential gains were evident. For the investors, such a scheme promised large returns if the Darien free-port could truly attract the trade of both hemispheres. (Paterson even speculated that it might be possible in due course to cut a waterway across the isthmus.) For the colonists who were to emigrate to Central America, the settlement offered fifty acres of land to plant and fifty feet of ground for a house. For the country as a whole, the Darien venture offered the chance to compete with the other trading nations of Europe as a colonial power, rich enough to defend itself and pursue policies independent of the unsympathetic English. Bolstered by West Indian wealth, the Scots would have the strength to escape the economic and constitutional stranglehold exercised by an English Parliament and a Dutch king more intent on pursuing their own economic agenda and an expensive European war than on improving the lot of the king's Scottish subjects.

The arguments for the venture were unimpeachable in their ambition and integrity, but those for the colony were also sadly naïve.

Paterson's critics pointed out that the proposed site of the settlement lay in territory claimed by the Spanish, though presently unoccupied by them. They would suffer no encroachment. Instead, the Scots' action could only affront William's main ally in his protracted war against France, and hence would also bring down the wrath of the English and of the King on their heads. The Company made every effort to keep its intentions and the location of its proposed colony secret, but it did not take long before their intentions became known. A concerted English propaganda campaign tried to prevent the Scots from attracting investment in northern Europe, though it could not stop Paterson and other agents of the Company from commissioning the core of a fleet from the shipbuilders of Hamburg. In due course, the English would also issue proclamations to all colonial governors in the Americas threatening punishment if they or any of their subjects aided the Scots, while the Spanish issued a fierce memorial reasserting their claim to Darien which the English enthusiastically supported.

Despite such opposition, the Scots sent two expeditions to Darien. The first left Leith in July 1698 and arrived the following October, carrying twelve hundred settlers including Paterson and his wife. The fleet of five ships sailed around the Orkneys to Madeira and thence to the Caribbean towards a destination that was still a well-kept secret. They anchored off the mainland of Panama in "Caledonia Bay" where they built Fort St. Andrew to defend the proposed settlement of New Edinburgh. International opposition to the plantation was immediate, yet sickness and starvation did more to dislodge the first settlement than the force of English proclamations or even of Spanish arms. After seven months the nine hundred surviving colonists abandoned the settlement. Only one of the four ships that had set out from Scotland made it back home: the other three only made it as far as Jamaica and New York. All suffered heavy loss of life.

Before news of the colony's abandonment reached Scotland, a second expedition set out for Darien in June 1699 propelled by the

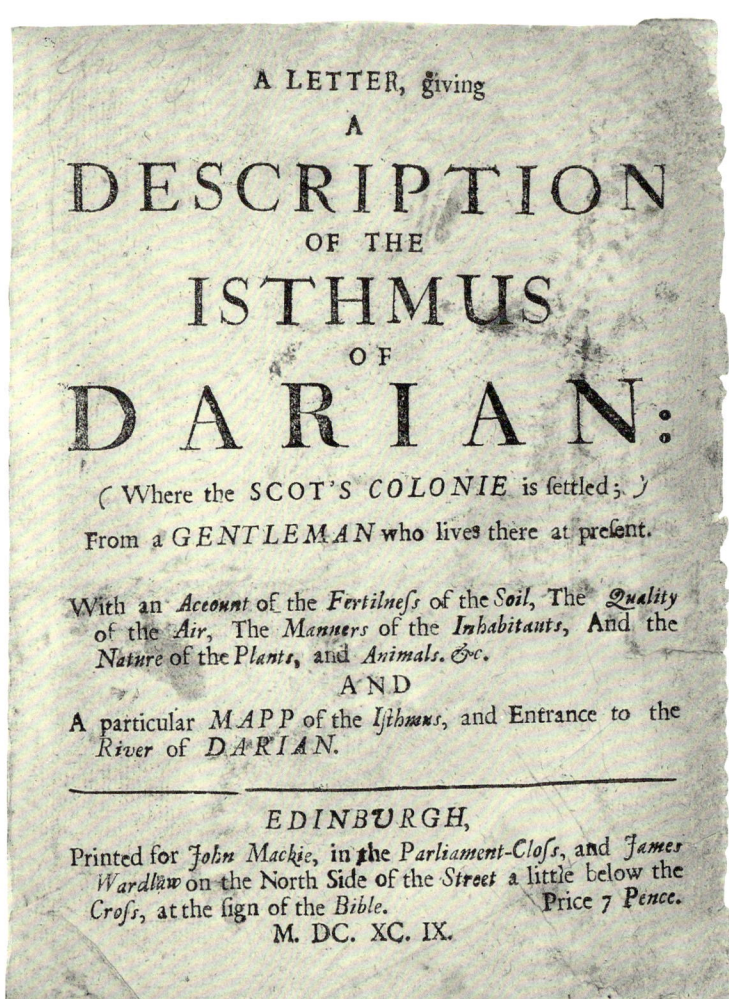

FIG. 3
A Letter, Giving a Description of the Isthmus of Darian, Edinburgh, 1699. This publication was the first comprehensive eye-witness account of the new settlement at Darien and full of false hopes concerning its suitability as a site. (Cat. no. 3).

enthusiasm that greeted the news of the first settlers' arrival. This second party found only a collapsed and deserted settlement. Nevertheless, they decided to stake a fresh and aggressive claim to Darien by routing a Spanish encampment at Toubacanti. Far from securing their position, this action enraged the Spaniards who sought a rapid military revenge. After two weeks under attack by the Spanish, the Scots capitulated and left Darien for good in April 1700.

The Scots made no further attempt to revive the colony but the claim to Darien, and the blame for the fiasco, were staples of bitter political debate until the Union of 1707. The site of the colony and the grievances exposed by its failure became counters in the larger political arguments which surrounded the successions to the thrones of England, Scotland, Spain, and France. William Paterson, among others, abandoned his commitment to a solely Scottish colony and proposed Darien as a British bulwark against the prospect of a Bourbon superstate that would include France, Spain, and the New World. Meanwhile, Scottish politicians, opposed to an English crown that had done so much to incapacitate the Scots venture, proposed that the crowns of England and Scotland should be uncoupled on Queen Anne's death to prevent any such collision in the future, unless Scottish independence in foreign policy and parliamentary sovereignty could be guaranteed. The trial and execution in Edinburgh in 1705 of Captain Thomas Green of the English ship the *Worcester*, which had been seized in retaliation for the English capture of one of the Company of Scotland's ships, embittered Anglo-Scottish relations still further. By the time that a Treaty of Union was being debated in 1706–07, the Darien venture remained as the memory of a grievance to be redressed and a sign that the structural relationship between England and Scotland as it had been set up in 1603 was no longer workable. The so-called "Equivalent" of £390,085 10s paid by the English to the Scots under the terms of the Treaty effectively dissolved the Company of Scotland. Scotland's most imaginative enterprise in the Americas had failed to found what Macaulay called "the Tyre, the Venice and the Amsterdam of the eighteenth century." Only the compensation payments to the investors and the memory of a new Scotland on a distant Panamanian shore remained as the monuments to its frustrated ambition.

1
An Act of Parliament, for Encourageing the Scots Affrican and Indian Company.
[Edinburgh(?), 1695].

The Scottish Parliament passed the Act which set up the Company of Scotland Trading to Africa and the Indies without the knowledge of King William, who was campaigning in the Low Countries at the time. Though touched with the royal scepter by the King's representative in Edinburgh, and hence technically assented to by the Crown, the Act incensed the King. He felt that the Scots Act granted "such powers, privileges and sovereignties as if there had been no King of Scotland," and pronounced himself "ill served in Scotland." The Act created Scotland's first joint-stock trading company with extensive privileges and protections, and biased its subscriptions heavily in favor of the Scots. At least ten different printed versions of the Act exist. This is a copy of the earliest known version, which misnames James Smith as "John Smith" and divides the Jewish merchant Joseph Cohen D'Azevedo into two people as "Joseph Cohaine. Dares Ovedo." (Fig. 2).

2
Andrew Fletcher of Saltoun.
Two Discourses Concerning the Affairs of Scotland.
Edinburgh, 1698.

Andrew Fletcher, the fiery republican laird of Saltoun in East Lothian, was probably the most creative and cosmopolitan political thinker in late seventeenth-century Britain. He was widely travelled in Europe, supported Monmouth's rebellion, and had been a member of the Scottish Parliament. In 1698 he published a cluster of discourses on the dangers of a standing army, on the Spanish Succession (in Italian), and on the social and economic problems of post-Revolutionary Scotland. Though the two *Discourses* on the affairs of Scotland have been most famous for their recommendation of domestic slavery as a temporary solution to Scotland's problems of poverty and economic underdevelopment, they were also the only major work in support of the Darien venture published between the official promotional tracts of the Company and the works that celebrated the arrival of the colonists. Fletcher himself subscribed for £1,000 worth of stock in the Company, and argued in the first of the *Discourses* that the Darien venture represented Scotland's last chance of becoming a "considerable" nation on the world stage. Once he became convinced that the venture had actually failed, he blamed the French and the English for conspiring to ruin the Company, and he argued that Scotland had "suffered so great a loss both in men and money, as to put us almost beyond any hope of having any considerable trade." He passionately opposed the idea of an incorporating union with England, and voted against the Union Treaty of 1707—a principled stand which, if it had succeeded, would have deprived him of any means of getting his investment back under the terms of the Equivalent.

3
A Letter, Giving a Description of the Isthmus of Darian. Edinburgh, 1699.

Sir William Alexander in 1624 had called for a "new Scotland" in the Americas, to sit alongside New England, New France, and New Spain. With the landing of the first Darien expedition in November 1698, Scotland had at last a "New Edinburgh" planted in the land newly-named Caledonia. Though short reports regarding the colony and its progress were received early in 1699 and absorbed into official documents and derivative travel-accounts drawn for example from the earlier works of William Dampier and Lionel Wafer, this *Letter* was the first comprehensive eye-witness account of the new settlement. It gave hope to the investors and potential settlers back home in Scotland with its detailed descriptions of the varieties of trees and animals, the friendliness of the local population, and the first planting of "*Tobacco* for Trade." The confidence that accompanied the second expedition was fuelled by such accounts, which nevertheless certainly misled their readers about the challenges presented to potential colonists by the environment of the intended plantation. (Figs. 3 and 4).

4
Alexander Pennecuik. *Caledonia Triumphans: A Panegyrick to the King.* Edinburgh, 1699.

An outpouring of encouraging, celebratory, and recriminatory verse, in Latin and English, accompanied the progress of the Darien colonists from their departure to the collapse of

FIG. 4
A New Map of the Isthumus of Darian appears in *A Letter, Giving a Description...of Darian*, 1699, and shows the city of New Edinburgh in the area of Caledonia. (Cat. no. 3).

Caledonia Triumphans:
A
PANEGYRICK
To the KING.

Thrice mighty PRINCE, Illustrious by thy Birth,
Bellona's Glory: Splendor of the Earth.
Wonder of Brav'ry, and of charming Parts,
Great Conquerour of Kingdoms and of Hearts,
All the fam'd Hero's in our Age that be,
Quite lose their Lustre, when compar'd with Thee.
Blessed Peace-maker in our Bloody Wars,
Wise Reconciler of Intestine Jarrs.
The Martial THISTLE budds, and no more withers,
The fragrant ROSE it's Scent again recovers.
The HARP is tun'd: And valiant SIR, to Thee,
The Conquering LILLIES bowe and humbled be.
The Ballance of all Europe SIR, is Your's,
Sole Help and Shelter of oppressed Powers.
No Mortal in his Veins bears nobler Blood,
Sprung from a Race, both Ancient, Great and Good,
Defenders of our Faith, to Pop'ry Foes,
This Holland, Flanders, and all Europe knows.
O! happy ORANGE-TREE, both Branch and Root,
That hath blest Britain with such cordial Fruit,
Yea, those that in the Northern World do dwell,
Are much refreshed by the very Smell.
Which perfumes all our European Costs,
Through Boreas Blasts and Hyperborean Frost.
To your own Thule, and the Orkney Isles,
And round cold Russia many thousand Miles.
Which rare Accomplishments that shine in You,
Makes CALEDONIA thus her Case renew.

Now if Great SIR, you list to lend an Ear,
From a far Countrey, joyful News we hear,
Zephyrus gently blows, and Whistling, Sings,
Here, my sweet Gales, delicious Tydings brings.
Fourth of November, that auspicious Day,
Your valiant SCOTS their Colours did display,
Into the Western World, where they did meet,
Thousands of Welcomes prostrat at their Feet.
The Soveraign Director was their Guide,
Neptune them favour'd; Earth, Seas, Wind and Tyde.
The Natives made their Joyes ring to the Skyes,
And them ador'd as Demi-deitys.
Kind harmless Heathens, whom through time we vow,
To train good Subjects both to GOD and You.
St. ANDREW our first Tutelar was he,
The UNICORN, must next Supporter be,
The CALEDONIA doth bring up the Rear,
Fraught with brave hardy Ladds, and void of Fear;

All splendedly equipt, and to the Three,
The Endeavour and Dolphin Hand-maids be.
Who to these Praises, this Addition have,
No Injuries they'l give, nor yet receive.
Both Ships and Men commanded Sir, it's true,
By Captains both of Sense and Honour too.
Nor are these Youths the Scum of this our Land,
But in effect, a brave and generous Band.
Inspyr'd with thirst of Fame, and fond to have,
Titles upon the Marbles of their Grave.
And though that hundreds in that Train do come,
Whose Vertues are eclipst with want at Home.
Yet were there Means but equal to their Mind,
In all the World you should not braver find.
But to allay Youths rash unwary Deeds,
They have their Orders sent from elder Heads.
Of a wise Senat, who Consult and Vote,
What is the Companys Int'rest, and what not.
At Landing, Fertile Fields and Golden Mountains,
Saluted them, with clear and christal Fountains;
Roots, Flowers and Fruits, for Physick, and to eat,
And neither pinching Colds, nor scorching Heat.
Rivers, safe Bayes, variety of Plants,
And useful Trees which our old Britain wants.
Here grows the Nicaragua, Manchtonell,
Vannileos also, that perfumes so well.
Our sable night is gone, the day is won,
The SCOTS are follow'd with the RISING-SUN.
The Ev'ning crowns the Day, and what remains?
Old ALBANY its antient Fame regains.
FERGUS 1st. } Your brave Ancestor gave the Scots of old
{ A Lyon rampant in a field of Gold.
When he our Coat-Armorial did dispense,
Which now is ours, in a true literal Sense.
And can our Breasts such swelling Joys contain,
WILLIAM the Lyon rules the SCOTS again:
A Nation who with hearts, with hands and head
Will serve you, Soveraign Sir, in time of need.
Warlike Gustavus, and Great Charl le maigno,
Did ne're employ our Martial Swords in vain.
The Brittons, Romans, Saxons and the Danes,
Did all invade us, but with fruitless Pains.
The treach'rous Picts did oft attempt the same;
But for Reward, lost Countrey, Life and Name.
The noble Race of Douglass did excell,
In Military Glory, all can tell.

At Home, and Forraign Shoars, yea, ever still,
Of all the Sirname, very few prove ill.
The antient Grahams are brave, and all confess,
True to their Sov'raigns, chiefly in distress.
The Danes who made our neighb'ring Nation Slaves,
Found here the Hays who beat them to their Graves.
Kind Mantua hath never yet forgot
Rare Creighton, call'd the Admiralle Scot,
Whose Life shews him a Miracle of Men:
As it is drawn by an Italian Pen.
Wallace and Bruce, I shall not now rehearse,
Least I offend you, Sir, with tedious Verse.
And hundreds more of undenyed Fame,
For Arts and Arms, whom I forbear to name:
And as our Valour flew all Europe round,
So now our Trade scarce both the Poles shall bound.
If You but own us, Mighty Sir. and then
No Devils we fear, nor yet malicious Men.
What humane Counter-plot can marr the thing,
That is protected by Great-Britains King.
Our Claim is just: and so we value not
The Brags of Spain, nor Thundrings of the Pope,
Who may well threaten; Yet Don dare not fight,
When he minds DARIEN, and old Eighty eight.
Their Cruelties were Catholick indeed,
Not Christian, to poor Indians and their Seed.
But those they call Hereticks of our Nation,
We hope will shew a meeker Reformation.
Nor shall insulting Neighbours henceforth taunt
The gen'rous SCOTS, for Poverty and Want.
Our Ships through all the World shall go and come,
Ev'n from the Rising to the Setting Sun.
Then shall we from the genuine Spring command,
What now we truckle at a second hand.
And we shall flourish by your Royal Rays,
With Honour, Riches, and old Nestors days:
And ever bless our GOD, and praise our KING,
And CALEDONIAs Triumphs gladly sing.

No mercenary thoughts, or base design
Of servile Flatt'ry, made these Verses mine.

By a Lover of Caledonia,
and the Muses.

Edinburgh, Printed by the Heirs and Successors of Andrew Anderson, Printer to the Kings most Excellent Majesty, 1699.

FIG. 5
Caledonia Triumphans, Edinburgh, 1699. This rare broadside has the coat-of-arms of the Darien Company at its head. The aspirations of the Scots are expressed: "Nor shall insulting Neighbours henceforth taunt/the gen'rous Scots for Poverty and Want./Our Ships through all the World shall go and come,/Ev'n from the Rising to the Setting Sun." (Cat. no. 4).

the settlement. *Caledonia Triumphans* (attributed to Alexander Pennecuik, M.D.) is the most handsome of all the broadside poems, and the most effusive of all the congratulatory verses. Its address to King William—who had done so much to block the Company of Scotland's plans—plays with the names of the colonists' ships (the Caledonia, the St. Andrew, the Unicorn, the Rising Sun) and projects a confident vision of future success for the settlement: "Our Ships through all the World shall go and come,/ Ev'n from the Rising to the Setting Sun." The rising sun was the central heraldic emblem in the Company's arms. It is strikingly reproduced on this broadside which was probably an official publication of the Company, printed by the King's printers in Edinburgh. (Fig. 5).

5
John Hamilton, Baron Belhaven.
A Defence of the Scots Settlement at Darien. Edinburgh, 1699.

Opposition to the embryonic Scottish settlement had come from two directions: from the Spanish, who protested that the Scots had planted their colony on land rightly held by the Spanish Crown, and from the English Parliament, which claimed that the colony threatened English overseas trade. *A Defence of the Scots Settlement at Darien* (attributed to John Hamilton, Lord Belhaven, the agricultural improver, orator, and later anti-Unionist) was the most sophisticated response to the arguments of the international opposition. It was

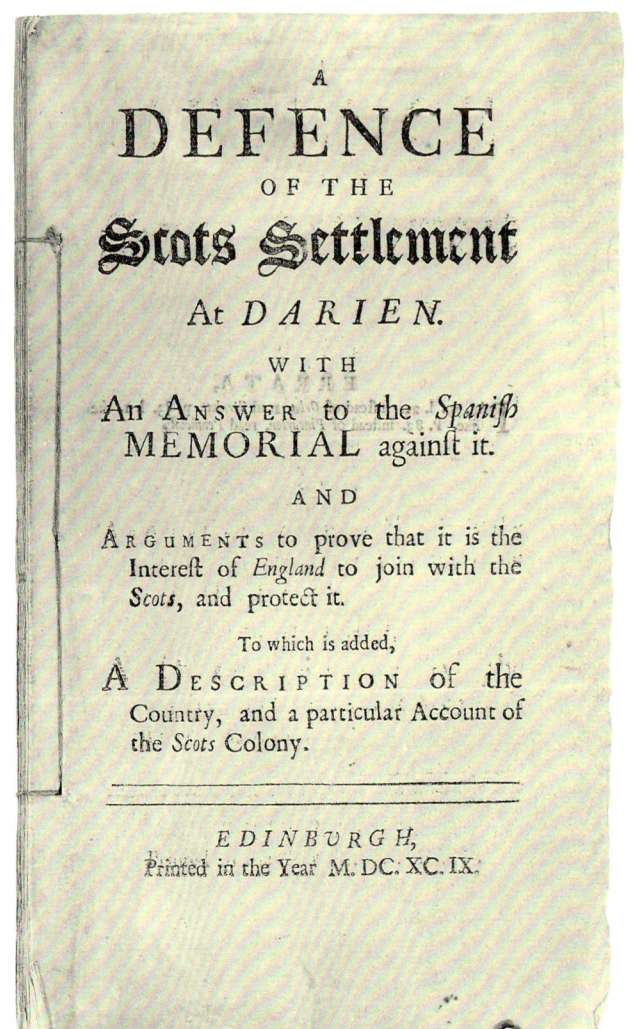

FIG. 6
A Defence of the Scots Settlement at Darien, Edinburgh, 1699. Whatever the actual realities of power, both the Scots and the Spanish attempted to legitimize their claim to settlement in Panama. This pamphlet is the best of the printed arguments in favor of the Scots. (Cat. no. 5).

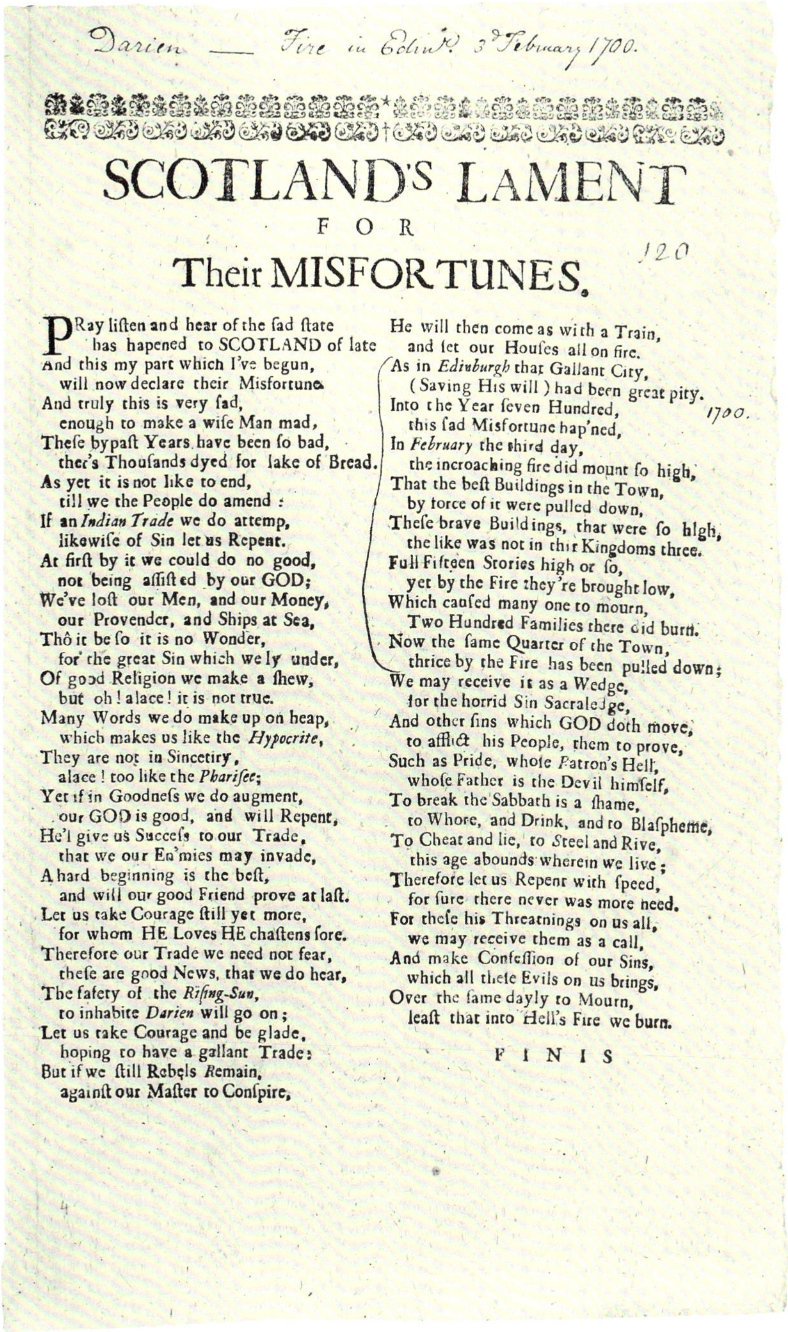

Darien — Fire in Edinr. 3d February 1700.

SCOTLAND'S LAMENT
FOR
Their MISFORTUNES.

120

PRay listen and hear of the sad state
    has hapened to SCOTLAND of late
And this my part which I've begun,
    will now declare their Misfortune.
And truly this is very sad,
    enough to make a wise Man mad,
These bypast Years have been so bad,
    ther's Thousands dyed for lake of Bread.
As yet it is not like to end,
    till we the People do amend:
If an *Indian Trade* we do attemp,
    likewise of Sin let us Repent.
At first by it we could do no good,
    not being assisted by our GOD;
We've lost our Men, and our Money,
    our Provender, and Ships at Sea,
Thô it be so it is no Wonder,
    for the great Sin which we ly under,
Of good Religion we make a shew,
    but oh! alace! it is not true.
Many Words we do make up on heap,
    which makes us like the *Hypocrite*,
They are not in Sincetiry,
    alace! too like the *Pharisee*;
Yet if in Goodness we do augment,
    our GOD is good, and will Repent,
He'l give us Success to our Trade,
    that we our En'mies may invade,
A hard beginning is the best,
    and will our good Friend prove at last.
Let us take Courage still yet more,
    for whom HE Loves HE chastens sore.
Therefore our Trade we need not fear,
    these are good News, that we do hear,
The safety of the *Rising-Sun*,
    to inhabite *Darien* will go on;
Let us take Courage and be glade,
    hoping to have a gallant Trade:
But if we still Rebels Remain,
    against our Master to Conspire,

He will then come as with a Train,
    and set our Houses all on fire.
As in *Edinburgh* that Gallant City,
    (Saving His will) had been great pity.
Into the Year seven Hundred,   1700.
    this sad Misfortune hap'ned,
In *February* the third day,
    the incroaching fire did mount so high,
That the best Buildings in the Town,
    by force of it were pulled down,
These brave Buildings, that were so high,
    the like was not in thir Kingdoms three.
Full Fifteen Stories high or so,
    yet by the Fire they're brought low,
Which caused many one to mourn,
    Two Hundred Families there did burn.
Now the same Quarter of the Town,
    thrice by the Fire has been pulled down;
We may receive it as a Wedge,
    for the horrid Sin Sacraledge,
And other sins which GOD doth move,
    to afflict his People, them to prove,
Such as Pride, whose Patron's Hell,
    whose Father is the Devil himself,
To break the Sabbath is a shame,
    to Whore, and Drink, and to Blaspheme,
To Cheat and lie, to Steel and Rive,
    this age abounds wherein we live;
Therefore let us Repent with speed,
    for sure there never was more need.
For these his Threatnings on us all,
    we may receive them as a call,
And make Confession of our Sins,
    which all these Evils on us brings,
Over the same dayly to Mourn,
    least that into Hell's Fire we burn.

FINIS

FIG. 7
Scotland's Lament for Their Misfortunes, [Edinburgh, 1700]. As the manuscript note across the top of this broadside shows, the disaster at Darien and the Edinburgh fire of 1700 were together considered divine punishments meted out to a sinful nation. This is the only recorded copy of this work. (Cat. no. 6).

published in the late summer of 1699 as a direct reply to the Spanish memorial of May 1699 which condemned the Scottish invasion of Spanish territory. The author, writing anonymously, dedicated his work to King William to remind him of the "Sovereignty and Dignity of Your Crown as King of Scots," and proceeded to attack the legal foundations of the Spanish claim to Darien, and to reassure the English that it would be to their advantage, nationally and internationally, for the Scots to prosper in their new venture. As well as a comprehensive account of the Scottish claim, the author provided a detailed description of Darien, and an account of the current state of the colony. When Andrew Fletcher received a copy in London in September 1699 he thought it "so well writ that I wish you had a 1000 copies of it in S[cotland]." The pamphlet was to be the most influential of all those published in the wake of the settlement, and was the first shot in the war of words which was to follow the final confirmation of the colony's desertion in the spring of 1700. (Fig. 6).

6
Scotland's Lament for Their Misfortunes. [Edinburgh, 1700].

Beyond the recriminations of the pamphlet war which succeeded the collapse of the Darien colony, the main response to the failure seems to have been a period of national self-searching. The notion that Scotland was a nation bound by a particular covenant to God was still potent, and any signs of His wrath had to be accounted for: "If an *Indian Trade* we do attempt,/ likewise of Sin let us repent." As the manuscript note on this, the only known copy of this broadside, shows, the retreat from Darien was particularly associated with the Edinburgh fire of February 1700 as a manifestation of divine displeasure. A spate of unofficial calls to repentance, such as this one, appeared that spring, when the General Assembly of the Church of Scotland also called for national days of fasting and repentance as God's purposes in dashing the colony and burning the capital city of His people were vainly sought, contributing to the general feeling that the national malaise was as much moral as economic or political. (Fig. 7).

7
John Clerk.
An Essay upon the XV. Article of the Treaty of Union. [Edinburgh(?), 1706].

The career of the noted antiquarian, lawyer, and economic improver John (later Sir John) Clerk of Penicuik, touched the progress of the Company of Scotland in three very different ways. Though neither he nor any of his immediate family invested capital in the Company of Scotland, Clerk had a family connection with the venture in that his brother Robert had sailed with the first expedition to Panama. Later, while on the Grand Tour in Europe in late 1699 or early 1700, Clerk composed a martial cantata (to a libretto by the Leyden medical professor Herman Boerhaave) entitled *Leo Scotiæ Irritatus* which urged Scots defiance of the Spanish in Darien. Some six years later, he was enlisted as one of the commissioners of the Union between England and Scotland whose job it was to calculate the so-called "Equivalent" guaranteed by the 15th Article of the Treaty of Union. The Equivalent recompensed the Scots for their liability for the higher rates of excise imposed by the English, but it also undertook to repay the Darien investors for their losses with accumulated interest. This was a calculated attempt to draw the sting of perhaps the greatest grievance occasioned within recent memory by the Union of the Crowns. It was the Equivalent—rather than the promise of free trade and hence entry into England's commercial fold in the Americas—which was exchanged for the possibility of Scotland's own independent colony in the Americas. Clerk's essay defends the provisions of the Equivalent, and recommends that any lingering resentment against the English for their treatment of the colony should be forgotten: "Darien is lost, and... nothing does properly remain of our Company, but the Name." Once the Treaty of Union was ratified, and the provisions of the 15th Article were thereby put into effect, the Company of Scotland was officially dissolved and the Darien venture passed into history.

FOR FURTHER READING

David Armitage, "The Scottish Vision of Empire: Intellectual Origins of the Darien Venture," in John Robertson, ed., *A Union for Empire: Political Thought and the British Union of 1707* (Cambridge, 1995).

George Pratt Insh, *The Company of Scotland Trading to Africa and the Indies* (London, 1932).

Gordon Marshall, *Presbyteries and Profits: Calvinism and the Development of Capitalism in Scotland, 1560–1707* (Oxford, 1980).

John Prebble, *The Darien Disaster* (London, 1968).

John Robertson, "Union, State and Empire: The Britain of 1707 in its European Setting," in Lawrence Stone, ed., *An Imperial State at War: Britain from 1689 to 1815* (London, 1993).

John Scott and George P. Johnston, *A Bibliography of Books Relating to the Darien Company* (Edinburgh, 1906).

FIG. 8
Sir William Alexander in 1621 received a charter from James I for possession of vast territory in North America to establish a New Scotland that would rival New England and New France. This portrait is the frontispiece in *An Encouragement to Colonies*, 1624. In 1633, Alexander was created Earl of Stirling. (Cat. no. 8).

CHAPTER TWO: *Immigration and Settlement*

NED C. LANDSMAN

THE SCOTS HAVE long been known as a nation of emigrants. Long before the first native of Scotland embarked for England's new colony at Jamestown, Scots demonstrated a propensity to travel far from home. Scottish students and churchmen had traveled and studied on the European Continent since the Middle Ages, to Italy or Spain or especially France, with whom an independent Scotland maintained an "Auld Alliance." Following the Scottish Reformation, they shifted more often to the centers of Continental Protestantism, to Geneva and the Netherlands. Scottish traders in abundance were found in France, at Göttingen, and at Rotterdam, where a Scottish community of a thousand or more persons resided in the seventeenth century. Especially important were Poland and Ireland; Scottish pedlars traversed the former country in such numbers that English observers at the time of the Union of Crowns in 1603 feared being "over-run with them…witness the multiplicities of the Scots in Polonia." Perhaps 40,000 Scots ventured to Poland during the first half of the seventeenth century, while the plantation of Ulster, beginning in the first decade of that century, would attract a greater number of settlers from the north of Britain over the next hundred years. Scotland provided early modern Europe with two of its best-known figures: the regimental soldier and the pedlar. Soldiers from Scotland were vital participants in Continental battles during the age of religious wars; pedlars in general were often referred to as "Scotsmen" in the records of the day.

Against that background, it is hardly surprising that Scots would become among the most prominent European groups to settle in early America. Even as English Pilgrims were establishing their settlement in Plymouth Colony, Scots were planning colonies of their own, at Nova Scotia (1622) and New Galloway (1629). But the largest Scottish efforts took place within English or—after the Union of Parliaments in 1707—British dominions. By the era of the American Revolution, Scots in America would be ubiquitous and notorious; colonials, from the Tidewater of Virginia to the back country of New York, would lament their seemingly universal presence, their prominence, and the pronounced clannishness that set Scots apart from their neighbors even as they flocked to the frontiers in ever-increasing numbers.

The willingness of Scots to depart their homeland was rooted in the nature of Scottish society. As a poor country with an inhospitable climate on the European periphery, the land itself had little hold on its inhabitants. Its limited productive capacity combined with a small domestic market to provide few employment alternatives at home. Scots who sought to better themselves, or even just to secure themselves against want, had to be prepared to leave their homes. Even those who never left their native country were apt to move about within the countryside with a regularity that those from more prosperous and settled lands would find startling. Conversely, the very propensity of Scots to migrate made such movements easier for individuals to undertake; they were never at a loss to find whole communities of their countrymen in all of the principal places to which they went. Especially striking among the Scots was the number of prominent individuals who lived and worked abroad, as merchants, ministers, and educators. The limited Scottish market meant that the necessities of foreign trade were only provided by Scots who left home to seek it; few foreign traders were attracted to Scotland. And from the time of the Renaissance, Scotland maintained a consistent and pronounced identification with the Continental world of letters, which insured the continuing European travels of Scottish scholars.

Despite the seeming omnipresence of Scots in eighteenth-century America, natives of Scotland in fact were rather slow to respond to the opportunities America provided. Strenuous efforts to promote the settlement of Nova Scotia and New Galloway produced a meager response with the majority of settlers probably coming from England rather than Scotland. An attempted Scottish voyage to New York in 1669 failed, as did a small Scottish colony in South Carolina during the 1680s and the much larger effort at Darien during the following decade. Their only modest success in the seventeenth century was the 1682 settlement of East New Jersey, where active promotion persuaded about seven hundred settlers to venture only a small fraction of the simultaneous and related English settlement of the neighboring Delaware Valley Colonies of West Jersey and Pennsylvania. And while the Union of 1707 gave Scottish merchants the right to trade with England's overseas colonies, it did little to stimulate a surge in settlement; probably fewer than 30,000 Scots settled anywhere in the Americas before 1760. That was not the result of an unwillingness to emigrate; the same decades that witnessed the Nova Scotia failures saw tens of thousands of Scots depart for Ulster, for Poland, and for service in the Continental regiments. Rather, it was the easy accessibility of places of long established opportunity for Scots abroad on the European Continent that deterred any early desire to travel to the New World.

Even as the majority of Scottish emigrants were choosing movement across the Irish and North Seas over crossing the Atlantic, an increasing number of prominent and educated Scots began to cash in on the opportunities the Americas provided. Scottish merchants began to turn up everywhere—in the colonial ports, back country crossroads, and especially the Chesapeake, where before the American Revolution Glasgow merchants capitalized on their advantageous west coast location in Scotland and their innovative business practices to dominate the tobacco trade. Scottish tobacco factors and storekeepers were ubiquitous figures throughout the region. Elsewhere, Scottish imperial officials, doctors, clergymen, and educators all flocked to colonies from New England to the West Indies in numbers all out of proportion to their percentage in the overall migration. The presence of so many prominent Scots was a principal reason for the perception among Americans of Scottish presence and power.

Gradually, increasing communities of common settlers began to appear in particular areas of colonial America. One was central Jersey's commercial corridor, an outgrowth of the East Jersey colony, where Scottish landlords, farmers, and traders established an important presence, which became as well a homeland for the Presbyterian Church. Another was the British West Indies, including Jamaica, Antigua, and St. Kitts, where Scots established important family dynasties as planters and as merchants. There were significant settlements of Highlanders also in New York's Ulster County, in Georgia, and especially in North Carolina in and around Cape Fear.

The turning point in Scottish emigration was the Seven Years' War, known as the French and Indian War in America, which attracted large numbers of Scottish soldiers after mid-century. Just as the Scottish regiments on the European Continent had acclimated Scots to a life in Europe, so would the war experience induce many Scots to stay in America, and to persuade their families and neighbors to join them. The end of hostilities in 1761 opened up a flood of settlement into the American back country, and then into the new British possessions of Canada and Florida. Perhaps 40,000 Scots ventured to America during the next dozen years, including as many as 15,000 Highlanders. Scottish promoters actively publicized the movement. Among them were several leading Glasgow merchants and such Presbyterian clergymen

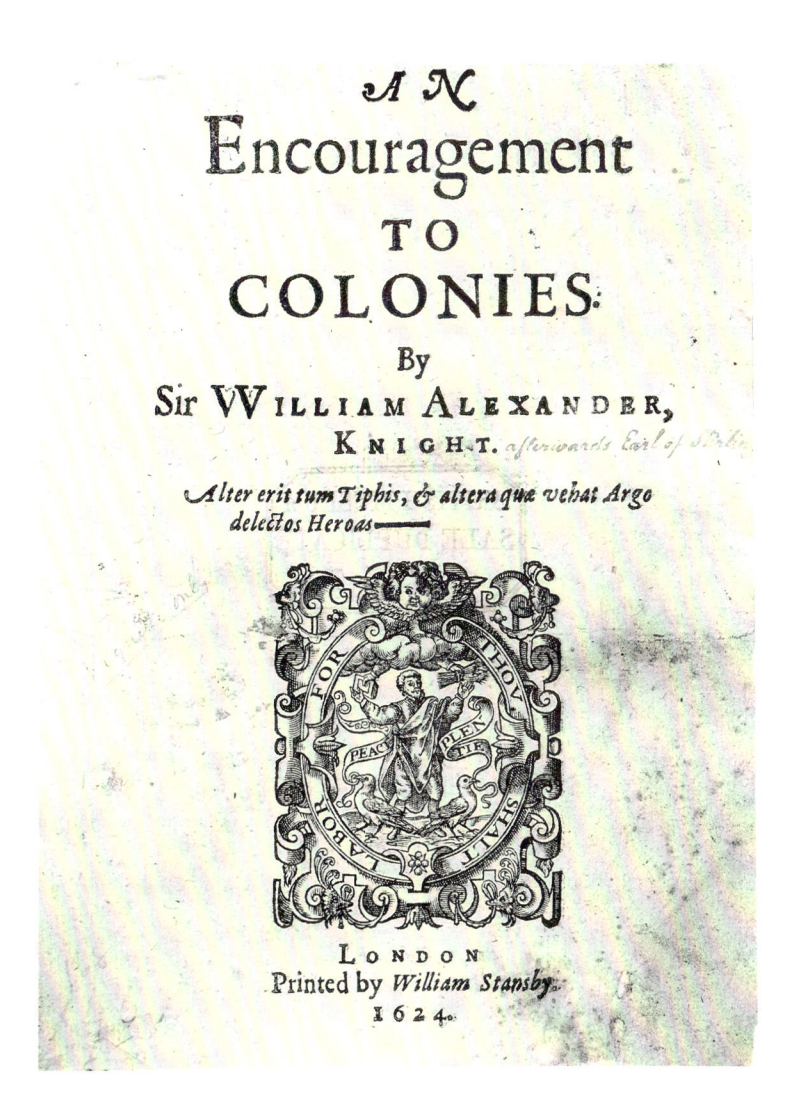

FIG. 9
William Alexander, Earl of Stirling, *An Encouragement to Colonies*, London, 1624, the first tract promoting Scottish colonization in America. (Cat. no. 8).

as William Thom of Govan, the reputed author of five tracts promoting emigration to America, and John Witherspoon, who left his Parish in Paisley, Scotland, in 1768 to head the College of New Jersey, later Princeton, where he became the leading spokesman for Scottish and Presbyterian interests in America. By 1771, emigration from the western Highlands and among the artisan communities of Glasgow and Paisley reached such proportions that Scottish landlords and officials began to fear depopulation. Johnson and Boswell described that "emigration mania" on their famous tour of Scotland's Western Isles.

The American Revolution provided only a temporary halt to that movement. Once again, Scots broadened their course of migration. After the war ended, Scots resumed their movements to the newly-independent United States. Even larger numbers migrated north into Nova Scotia and Quebec, building upon the momentum of a movement that had begun shortly before the war. By the end of the century, Scottish workers in Halifax were considered a glut on the market, while merchant investors began to promote trade and settlement far to the west, eventually reaching the Pacific Coast. Probably 8,000 Scottish Highlanders emigrated to what would become Canada during the first decade and a half of the new century, and many thousands more thereafter. Other groups would branch out in a different direction, investing and settling in Latin America, where Scottish settlements appeared at Poyais on the Mosquito Coast between Nicaragua and Honduras, at Topo in Venezuela, and at Monte Grande in Argentina, all by the early 1820s.

Those Scots who moved into English and then British colonies did not abandon their Scottish identities. Everywhere they retained a reputation for a clannishness that made them often unpopular within the American colonies. Scottish merchants in the Americas retained their trade connections with an ever-growing Scottish commercial empire. And those prominent Scots who went to the Americas as British imperial officials worked actively to promote a conception of empire in which the rights of provincial citizens matched those of metropolitans, and all were linked together by ties of commercial interest. Indeed, more than anyone else, those Scots promoted a vision of provincial growth leading to enhanced provincial status and power that they would share with such prominent colonials as Benjamin Franklin, and which would play an important role in the formation of an American identity.

8

William Alexander, Earl of Stirling. *An Encouragement to Colonies.* London, 1624.

From its very beginnings, Scottish colonization was closely intertwined with the history of the literary classes. Among the most important of that group was Sir William Alexander of Menstrie, later Earl of Stirling, an educated Scottish gentleman who had traveled on the Continent and was one of the leading Scottish poets of the day. (Fig. 8). Alexander, a personal favorite of James VI of Scotland and I of England, received a charter for the lands of "new Scotland in America" in 1621 and soon began efforts to explore and

FIG. 10
A map of "New Scotlande" in Lord Stirling's *An Encouragement to Colonies*, 1624, which is more or less present-day Nova Scotia. (Cat. no. 8).

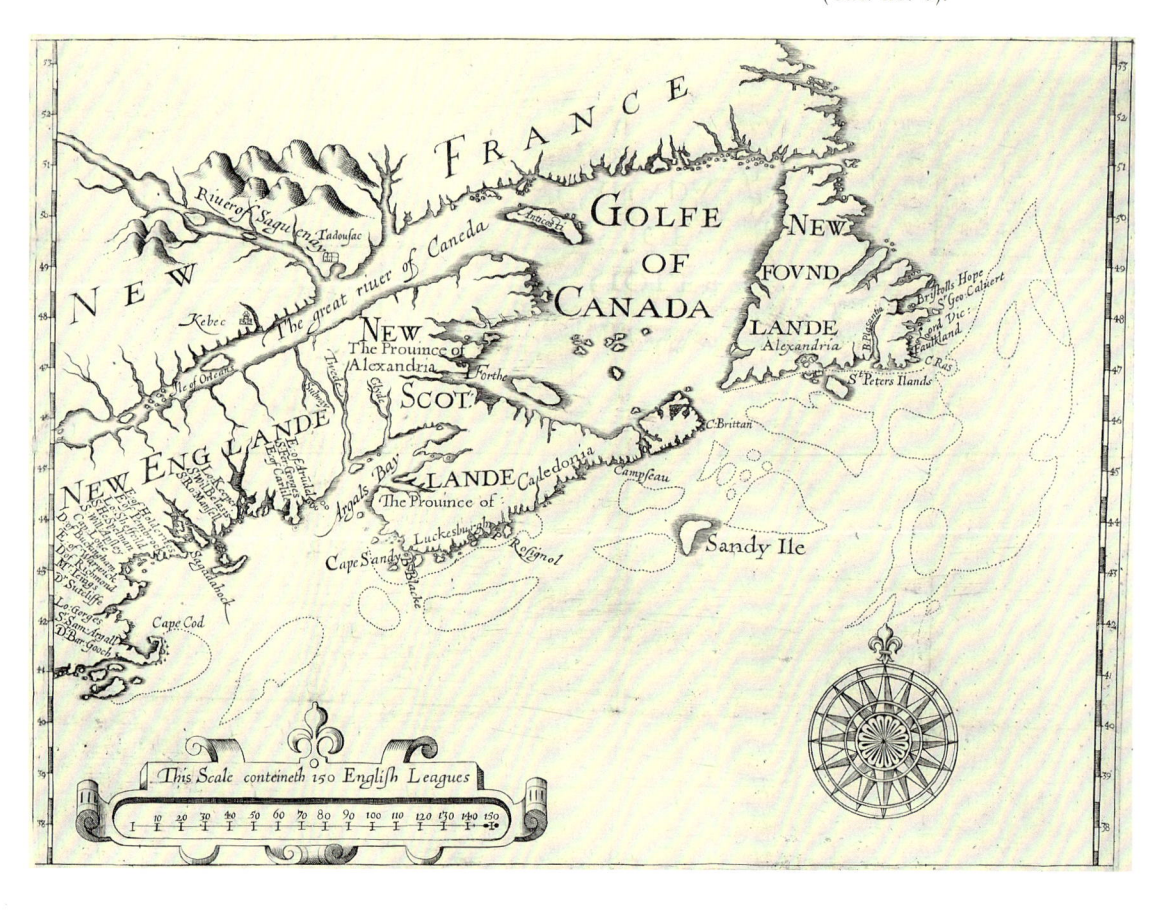

18 IMMIGRATION AND SETTLEMENT

plant those northern lands. After two preliminary expeditions, Alexander published his *Encouragement to Colonies*, which can be considered the first promotional work in favor of Scottish colonization in America. (Fig. 9).

The pamphlet was dedicated to James and quickly displayed Alexander's learning. It began with a lengthy discussion of the history of colonies, from Biblical times through the Phoenicians, Greeks, Romans, and Babylonians, ending with Europeans in earlier as well as recent times. He followed that with a patriotic appeal. Scotland, "by reason of her populousnesse" did every year send out "swarmes" to Poland and to the Continental armies, who might better be employed in the service of their prince, bringing their country "both Honour and Profit." (Fig. 10).

Alexander sent three further expeditions to New Scotland, one, under his son, in 1628, two the following year to Cape Breton and Port Royal. The colony gave signs of flourishing for a time, but it was not to be. In reaction to French complaints of impingement upon their Canadian territories, the Scots were told to evacuate Port Royal in 1632, with the proviso that Alexander could settle them elsewhere in New Scotland. The removal left Alexander deeply in debt, and no further expeditions were sent during his lifetime. Alexander was compensated for his losses, and in 1633 he was created Earl of Stirling.

9
George Scot.
The Model of the Government of the Province of East-New-Jersey in America. Edinburgh, 1685.

A more successful colonial venture than the Nova Scotia settlements was the colony of Scots at East New Jersey, founded in 1683 by a group of Scots proprietors, who purchased a one-half share in the colony from an English Quaker group that included William Penn. (Fig. 11). Penn was turning most of his energies towards his own Pennsylvania settlement; so the leadership of the Jersey colony devolved upon a mixed group of Quaker, Anglican, and Presbyterian Scottish proprietors, led by the renowned Scottish Quaker Robert Barclay, author of the famous *Apology for the True Christian Divinity of the People called Quakers*, one of the most important of Quaker theological tracts.

Over the next several years, the Scots proprietors sent more than six hundred of their countrymen to the colony, many of them attracted by a series of four promotional tracts that they published. By far the most substantial of those was George Scot's *Model*, which ran to more than 270 pages. (Fig. 12). Scot was the owner of a small estate in the shire of Fife called Pitlochy. He was also a Presbyterian, at a time when the Scottish administration under the last of the Stuart kings (James VII of Scotland and II of England) was seeking to eradicate Presbyterianism from Scotland. Scot's *Model* appealed to his fellow Presbyterians to venture to East Jersey, in a vessel he had chartered, where they would be allowed to follow their faith with impunity. The *Henry and Francis* embarked for East Jersey in 1685 with about 100 passengers, most of them Presbyterians, and most of those religious prisoners granted to Scot as servants on the condition that he remove them from Scotland. Illness struck the ship and the majority of the passengers died, including Scot. The remainder of the prisoners sued for their release in the New World. Some of those remained in the Scottish colony, others moved on to New York or New England, and a few returned to Scotland.

10
Rules of the St. Andrew's Club, at Charlestown. Charlestown, 1762.

In addition to attempting colonies of their own, Scots began very early to settle within England's American colonies. After the Union of 1707, Scottish emigration to America accelerated, especially among prominent and educated groups, such as merchants, doctors, and public officials. By the middle years of the eighteenth century, clusters of prominent Scots settlers could be found in nearly every

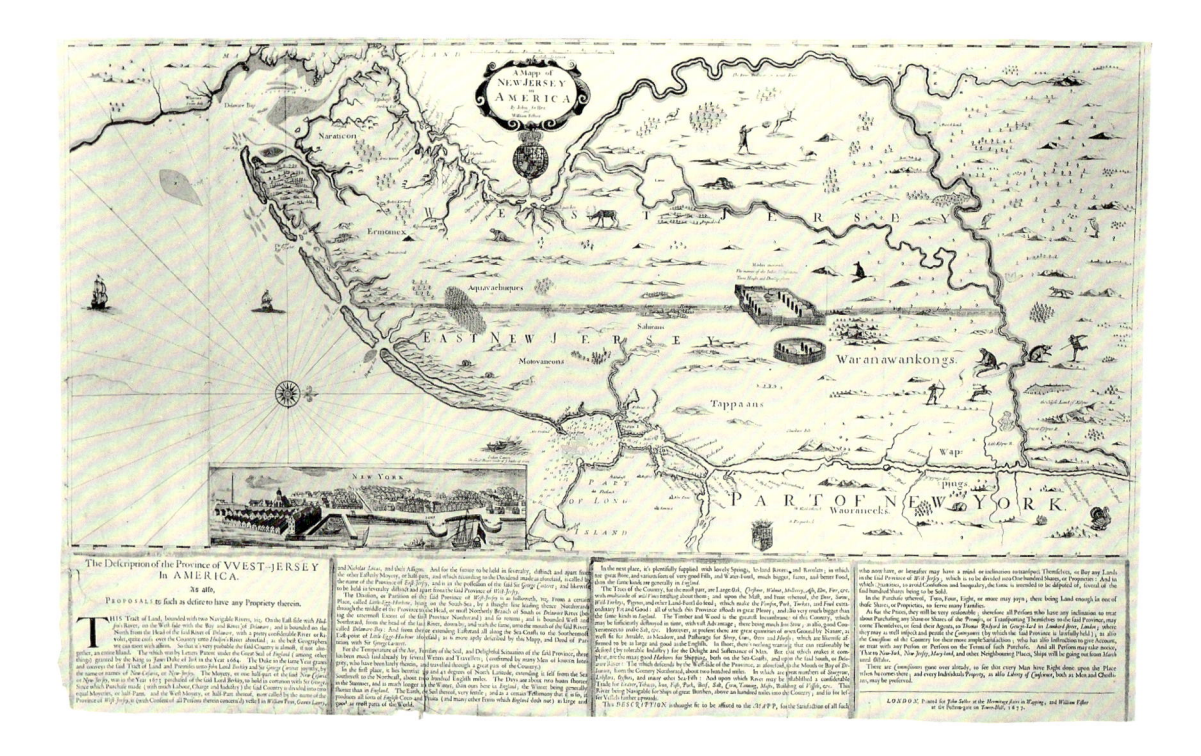

FIG. 11
A Mapp of New Jersey, London, 1677. (22½ 2 37 9). Organized Scottish settlement in the area of the present-day United States began in New Jersey, in the 1680s. This map from 1677, published by John Seller and William Fisher, shows the division of the land west of the Hudson River into West New Jersey, which was under the control of an English Quaker group that included William Penn, and East New Jersey, the site chosen by a group of Scots proprietors led by George Scot.

colony, and especially within the larger colonial cities of Philadelphia, Boston, New York, Norfolk, and Charleston. They were known especially for banding together for purposes of commerce, conviviality, and charity. Out of those associations grew a number of institutions, including the Saint Andrew's Societies of New York, Philadelphia, and Charleston, composed of men, mostly Scottish immigrants, who were "well-disposed to charitable actions."

Among the first such societies was the Saint Andrew's Club of Charleston, founded in 1729. (Fig. 13). Scottish merchants, public officials, and especially doctors played a prominent role in the Carolina colony from an early date, and the society, dedicated to the "relief of indigent and poor people," included some of the most prominent men in the colony. Among the names of the members included in the published *Rules* of the society can be found such prominent individuals as the governors Robert Johnson and James Glen of Carolina, James Grant of East Florida, and James Wright of Georgia. Other prominent early members included Lord Adam Gordon, Sir Alexander Nesbit, Baronet, the prominent colonial agent James Abercromby, and several ministers of the Episcopalian and Presbyterian churches. Perhaps the most important Scottish influences in Charleston would come from the doctors, such as John Moultrie, John Lining, and Alexander Garden; Moultrie was among the founding members of the Society. (Fig. 14). With the rise of Edinburgh's medical school to world renown in the second quarter of the eighteenth century, Scottish and Scottish-trained doctors would form the most prominent group of medical men throughout the American colonies.

11
Scotus Americanus [William Thom]. *Informations Concerning the Province of North Carolina, Addressed to Emigrants from the Highlands.* Glasgow, 1773.

The end of the Seven Years War led to an explosion of emigration from Scotland to America. Of particular importance were the Highland soldiers who remained in America after the war had ended, or who returned and spread stories of what they had seen. By the early 1770s, Johnson and Boswell, touring Scotland's Western Isles, depicted within the region a veritable emigration mania with whole communities packing up and departing for America, to the point that landholders in those areas began to fear a general depopulation. Much of the impetus to emigration came from word-of-mouth reports; also important were the frequent letters appearing in the public papers, and especially a series of five pamphlets published in Glasgow between 1770 and 1774 extolling the virtues of emigration, including this work. (Fig. 15). Written under the pen name of "Scotus Americanus", and addressed to Highlanders, the purpose of the publication was to promote movement to the Highland settlements in North Carolina.

The authorship of this tract is uncertain. All five pamphlets were published without attribution. The other four can definitively be assigned to the Reverend William Thom of Govan near Glasgow, a somewhat irascible minister of the orthodox or Popular Party in

FIG. 12
George Scot, *The Model of the Government of the Province of East-New-Jersey*, Edinburgh, 1685. This work, a major piece of promotional writing encouraging settlement by Scots in New Jersey, featured letters of testimony from early settlers in the province. Scot himself died in 1685 on shipboard leading a group of colonists. (Cat. no. 9).

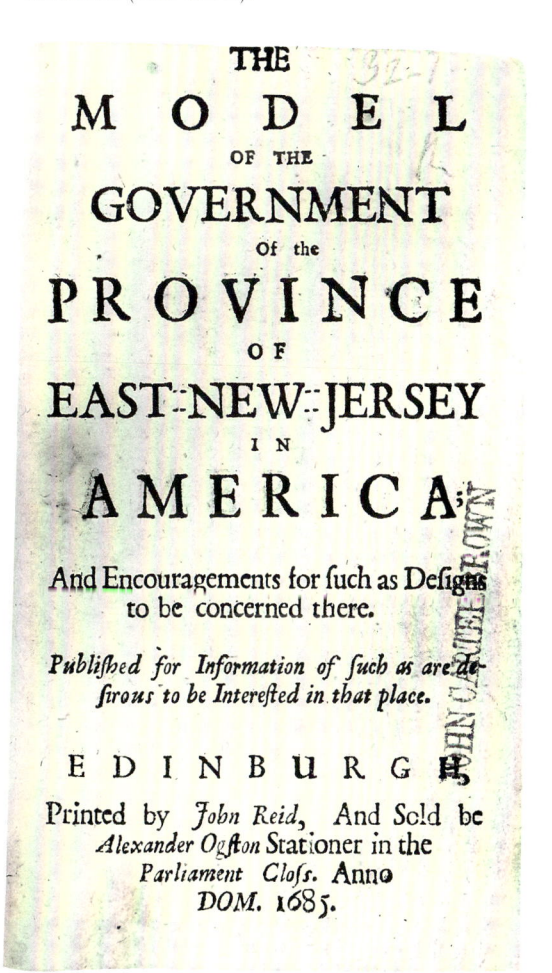

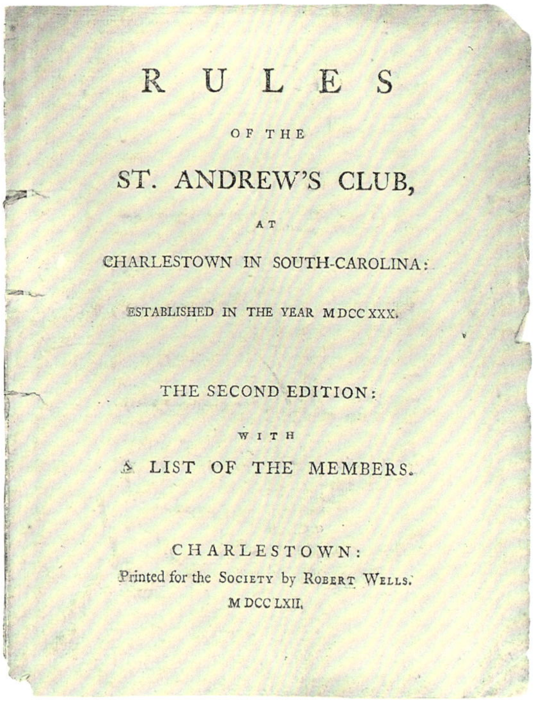

RULES

OF THE

ST. ANDREW'S CLUB,

AT

CHARLESTOWN IN SOUTH-CAROLINA:

ESTABLISHED IN THE YEAR MDCCXXX.

THE SECOND EDITION:

WITH

A LIST OF THE MEMBERS.

CHARLESTOWN:

Printed for the SOCIETY by ROBERT WELLS.

MDCCLXII.

FIG. 13
Rules of the St. Andrew's Club, at Charlestown in South-Carolina, Charlestown, 1762. The Charleston St. Andrew's Club, founded in 1729, was among the first in America. This little booklet, one of only two copies known to exist, includes a list of members in addition to the rules. (Cat. no. 10).

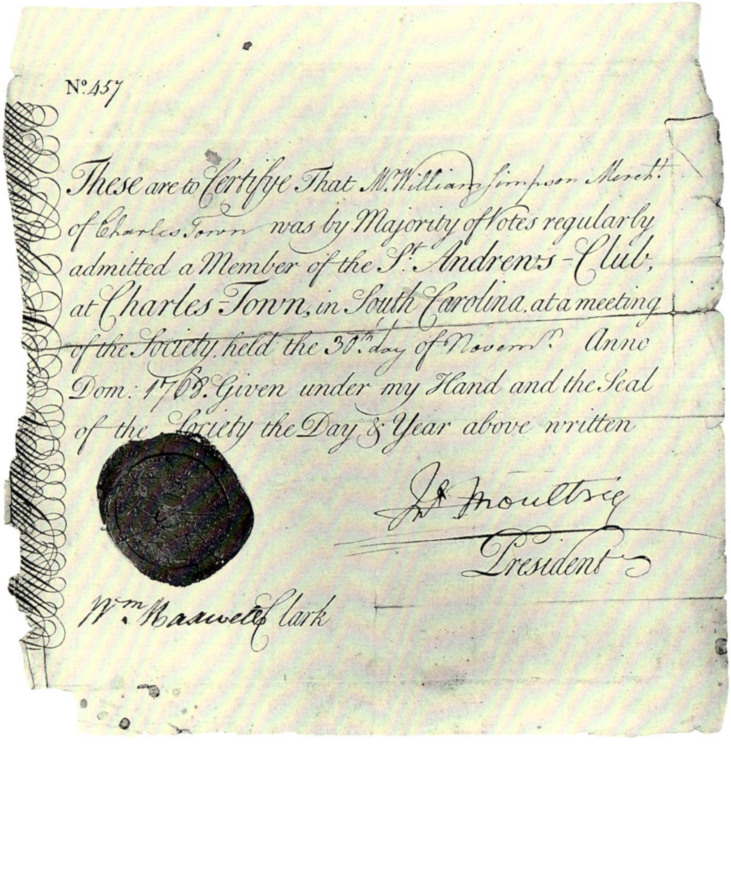

N.o 457

These are to Certifye That M.r William Simpson Merch.t of Charles Town was by Majority of Votes regularly admitted a Member of the S.t Andrews-Club, at Charles Town, in South Carolina, at a meeting of the Society, held the 30.th day of Novem.r Anno Dom: 1768. Given under my Hand and the Seal of the Society the Day & Year above written

Jn.o Moultrie
President

W.m Maxwell Clark

FIG. 14
Certificate of membership in the St.Andrew's Club of Charleston. Very few St. Andrew's Club documents of this vintage have survived from the colonial period. This certificate dates from 1768. (Cat. no. 10).

the Church of Scotland and, later, a defender of the American side in the quarrel with Britain. All five can be found together in an old leather-bound volume in the National Library of Scotland labeled as pamphlets by William Thom, which also includes several other works Thom published anonymously. The attribution of four of the pamphlets can be confirmed from some later printed advertisements by Thom's publishers but not the *Informations Concerning the Province of North Carolina*. We can only note some similarities in theme to Thom's other emigration pamphlets, such as his referring to Highland landlords as Egyptian taskmasters (p. 11). On the other hand, the pamphlet contains a description of Carolina based upon first-hand observation. Thom never visited America, although the author of the pamphlet does refer to many descriptive letters received from Carolina emigrants, so it could have been a composite work. In another emigration pamphlet, entitled *Information to Emigrants, being the Copy of a Letter from a Gentleman in North-America*, Thom did combine his own declarations in favor of emigration with a descriptive letter from a resident of New York, although in that pamphlet Thom acknowledged his borrowing from the letter.

Regardless of authorship, the tract contains much of interest. The author attributes Highland settlement in America to providential design—a favorite theme of Thom's—contending that Highland soldiers had been allowed to prosper in the recent war against France in order to open up to themselves "an agreeable and happy retreat, and a large and fertile field for them and their posterity to flourish in" (p. 10). The author also viewed Carolina as a retreat from the corruption he saw enveloping Britain: it was a land of "liberty and plenty"; there they could "carry over with them some remains of the true old British spirit before it be totally vitiated and extinguished" (pp. 9, 32).

12
Thomas Tod.
Consolatory Thoughts on American Independence; Shewing the Great Advantages that Will Arise from It to the Manufactures…of Britain.
Edinburgh, 1782.

The rebellion of the American colonies against British rule threatened to strike a serious blow to Scottish emigration and trade. While Scots both in Britain and in America divided in their positions on the war, nearly all hoped until the end for some means of reconciling the colonies to Britain. As it became clear that that would not happen, and that the thirteen colonies would be lost to Britain, Scottish merchants began to cast about for other ways to direct their commerce. Some tobacco merchants shifted their investment to the sugar trade with the still-dependent colonies of the British West Indies. Others suggested more ambitious ideas.

One such merchant was Thomas Tod of Edinburgh, a public-spirited commercial man with a long involvement with charitable causes, such as Edinburgh's Orphan Hospital. As the war drew to a close, Tod offered what he called "consolatory thoughts" to his countrymen on the ramifications of the loss of America. Perhaps, Tod suggested, the loss of America would not be disastrous for Scotland. A newly-independent America, as the leading commercial nation in the western hemisphere, was likely to extend its trade throughout the region, a full quarter of the globe. And since Britain was America's leading trading partner, it too would benefit from that greatly-expanded trade. Tod finished with an almost millennial conclusion, envisioning nations beating their swords into plowshares in an unencumbered era of free trade. Tod's pamphlet reflected in part the growing Scottish belief in the ability of commercial forces to dictate power relationships among nations, a position reflected in the early development of political economy in Scotland associated with such names as David Hume and Adam Smith. It also prefigured the expansion of Scottish interests in the Americas beyond the eastern seaboard of North America into the farther reaches to the north, the south, and the west during the first quarter of the nineteenth century, culminating in the Canadian settlements and the three Latin American colonizing ventures.

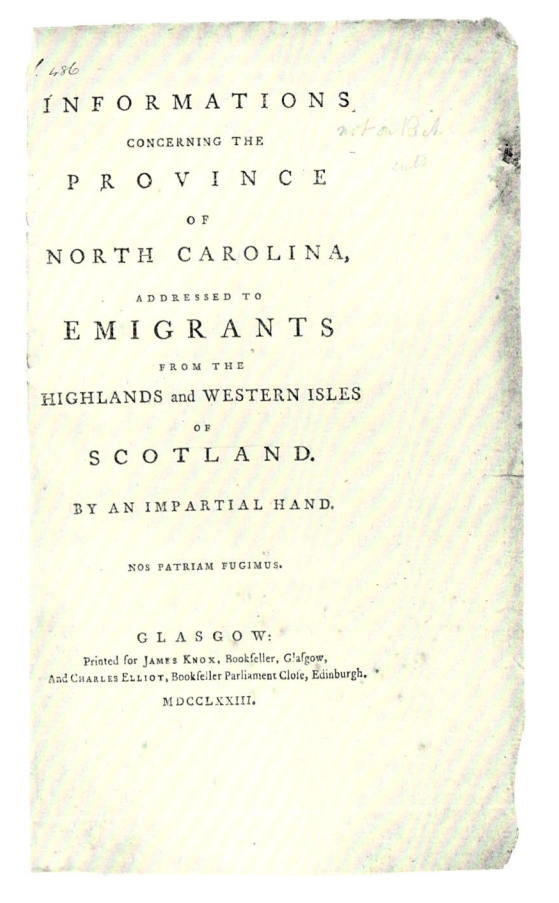

FIG. 15
Scotus Americanus, *Informations Concerning the Province of North Carolina*, Glasgow, 1773. This promotional tract encouraging Highlanders to settle in North Carolina was probably written by William Thom. The service of Scottish soldiers in the French and Indian War in America was providential, the author believed, in that it made known to so many Scots the blessings of residence in America. (Cat. no. 11).

13
Samuel Hull Wilcocke.
A Narrative of the Occurrences in the Indian Countries of North America, Since the Connexion of the Right Hon. the Earl of Selkirk with the Hudson's Bay Company, and His Attempt to Establish a Colony on the Red River. London, 1817.

The most fertile area for further Scottish settlement in America were the northern provinces that would become Canada. Even before the outbreak of the Revolutionary War, Scottish merchants were assuming substantial positions in Quebec and in Halifax; in the latter Scottish merchants organized a "North British Society." In 1779, a predominantly Scottish investment group in Montreal launched the "North West Company" of fur traders. The biggest obstacle to the success of that firm would be another Scot, Thomas Douglas, fifth Earl of Selkirk, an ambitious politician with even more ambitious colonial plans. He was the author of an important emigration tract, *Observations on the Present State of the Highlands of Scotland, with a View of the Causes and Probable Consequences of Emigration* (London, 1805). After some early settlement ventures on Prince Edward Island, Selkirk turned his attention to the Red River area in Central Canada and began actively to recruit Scottish Highlanders to settle there. Not everyone supported Selkirk's settlement plans. The North West Company saw him as interfering with their main business, which was the fur trade. In a series of published attacks, including the one shown here, the traders suggested that settlement in so remote an area as Red River was impractical and based upon misrepresentations in the printed advertisements of both the location and the climate, as well as impinging upon North West Company claims. The colony grew slowly, hampered by frequent attacks by agents of the rival company, with a population combining French Canadians, natives, and Scots Highlanders.

24 IMMIGRATION AND SETTLEMENT

FOR FURTHER READING

Bernard Bailyn, *Voyagers to the West: A Passage in the Peopling of America on the Eve of the Revolution* (New York, 1986).

William R. Brock with Dr. C. Helen, *Scotus Americanus: A Survey of the Sources for Links Between Scotland and America in the Eighteenth Century* (Edinburgh, 1982).

J. M. Bumsted, *The People's Clearance: Highland Emigration to British North America 1770–1815* (Edinburgh, 1982).

R. A. Cage, ed., *The Scots Abroad: Labour, Capital, Enterprise, 1750–1914* (London, 1985).

T. M. Devine, ed., *The Tobacco Lords* (Edinburgh, 1975).

T. M. Devine, *Scottish Emigration and Scottish Society* (Edinburgh, 1993).

Gordon Donaldson, *The Scots Overseas* (London, 1966).

Ian Charles Cargill Graham, *Colonists from Scotland: Emigration to North America, 1707–1783* (Ithaca, 1956).

Ned C. Landsman, *Scotland and its First American Colony 1683–1765* (Princeton, 1985).

Duane Meyer, *The Highland Scots of North Carolina, 1732–1776* (Chapel Hill, 1961).

John Reid, *Acadia, Maine, and New Scotland: Marginal Colonies in the Seventeenth Century* (Toronto, 1981).

Richard B. Sheridan, *Doctors and Slaves: A Medical and Demographic History of Slavery in the British West Indies, 1680–1834* (New York, 1985).

T.C. Smout, N.C. Landsman, and T.M. Devine, "Scottish Emigration in the Seventeenth and Eighteenth Centuries," in Nicholas Canny, ed., *Europeans on the Move: Studies on European Migration, 1500–1800* (Oxford, 1994).

A MAP of the CARIBBEE ISLANDS and GUAYANA, from the best Authorities.
Western Longitude from the Lizard, Computed at 5°.32 from London.
Western Longitude from the Meridian of Ferro.
ATLANTIC
OCEAN
THE CARIBBEE ISLANDS Named by the Spaniards ANTILLAS and WINDWARD ISLES
THE VIRGIN ISLANDS
THE LEEWARD CARIBBEE ISLANDS
THE GALLIONS PASSAGE
Anegada
Anguilla
St. Martins
Barbuda
Saba
ANTIGUA
GUADALOUPE
DOMINICA
MARTINICO
St. LUCIA
St. VINCENT
BARBADOS
GRANADA
Tabago
C. de Tres Puntas
TRINIDAD
GUAYANA
Aruacas
Carivas
Quirquiripas
MISSIONS OF THE CAPUCHINS from Catalonia
las Sierras de Orinoco
Cape Nassau
Mercioux
LAKE PARIMA

CHAPTER THREE: *Trade*

DAVID HANCOCK

Throughout the seventeenth century, Scotland was looked upon as one of the most impoverished regions of Europe. A stagnant economy was troubled by chronic famine and repeated commercial crises in export markets. In contrast, one hundred years later, at the outset of the Industrial Revolution, Scotland was at the center of Britain's economy. How this happened was, and is, much debated. One group of contemporary observers looked upon trade as "the conduit of riches" and, in hindsight, it appears that they may have been right: some of the most important underpinnings of Scotland's "modernization" were found in "an enriching Trade" with Britain's American colonies.

At least as early as 1650, Scots were trading with the colonies, although they could do so legally only under the cover of residence in England. Scots' share in Britain's foreign trade did not grow until the founding of the Company of Scotland Trading to Africa and the Indies in 1695, and the Union of Parliaments in 1707 that allowed Scots full right to trade and hold office in the empire. After permission to trade was granted, there ensued a rapid and sustained rise in commerce and a similar, if somewhat delayed rise in emigration, first of merchants and other profession als, later of settlers generally.

Scotland's shares of Britain's legal exports and imports were negligible at the turn of the eighteenth century, but rose to 11 percent by the 1740s—the same percentage as Scots in the overall population of the British Isles. The Scottish share of British exports remained at that level until the American Revolution, and its share of imports rose to 29 percent. Because the base of this success was Scotland's trade with the Thirteen Colonies, the American Revolution ravaged Scotland's overseas trade. By cutting Britain off from a monopoly commerce with her colonies, independence reduced Britain's trade. Scotland fell more than England, reducing its share of Britain's exports to 5 percent by 1791, and nearly halving its share of imports. As a result, Scottish traders turned their attention to the Caribbean, building new connections in the process.

The Act of Union in 1707 gave Scots access to the lucrative business of buying tobacco in the tobacco-producing regions of British America, and reselling it to the tobacco-loving peoples of continental Europe. Scots' overseas trade concentrated primarily on the three colonies of Virginia, Maryland, and North Carolina. The Scots began tobacco trading with the natural advantage, compared to English ports, of having easy access to a route to North America that was shorter and quicker

FIG. 16
This *Map of the Caribbee Islands and Guayana* (17 × 13″) from *Candid and Impartial Considerations on the Nature of the Sugar Trade*, 1763, by John Campbell, with its effort at meticulously detailing places in the West Indies, suggests something of the economic importance of the islands in the eighteenth century. Because of the enormous value of the sugar trade, West Indian islands were coveted far out of proportion to their size as imperial territories. (Cat. no. 17).

and, at least until 1755, relatively untroubled by privateers. Moreover, Scots went after the market for tobacco with extreme vigor and enthusiasm. The trade, in particular, spurred them to innovate in the technology and management of trans-oceanic shipping and in the handling of trade in the American hinterland. Glasgow merchants squeezed more goods into their holds, improved upon the time that their English competitors' ships spent in transit and in port, and used their ships more frequently each year than did competitors in London. Quintessentially frugal, Glasgow merchants also excelled in keeping operating costs low.

Lastly, and most importantly, Scots developed a distinctive banking and commercial practice that supported their trade. Glasgow's "tobacco lords" established the city's first three banks during the 1750s and 1760s and these provided ancillary sources of capital and credit to North American traders and planters. But they made their greatest innovation in the store system that they introduced in the 1740s and which prevailed over the supercargo system from the 1760s onward. In the supercargo system, American planters consigned their crops to English merchants from whom they also ordered European manufactures. In the factory system, by contrast, Glasgow partnerships consigned goods to employees living in the colonies and working out of firm "stores." Each partnership placed a chief factor (often a partner) over the entire operation in the colony, a subordinate salaried factor over one or more stores and, in each store, storekeepers and clerks. Each store dealt with local planters who, with their perennial need for equipment and slaves, bought goods on credit and tendered their tobacco as payment in advance of harvest. With chains of stores stretching deep into the interior and reaching previously ignored small and middling retail customers, the Scottish credit, marketing, and supply arrangement allowed merchants to penetrate the hinterland more deeply and thoroughly than any group of merchants had done before.

The results of the Scots' technological innovation in shipping, their commercial frugality, and their approach to handling and marketing were dramatic. Scottish imports of North American tobacco rose from 10 percent of total British imports of North American tobacco in 1738 to 50 percent in 1768–1770; in 1769, Scotland 's share (52 percent) actually outstripped England's share. Since Scotland and England together constituted a limited home market, most of the crop was re-exported to Europe, mainly France and the Netherlands.

To emphasize the importance and rise of tobacco in Scotland's trading relations with British America is not to ignore the growing significance of other commodities. Two—people and Caribbean crops—stand out. The growth in a Scottish-American trade in tobacco was linked, in many ways, to the exchange of people. Before 1700, Scotland experienced high levels of emigration, but most emigrants settled in Ireland and to a lesser extent, Poland and Scandinavia; only 7,000 emigrated to America. It was not until the eighteenth century that Scots went to British America in significant numbers, and most of them seen to have come after 1763. Migration totals for the eighteenth century are still uncertain; recent estimates suggest that 75,000 Scots left their homeland for America between 1700 and 1775. Scots constituted a substantial portion of the settlers of Britain's undeveloped territories in America. Nearly half of the grants of 100 acres or more in St. Christopher's French Quarter, for instance, went to Scots, after Britain finally acquired title to the island in 1713. To the west in Jamaica, some 20 percent of all land patentees who received governmental grants of land between 1714 and 1754 were Scots; in the latter year, Scots constituted nearly a quarter of all landholders. A new wave of Scots swept over British America in the aftermath of the Seven Years War, especially in the newly-acquired sugar-producing Ceded Islands. Well over a third of the purchasers of land in Tobago, Grenada, St. Vincent, and Dominica were Scots. Only 11 percent of the combined population of England, Wales, Scotland, and Ireland, Scots thus formed a disproportionately large group of settlers in the empire's new lands. Given their tendency to do business with kin and

The present State of the Tobacco-Plantations in *America*.

Before the present War, *France* and *Spain* annually took off near 20000 Hogshead of *Virginia* and *Maryland*-Tobacco; but of late both those Kingdoms have been otherwise supply'd.

The Troubles in *Sweden*, *Poland*, *Russia*, &c. have prevented the usual Exportations of great Quantities of Tobacco to those Parts.

Virginia and *Maryland* have severely felt the Loss of such Exportations, having so far reduc'd the Planters, that for several Years past, the whole Product of their Tobacco would hardly clothe the Servants that made it, notwithstanding the ready and earnest Endeavours of the Lords Commissioners of Trade, &c. to prevent such Mischiefs, and encourage the Tobacco-Trade.

This hath produc'd two Effects.

Ist. Some, in hopes of better Success, have continued Planting, till they have run themselves so far in Debt, that they have been forc'd to sell part of their Land and Servants, to secure the rest.

IId. Others, out of meer Necessity, have fallen into the Manufacturing of Woollen, Cotton, Flax, Leather, &c. Which they have brought to such Perfection, that four whole Counties, and part of several others, not only clothed themselves, but sold great Quantities of the same Manufactures to other neighbouring Counties.

These Plantations of *Virginia* and *Maryland*, in Times of Peace, yearly; (and in the War, in Fleets) have taken off not less than the Value of 300000 *l. Sterl.* in the Woollen and other Manufactures of this Kingdom; and, in return, send the Product of their Labour, Tobacco; which pays annually to the Crown above 400000 *l.* Customs, exclusive of what is drawn-back, by Debenture, on Exportation.

Wherefore it is humbly hop'd, a general Liberty, and further Encouragement may speedily be given, for the Exporting of Tobacco, and all other Products of the Plantations, and Manufactures of *Great Britain* not counterband, for *France*, &c. to prevent the impending Ruin of the Plantations, and regain the advantagious Trade of sending the Woollen and other Manufactures of *Great Britain* to those Colonies, which otherwise must annually decrease.

Note, Establishing of Woollen, and other Manufactures in *America*, will not only lessen the Planting Tobacco, but consequently very much diminish the Revenue and Navigation of this Kingdom.

FIG. 17
The Present State of the Tobacco-Plantations in America. [London(?), 1708?]. Tobacco, along with sugar, was a prime commodity in the colonial period, and in the commerce of both, Scots were major players. (Cat. no. 15).

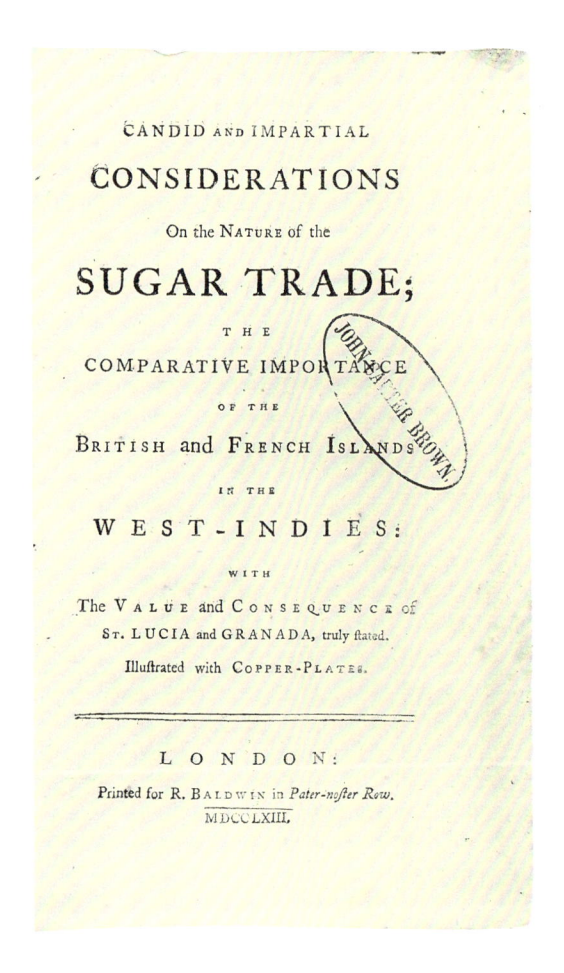

FIG. 18
John Campbell, *Candid and Impartial Considerations on the Nature of the Sugar Trade*, London, 1763. Campbell was a highly regarded authority on imperial trade, one of a number of Scots who helped the British empire to function. He ended his career as the agent of King George III in Georgia. (Cat. no. 17).

countrymen over others, the increased presence of Scots in British America reinforced the expansion of Scottish-American trade.

Many of the links between emigrants and traders were severed by the American War for Independence; the tobacco trade, for instance, never fully recovered. Yet other forms of trade with other parts of America rose in their stead. Throughout the century, sugar figured as the most important British import from any region, and it became an increasingly significant commodity in Scotland's trading portfolio. Most major Glasgow tobacco houses also traded in sugar and rum. Richard and Alexander Oswald, for instance, traded in sugar and rum as early as 1723 and, over the years, they increased the amount of the sweet stuff they imported from the British West Indies. By 1764, they were annually importing 195 hogsheads of sugar, on top of 890 hogsheads of tobacco. In the Scottish economy overall, sugar and rum accounted for 9 percent to 15 percent of the imports from the colonies between 1750 and 1770, a period when Britain's sugar-producing capacity increased with the acquisition of the Ceded Islands.

Despite these gains, however, it was not until the last decades of the eighteenth century that Glasgow sugar-trading rose to real importance. By that time, there were eight sugar refineries in the Glasgow area. With the tradition of sugar importing long established, the facilities for processing it ready to use, and the commercial lines for North American tobacco temporarily cut and permanently reduced by American independence, Scotland's trade in West Indian sugar and rum took off. In the seven years that succeeded the Peace of Paris, for instance, sugar-related imports to Scotland increased more than 200 percent and exports to sugar-producing colonies rose more than 150 percent. By 1790, British West Indian imports constituted 22 percent of Scotland's total imports from around the world, and exports to the West Indies 26 percent. The move to sugar, and similar shifts to other American crops like cotton, evidence the resilience of the Scottish-American trade connection. (Fig. 16).

Although we know something about the scale of Scotland's trade with America, we still do not have a very full understanding of the role that trade played in the modernization of Scotland and America. The answer, of course, will lie not solely in trade, but in some combination of trade and other factors. Glasgow merchants, we now know, invested heavily in manufacturing and industrial ventures of the eighteenth century, yet this leaves many questions unanswered: Were these ventures profitable for their sponsors, or were they largely charitable ways to spend the wealth generated by foreign trade? What was the relationship between the ups and downs of trade and the increase in ancillary investments like road-, bridge-, and canal-building? And how did such modernizing improvements affect the outward flow of Scots to the empire?

The effects of trade on the colonies are even less clear. What impact, for instance, did the innovative factory system have on the economic and social development of Maryland, Virginia, and North Carolina? Some have found that it encouraged a state and *mentalité* of indebtedness among many planters, but it may also have been a principal source of tools and consumer goods to smaller farmers, as well as a means of disseminating new agricultural technologies. Could it have shifted, for instance, the economies of tobacco-growing in favor of smaller farms or different crops? What influence, moreover, did the Scots in British America—Scots from all walks of life, and not just from the merchant classes—exert on the conduct of inland commerce? The contribution of Scots, distinct from that of the English, awaits further study.

14
William Paterson.
An Essay Concerning Inland and Foreign, Publick and Private Trade.
[Edinburgh(?), 1705].

Throughout the seventeenth and eighteenth centuries, Scotland's trade with America was conducted in accordance with the precepts of mercantilism. According to this theory, national power and wealth were best augmented by increasing exports and collecting bullion, especially gold. Under mercantilist thinking, a state strove to sell more than it bought so as to stockpile precious metals and raw material. As a result, foreign trade was favored above domestic trade, and manufacturing above agriculture. At the beginning of the eighteenth century, amidst difficulties in the commercial sector and calamities of famine, enterprising Scots eager for economic growth and "sensible of their poverty" believed they could alleviate their suffering with "an enriching Trade." According to this *Essay* of 1705, the best opportunities for enrichment lay in the colonial trades England already enjoyed. To many, the establishment of "a Scheme of Trade" wherein Scots would gain "free and uninterrupted commerce with all the American Plantations" would stimulate Scottish manufacturing and increase exports.

15
The Present State of the Tobacco-Plantations in America.
[London(?), 1708?].

From a mercantilist standpoint, a trade in tobacco was ideal for a developing economy. Through it, Scots acquired a commodity import that came from a friendly colony, rather than a competing state; that required packaging and processing at home; that produced an extremely valuable re-export to the Continent; and that caused men and development capital to flow overseas. For most of the seventeenth century, the amount produced by North American planters rose, albeit at a decreasing rate, even as prices fell. But, from 1680 onwards, output levelled off and remained steady through 1710. Slowdown and stagnation took their toll on the planters, who fell in debt or adopted alternative pursuits. As *The Present State* suggests, contemporaries blamed the restrictive nature of mercantilist policy, especially in time of war. (Fig. 17). War closed many European markets to American tobacco; in the early 1700s, it closed France, Spain, Russia, and Sweden to Scottish re-exports of American tobacco. The broadside bears witness to the costs of mercantilism. This copy is undated; but a copy in the British Library is dated, in a contemporary hand, 17 February 1708, and suggests London as the place of publication.

16
The Caledonian Mercury. Edinburgh, 1753.

Scottish newspapers complement shipping records in reconstructing trade between Scotland and America. When shipping records are incomplete or non-existent, newspapers often offer the only form of data. They provided merchants, customers, and emigrants with three sorts of information. First they recorded the arrival and departure of merchant vessels. Second, they provided subsequent information about the affairs of these vessels and their passengers, such as the Scottish encounters with Spanish privateers in Honduras Bay, recorded here as "Plantation News." They also relayed relevant information about Scots abroad—their harvests, misfortunes, promotions, or deaths. Finally, they advertised the availability of berths to would-be emigrants, as in the case of the sloop *Dolphin*, lying in Dundee harbor and bound for Jamaica.

17
John Campbell. *Candid and Impartial Considerations on the Nature of the Sugar Trade; The Comparative Importance of the British and French Islands in the West-Indies: with the Value and Consequence of St. Lucia and Granada, Truly Stated.* London, 1763.

John Campbell (1708–1775) was one of the most prolific Scots writing about the connections between empire and commerce in the middle decades of the eighteenth century. Both his experiences and subjects evidenced the opportunities open to Scots during the Hanoverian period. Born in Edinburgh, he

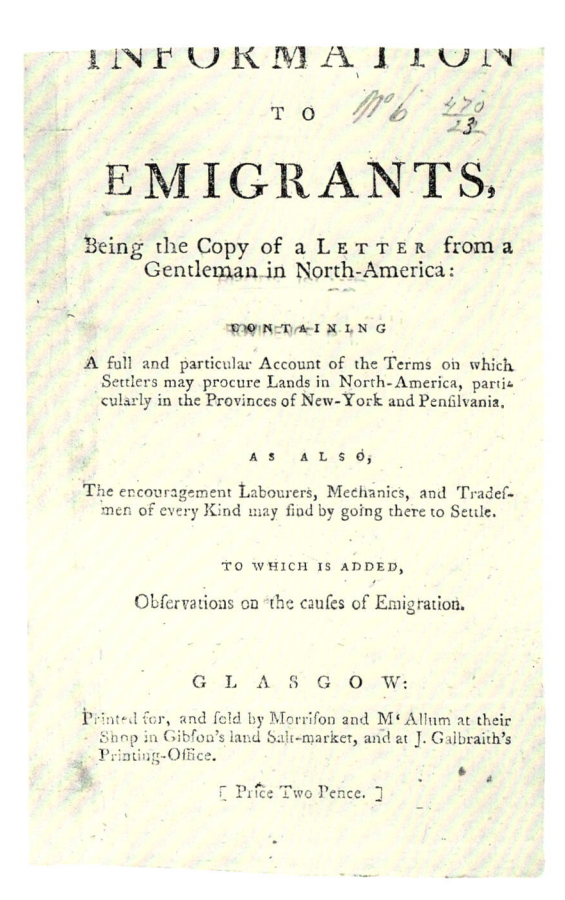

FIG. 19
William Smith, *Information to Emigrants*, Glasgow, [1773]. Smith was a prominent lawyer in colonial New York, a Presbyterian, and an active writer who published among other works a history of the colony. This copy was badly trimmed at the top, but the pamphlet is so rare one must be grateful even for a copy in poor condition. (Cat. no. 18).

moved to Windsor as a child and trained as a clerk in a London attorney's office, after which he left law for literature. His early works included a history of the campaigns of Prince Eugene of Savoy and the Duke of Marlborough and the relatively unstudied *Travels and Adventures of Edmund Bevan, Esq. formerly a Merchant in London*. But imperial commerce was his specialty. In 1762, at the request of Lord Bute, he penned an extensive history of the Caribbean islands ceded to Britain by France in the Seven Years War. The following year, he issued *Candid and Impartial Considerations on the Nature of the Sugar Trade*, a treatise that applied the ideas of the Enlightenment and its agricultural Improvers to the Ceded Islands rapidly filling up with fellow Scots. (Fig. 18). In 1765, George III appointed Campbell his agent in Georgia, a post he held until death. Samuel Johnson considered him "the richest author that ever grazed the common of literature"; Horace Walpole later described him as "one of the ablest and most beautiful writers of his country."

18
William Smith.
Information to Emigrants.
Glasgow, [1773].

The emigration of Scots to British-America is an often neglected factor in the history of Scottish-American trade. It was especially significant in the decades following the Peace of 1763 when a manic "Spirit of Emigration" prevailed "in several parts of Scotland." In the years 1769–1776, as many as 20,000 moved to the Thirteen Colonies. This supply of potential laborers was, in many instances, organized by Scottish merchants and their shipmasters, agents, and correspondents. Driven by a desire for profits, trans-Atlantic merchants like George and John Buchanan of Greenock pursued a lively trade in gathering, transporting, and marketing settlers, servants, and convicts. To attract the right kind of laborers, such merchants relied primarily on public information distribution networks: they posted notices in pubs and marketplaces,

FIG. 20
Adam Smith, *An Inquiry into the Nature and Causes of the Wealth of Nations*, London, 1776. A foundation stone of all economic theory by one of the great geniuses of the Scottish Enlightenment, this book was to some degree the product of the historical experience of Scotland in matters of commerce and industry. It includes much commentary on trade with America. (Cat. no. 20).

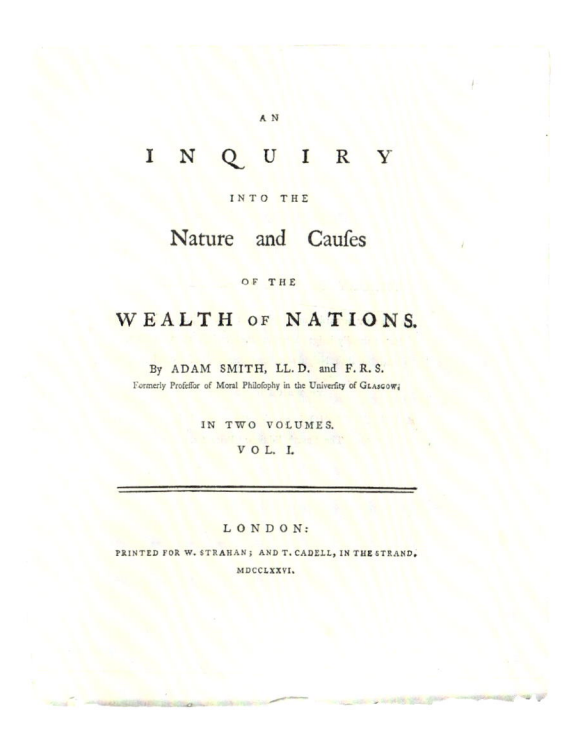

[To face Page 37.]

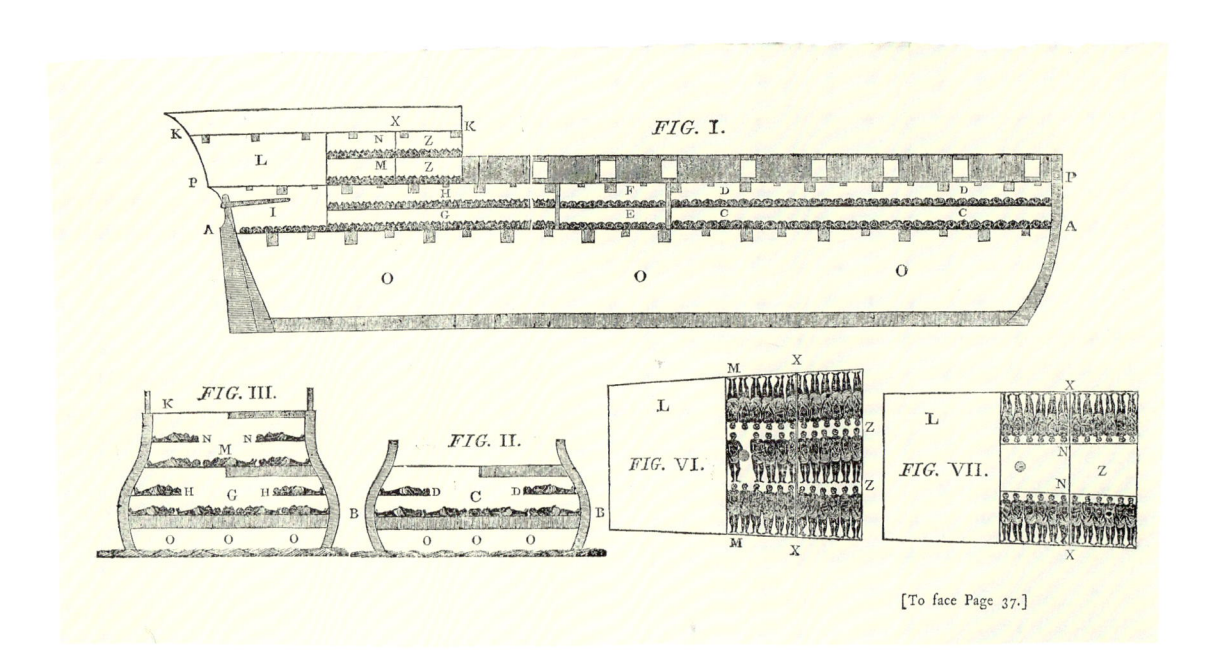

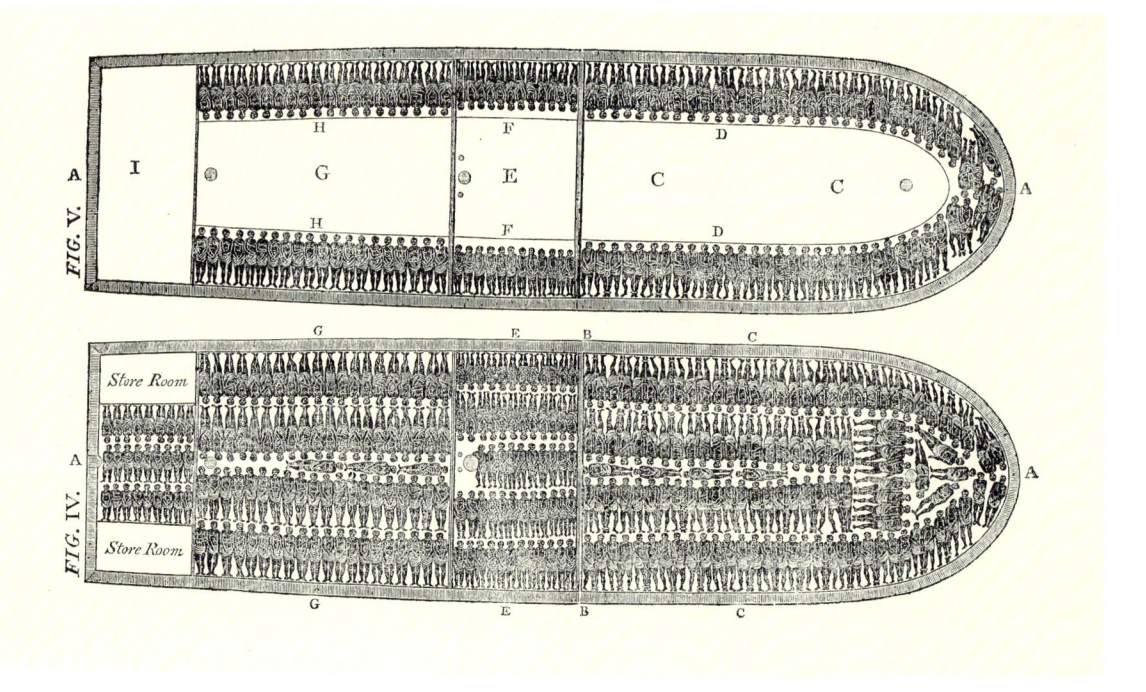

printed ads in newspapers, and in the countryside distributed leaflets and pamphlets, such as the one exhibited here advertising the wonders of New York. (Fig. 19).

19
David Loch.
Essay on the Trade, Commerce, and Manufactures of Scotland.
Edinburgh, 1775.

Having trained as a sailor, risen to the command of a vessel, and settled in Leith as a shipowner and merchant, the Scot David Loch (d. 1780) was one of Hanoverian Scotland's most well-informed and influential observers of commercial practice. His *Essay* of 1775, written at the outset of the War with America, typically paid the conflict little attention. He himself had twice visited the colonies and traded there "but not to advantage," because he "could not get payments." His chief concerns, like those of most Scots merchants of the day, were the debts owed by colonists to Scotsmen. "When the Americans come to their senses," he believed, "they will find it for their interests as well as their safety and conveniency, to strengthen the bond of friendship with the Mother Country." One year after the publication of this treatise, Scotland's Trustees for Fisheries, Manufactures, and Improvements named Loch Inspector-General for Woolen Manufacture.

20
Adam Smith.
An Inquiry into the Nature and Causes of the Wealth of Nations.
London, 1776.

There is perhaps no more incisive or influential commentary on the course of economic development in Britain and her colonies than Adam Smith's *Wealth of Nations*. The only child of the Comptroller of Customs at Kirkcaldy, Smith (1723–1790) was schooled in Kirkcaldy, Glasgow, and Oxford. Returning to Kirkcaldy in 1746, he gave a series of lec-

FIG. 21a and 21b
A cargo of slaves as transported from Africa to the West Indies. For millennia human slavery had been a totally unquestioned social and economic institution throughout virtually the entire world. It was only in the eighteenth century that organized protest against it arose, in particular against the horrific suffering caused by the Atlantic slave trade. Scots were deeply implicated in the slave trade, but they were also in the forefront of opposition to it. Agitation against the trade and works such as James Ramsay's led to Parliamentary hearings. These engravings appeared in *An Abstract of the Evidence Delivered before a Select Committee of the House of Commons in the years 1790, and 1791; on the Part of the Petitioners for the Abolition of the Slave Trade* (Edinburgh, 1791). (Cat. no. 22).

tures in political economy and English literature. In 1751, he was elected to the chair of logic at the University of Glasgow and the following year, he was granted its chair of moral philosophy. The lectures he gave at Glasgow laid the foundation for his argument in the *Wealth of Nations*. In 1763, he resigned his professorship and accepted a position as tutor to the young 3rd Duke of Buccleuch, which post he held for three years. Back in Kirkcaldy, he began work on the *Wealth of Nations*. In writing this treatise, Smith aimed to provide an analytical system which would demolish governmental regulations binding the metropolitan center to the colonial periphery and would explode mercantilist assumptions linking state management to a rise in colonial "wealth and greatness." Personal interests and unfettered energies, Smith believed, would better increase such wealth. In general, government should repeal legislative regulations that impeded individual endeavor, because they artificially restricted the workings of the market and impeded the division of labor. In short, he objected to forcing "part of the industry of the country into a channel less advantageous than that in which it would run of its own accord." (Fig. 20).

21
James Tweed.
Considerations and Remarks on the Present State of the Trade to Africa.
London, 1771.

While at first glance it may appear that before the American Revolution Glasgow's African trade was insubstantial, closer study of the matter reveals the contrary. Elusive scraps scattered about the Port Glasgow and Greenock port books suggest typical shuttle operations of the 1730s: merchants leaving Port Glasgow, shuttling between Virginia and Jamaica several times (bringing lumber, corn, and European manufactures from Virginia to Jamaica and, in return, slaves, sugar and wine to Virginia), before returning to Scotland with tobacco. More importantly, notwithstanding the denunciations uttered by the likes of intellectuals like David Hume, Scots slave traders flourished in England's slave-trading ports of London, Bristol, and Liverpool. One such trader was James Tweed, the author of this pamphlet. A native of Glasgow, he had served for fifteen years as the chief agent of a Sierra Leone slave "factory" owned and operated by the London Scots Richard Oswald, Alexander Grant, John Mill, and Augustus and John Boyd. Returning to London in the late 1760s, Tweed established his own independent African trading house and, in this pamphlet, he described in rare detail "the miserable Condition of the Forts, the Acts of the Governors, and other Abuses worthy attending to" along the Windward Coast. The pamphlet was published anonymously, but the attribution to Tweed was made one year later by "An African Merchant" in *A Treatise upon the Trade from Great Britain to Africa*.

22
James Ramsay.
An Essay on the Treatment and Conversion of African Slaves in the British Sugar Colonies.
London, 1784.

Scots were in the vanguard of slave-trading, but they also led the charge for abolition. James Ramsay (1733–1789), a native of Fraserburgh and a medical graduate of King's College, Aberdeen, enlisted in the Royal Navy as a surgeon. On one of his voyages, he was called upon to provide medical assistance to a slaver that had fallen in with the fleet; he went on board the vessel and ministered to both white and black patients but, on returning, broke his thigh bone. The injury led him to leave the Navy and don the cloth. Admitted to orders in 1762, he returned to the Caribbean and took up a living in St. Kitts, where he took a strong interest in the welfare of slaves. Eventually tiring of the struggle with the planters over their barbarous treatment of slaves, he returned to Britain. His *Essay* stands as the opening salvo in his campaign for the amelioration of the slave condition. (Figs. 21a and 21b). In essence, it argues that the advancement of slaves improves their social and religious importance; the capacity for the advancement of blacks is full and on a par with whites; and their improvement should comprehend general education, religious training, legal justice, governmental participation, and family life. Africans, in Ramsay's view, were not an inferior group. Although he did not call for immediate abolition, his essay sounded an alarm that planters and slavers did not ignore.

FOR FURTHER READING

T. M. Devine, *The Tobacco Lords: A Study of the Tobacco Merchants of Glasgow and their Trading Activities, c. 1740–90* (Edinburgh, 1975).

T. M. Devine, "Glasgow Merchants and the Collapse of the Tobacco Trade, 1775–1783," *Scottish Historical Review*, v. 52 (April 1973), 50–74.

T. M. Devine, "An Eighteenth-Century Business Elite: Glasgow-West India Merchants, c. 1750–1815," *Scottish Historical Review*, v. 57 (April 1978), 40–67.

Jacob Price, *Capital and Credit in British Overseas Trade: The View from the Chesapeake, 1700–76* (Cambridge, Mass., 1980).

Jacob Price, "New Time Series for Scotland's and Britain's Trade with the Thirteen Colonies and States, 1740 to 1791," *William and Mary Quarterly*, v. 32 (April 1975), 307–25.

Jacob Price, "The Rise of Glasgow in the Chesapeake Tobacco Trade, 1707–1775," *William and Mary Quarterly*, v. 11 (April 1954), 179–99.

T. C. Smout, *Scottish Trade on the Eve of Union, 1660–1707* (Edinburgh, 1963).

T. C. Smout, "Where had the Scottish economy got to by the third quarter of the eighteenth century?" in Istvan Hont and Michael Ignatieff, eds., *Wealth and Virtue: The Shaping of Political Economy in the Scottish Enlightenment* (Cambridge, 1983), 45–72.

McINTOSH

A Creek Chief.

Philadelphia Published by E.C. Biddle

CHAPTER FOUR: # *Scots in Georgia and the British Floridas*

ROBIN FABEL

Of the famous thirteen colonies that declared their independence from Britain in 1776, only Georgia was founded as late as the eighteenth century. East and West Florida became British colonies in 1763, but were not involved in the independence movement. In addition to the Amerindians already there, immigrants peopled all three of these new British colonies. Many whites, willingly, and blacks, involuntarily, came from existing colonies, but many immigrants also came directly from the British Isles, particularly from Scotland.

The reasons for the huge eighteenth-century Scottish exodus to America are too well known to need elaboration here. Perhaps the most important were the economic hardship caused by an expanding population without gainful employment—population grew particularly fast in the quarter-century before the Revolution—and confidence that a better life was possible in America.

FIG. 22
The Creek Chief McIntosh in tartan fabric, from Thomas McKenney and James Hall, *History of the Indian Tribes of North America, with Biographical Sketches and Anecdotes of the Principal Chiefs*, Philadelphia, 1836–1844. The extensive Scottish involvement in back-country trade with the Indians is manifested in the appearance of Scottish tartan patterns in Indian dress, beginning early in the eighteenth century.

Bernard Bailyn has shown that, in proportion to total population, Scotland sent more emigrants to the American colonies than did England in the latter eighteenth century and that they originated, overwhelmingly, in the Northwest Highlands.

Highlanders enjoyed a reputation for military prowess. When, in Georgia's infancy, its Trustees sited a settlement on the colony's border with potentially hostile Spanish Florida, they recruited Highlanders for it. These Gaelic-speaking migrants sailed in 1735, establishing themselves at New Inverness, later renamed Darien, on the Altamaha River. A group of Lowland Scots settled, less permanently, at Josephs Town on the Savannah River. The Lowlanders soon moved downstream to the capital, Savannah, where, criticizing the Trustee style of government, under which Georgia fumbled and languished until 1754, they soon became known as Malcontents. Malcontents organized a St. Andrew's Club in Savannah to pursue conviviality as well as to pillory the establishment. Refounded in 1764, a new St. Andrew's Club concerned itself with charitable activities. Eating and heavy drinking were, however, the main preoccupations of Georgia's Scots every November 30, when they honored St. Andrew, Scotland's patron saint, in settlements throughout the province.

During the two decades of Trustee rule in Georgia, prohibitions on the importation of slaves and rum thwarted the creation of plantations and trade with the West Indies, which would otherwise have been natural economic developments. To the extent to which Georgia's economy thrived in these early years, it did so because of the deerskin trade.

That trade was dominated by Scots. Names like Campbell, MacDonald, McIntosh, and McQueen occur and recur in the partnerships of the backcountry Indian trade. But the name repeated most often is McGillivray. Even before Georgia obtained its charter in 1732, Archibald McGillivray, exiled from Scotland after the Jacobite rising of 1715, had traded in what would become Georgia from a base in South Carolina. He headed the largest of the several companies trading with the Creek Indians in that era. His younger kinsman, Lachlan McGillivray of Dunmaglass, arrived in Georgia in 1736. As trader, landholder, and diplomatic link between the colonial governments of Georgia and South Carolina and the local tribes, Lachlan was destined to outshine Archibald. Another kinsman, John McGillivray, would be Mobile's leading trader in the 1760s. Lachlan's marriage to Sehoy, a woman of the influential Creek Wind clan, explains in part his eminence. Their son, Alexander, would become even more famous than his father in the postcolonial era.

Marrying an Indian wife was all but universal among the backcountry traders. The practice served not only to perpetuate Scottish names among their descendants but also Scottish culture. One consequence was the "scotchification" of Indian clothing. Cloth and clothing were the commonest items traded for deerskins. Amerindians often copied or adapted what they saw. They particularly liked tartan patterns, sometimes wore the feathered bonnet and, with their detestation of breeches, saw merit in, and could identify with, the Scottish substitute for them. (Fig. 22). William Bartram, noted traveler of the southern colonies in the 1770s, likened the colored flaps the Creeks wore to the Highlanders' kilt.

In the Revolutionary era the Scots traders of Georgia realized that the new United States could not supply the manufactured goods on which their livelihoods depended. Many of them in consequence were Loyalists. In 1776, in response to the political crisis with Great Britain, the state legislature prohibited natives of Scotland from practicing commerce in Georgia or even settling there.

Scots were even more prominent in the British colonies of East and West Florida than they were in Georgia. Originally Spanish, these provinces, the spoils of victory in war, became part of the British empire in 1763. In the previous year, John Stuart, the Scottish earl of Bute, had become George III's chief minister. He appointed Scotsmen to both governorships in the Floridas.

To St. Augustine, East Florida's capital, he sent James Grant, a native of Banffshire and victor in a recently ended campaign against the Cherokees. To Pensacola, the capital of West Florida, went George Johnstone, a Dumfriesshire-born captain of the Royal Navy. Several of Johnstone's entourage were Scots. The best remembered, though not for what he did in Florida, from which he decamped after a year, is James MacPherson, who was celebrated in his day as the translator of the *Ossian* epic.

Enhancing Scottish influence in Britain's "Deep South" colonies was the man who, in 1762, at the age of forty-four, became Superintendent for Indian Affairs in the southern department. His name, like that of King George's favorite minister, the Earl of Bute, although they were unrelated, was John Stuart. A native of Inverness, Stuart had enjoyed a varied naval, military, and mercantile career.

FIG. 23a and 23b
A Map of South Carolina and a Part of Georgia, 1780. The original of this splendid two-piece map when put together measures 4 ft. high. Published in London by William Faden, "Successor" of the late Thomas Jeffrys as "Geographer to the King," the cartouche announced that the map was prepared with the guidance of "John Stuart, Esq., His Majesty's Superintendant of Indian Affairs." The Scottish administrator Stuart is credited with having kept the southern Indian tribes safely on the British side during the American war for independence.

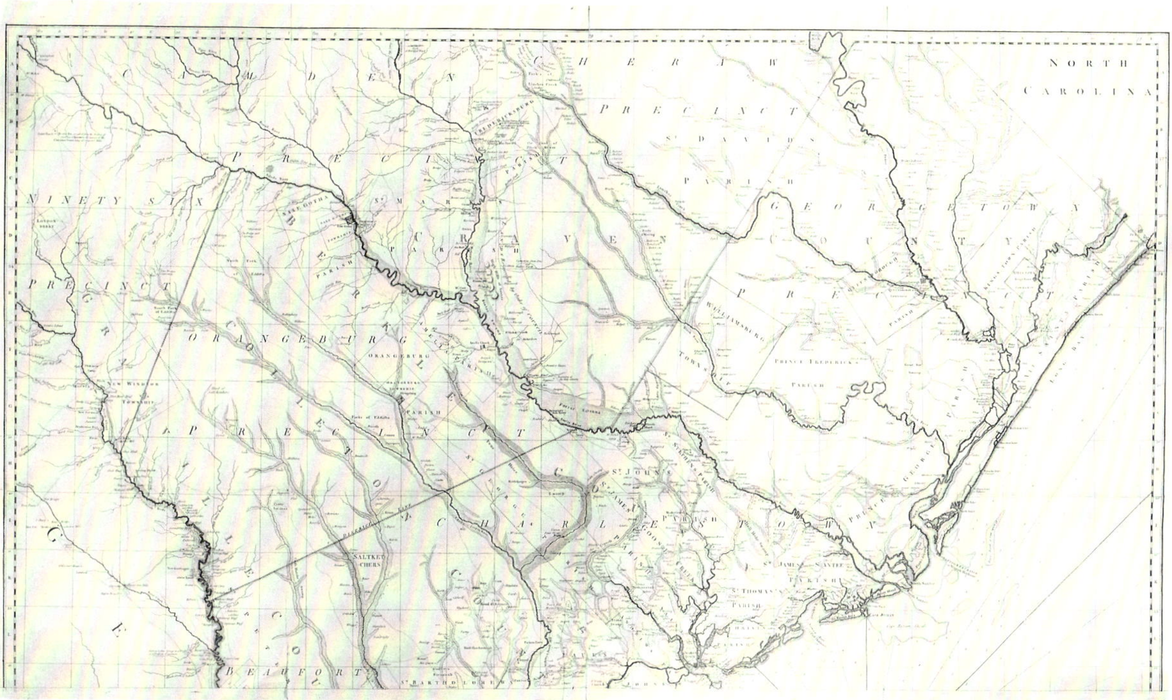
NORTH CAROLINA
NINETY SIX
PRECINCT
CHERAW
PRECINCT
ST DAVIDS
PARISH
GEORGETOWN
COUNTY
PRECINCT
WILLIAMSBURG
TOWNSHIP
PRINCE FREDERICKS
PARISH
ORANGEBURG
ORANGEBURG
NEW WINDSOR
TOWNSHIP
ST JOHNS
PARISH
ST JAMES SANTEE
PARISH
ST THOMAS'S
PARISH
SALTKETCHERS
BEAUFORT
ST BARTHOLOMEWS

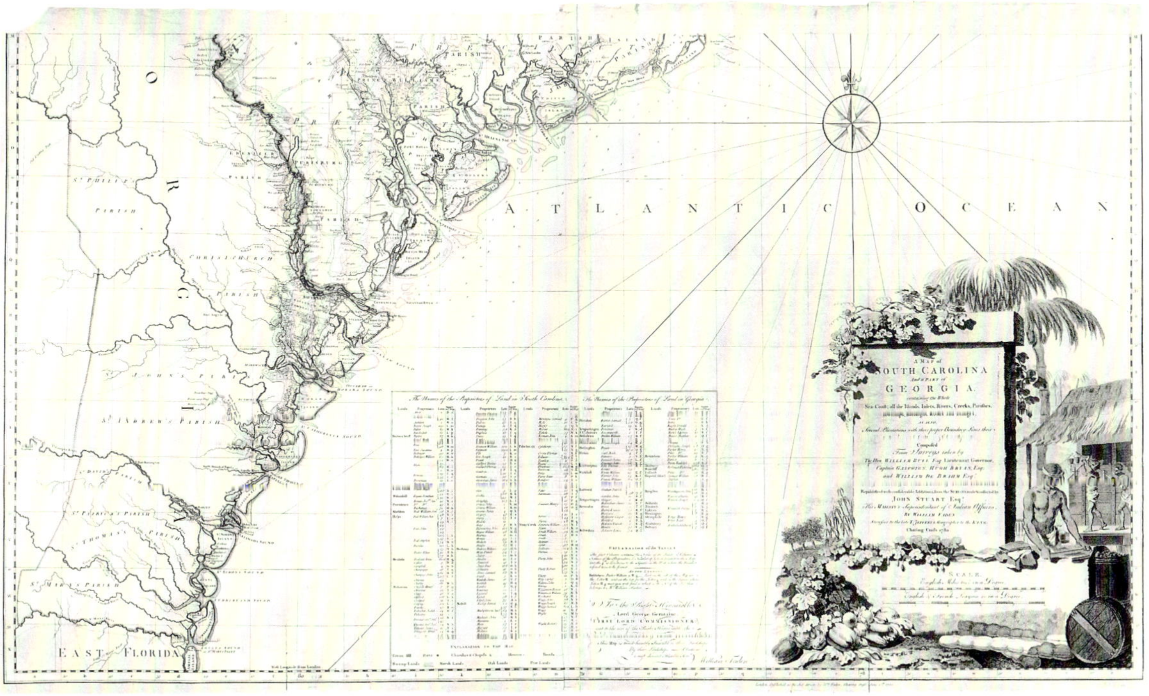
ATLANTIC OCEAN
ST PHILIPS
PARISH
CHRISTCHURCH
PARISH
ST ANDREWS PARISH
ST PATRICKS PARISH
ST THOMAS PARISH
ST MARYS PARISH
EAST FLORIDA
A MAP of
SOUTH CAROLINA
And a PART of
GEORGIA.
containing the Whole
Sea Coast; all the Islands, Inlets, Rivers, Creeks, Parishes,
AS ALSO
Compiled
From Surveys taken by
The Hon. WILLIAM BULL Esq. Lieutenant Governor,
Captain GASCOIGN, HUGH BRYAN, Esq.
and WILLIAM DE BRAHM Esq.
JOHN STUART Esq.
BY WILLIAM FADEN
Charing Cross 1780
SCALE.

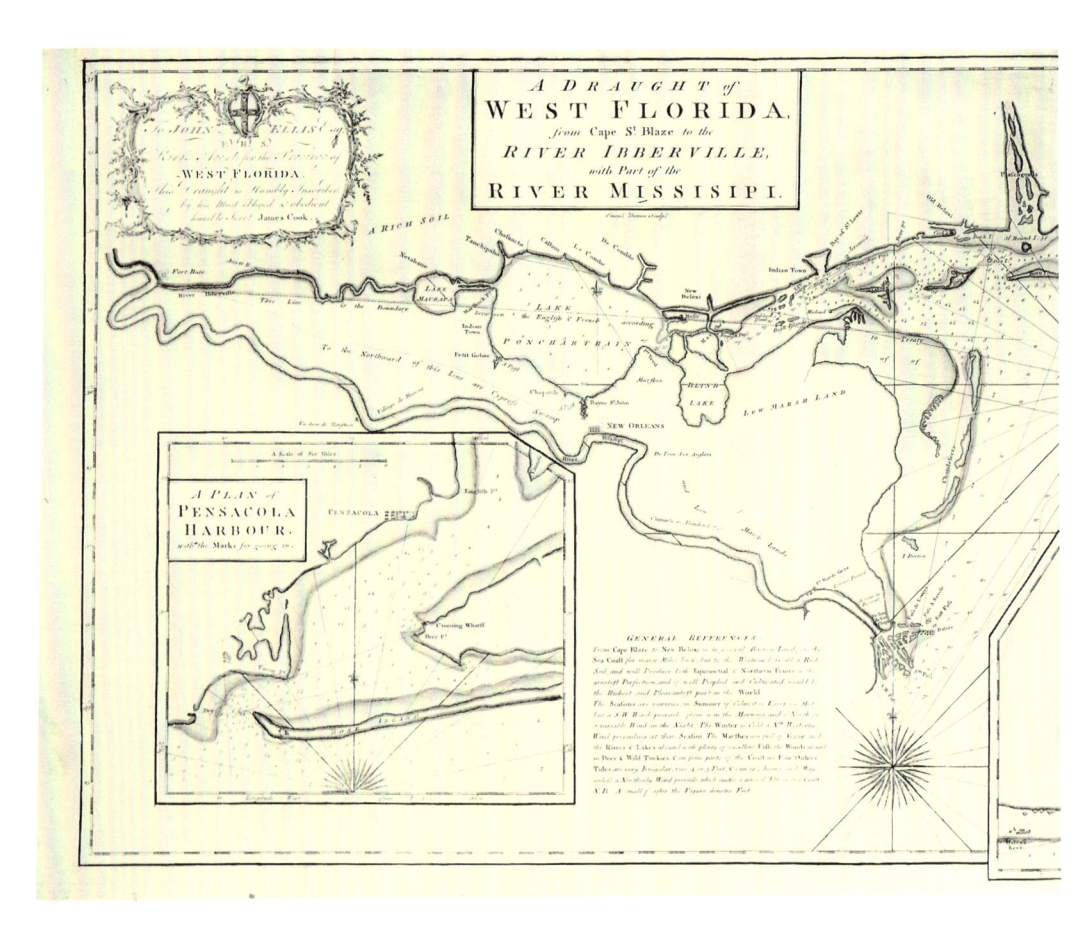

FIG. 24
James Cook, *A Draught of West Florida*, London, 1766 (20¾ × 50½"). The Floridas, originally Spanish, became part of the British empire in 1763. From the beginning, Scotsmen were the most influential figures in their history as British possessions. The first governor of West Florida, the Scot George Johnstone, successfully promoted British settlement in the colony, the area of which extended all the way to the Mississippi. Florida reverted to Spanish control in 1783.

It was, however, his close knowledge of the Cherokees that particularly fitted Stuart for the superintendentship he would hold for seventeen years. His opinions on policy often differed from those of colonial governors and his superiors in London. The high respect in which the southern tribes held him, however, enabled him to solve peacefully many problems that at the time were perplexing relations between whites and Amerindians. (Figs. 23a and 23b).

When Revolution came, he negotiated peace between the Choctaws and Creeks, who had been fighting for a decade, and used his influence, with almost total success, to ensure that the southern tribes stayed loyal to the British cause. While holding office, Stuart worked through deputy superintendents in the farflung area under his jurisdiction, and it is clear that he preferred them to be Scots and, if possible, members of his family.

Few Scots who became important in the southernmost colonies were of wealthy or aristocratic background. Lachlan McGillivray began his career in Georgia as an indentured servant; John Stuart had joined the Royal Navy as a mere ablebodied seaman in 1748. But there were rich and high-born Scots who took an interest in Florida and had a great influence over its development.

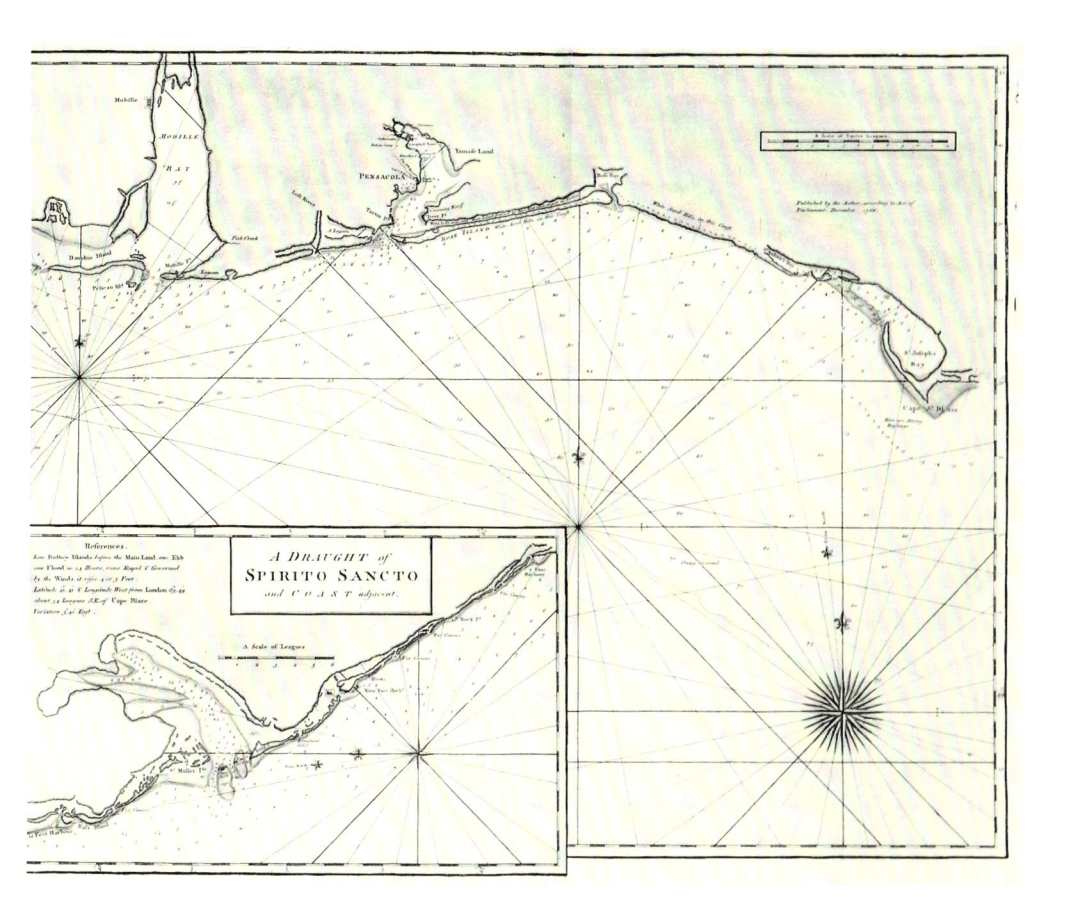

Lord Adam Gordon, a younger son of the duke of Gordon, after visiting both the Floridas, had decided that East Florida offered the best opportunities for profitable speculation. He headed the East Florida Society which aimed, through lobbying and influential connections, to gain title to substantial tracts of land for its members, designedly as plantations to be worked by other people. Another member was Richard Oswald, a Scottish merchant who had amassed a fortune from war contracts. Perhaps the most important member was James Grant, the governor of East Florida from 1763 to 1771, who could be counted on to support the Society's largely successful schemes. During the 1760s the privy council made 227 land grants in East Florida totalling 2.8 million acres, more than in any other colony. Although the bulk of the beneficiaries did nothing about their grants, thus excluding some of the best land in East Florida from cultivation, there were exceptions.

Dr. Andrew Turnbull, a Scot, spent, and ultimately lost, a fortune on the largest and most imaginative East Florida immigration scheme. After recruiting in the Mediterranean, Turnbull arrived in 1768 at his property on the Mosquito inlet with more than 1,400 Minorcans, Greeks, and Italians. The brutality of life as Turnbull's indentured servants and the ravages of disease ruined any chance of success that the so-called New Smyrna settlement might have had. By 1770 half of its settlers were dead.

Richard Oswald preferred to work his grant of 20,000 acres with blacks, which, as the chief importer of slaves to East Florida, he could easily obtain. On his principal plan-

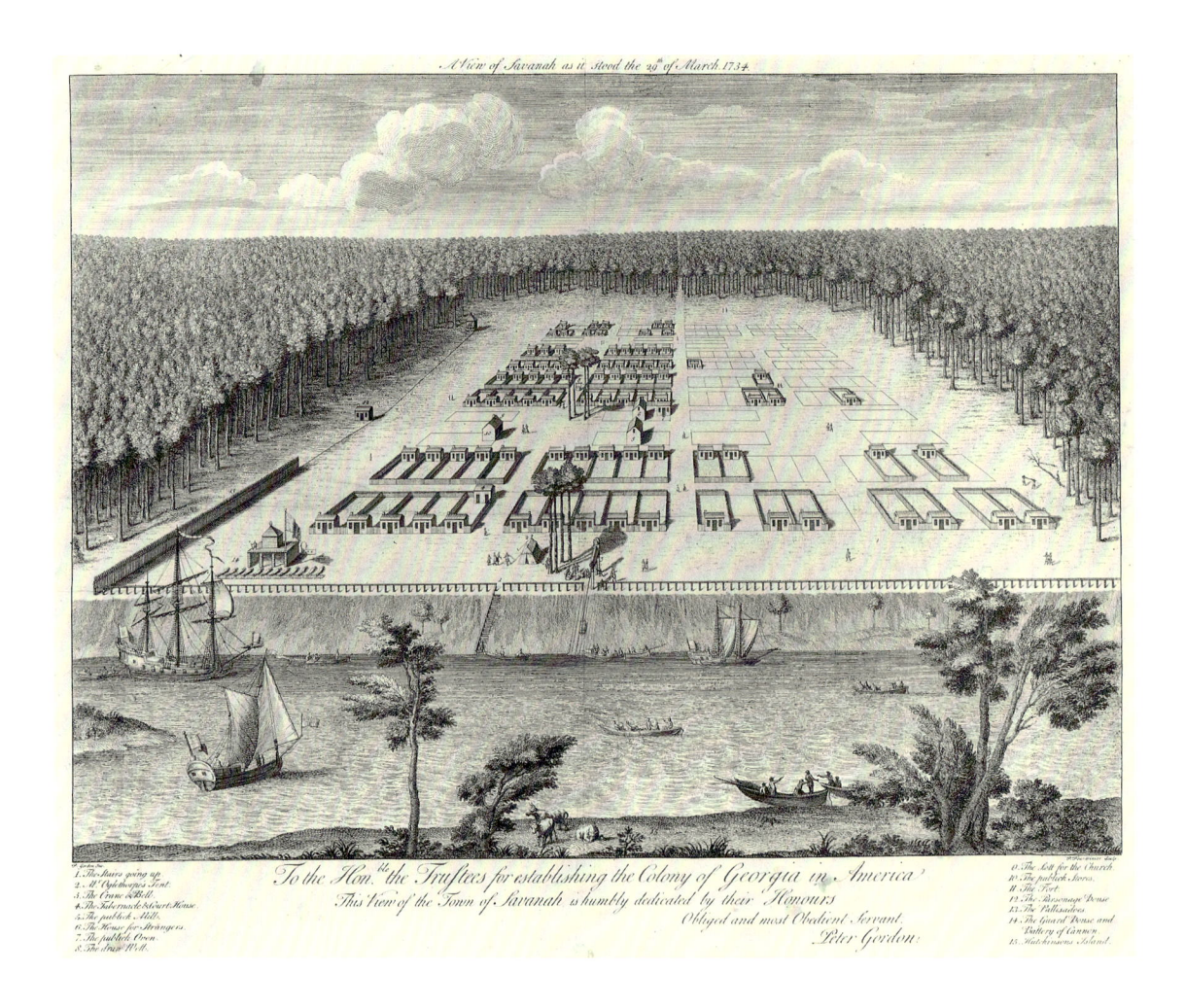

FIG. 25
Peter Gordon, *View of Savanah as It Stood the 29th of March, 1734*, London, 1734. Organized British settlement of Georgia began in 1733. This engraving, the earliest image of the colony, was made only a year later. Scots came to Georgia in substantial numbers but were generally opposed to the restrictive administrative policies of the Board of Trustees that ran the colony, in particular the prohibition of slavery and alcohol and the limitations imposed on land ownership. (Cat. no. 26).

tation, "Mount Oswald," he was one of the first to grow indigo, which was destined to be East Florida's most valuable export.

Unlike James Grant, West Florida's George Johnstone did not encourage huge land grants to absentee owners. He favored requests for much smaller grants which were available free to immigrants. How big they were depended on family size but most of them were less than 1,000 acres. One consequence was that, despite the greater difficulty of getting there, West Florida had a significantly larger settler population than East Florida before the Revolution. (Fig. 24). Once the Revolution broke out the preponderance swung in the other direction, because East Florida became a major haven for Loyalists.

Another reason for West Florida's greater popularity among immigrants was the discovery, in the early 1770s, that the land of West Florida's Natchez district, especially along the Mississippi River, was extraordinarily fertile. It was there, at his plantation, New Richmond, that William Dunbar lived.

A son of Sir Archibald Dunbar of Westfield (Morayshire), Dunbar was one of the few Floridians of the day with a university education. His lifelong interest in science involved him in correspondence with Thomas Jefferson, who nominated him to the American Philosophical Society.

Because he was a successful planter, Dunbar could keep up a lifestyle that was uncommonly cultured and opulent for the Florida frontier. Seeing no wrong in slavery, he worked the slaves he imported from Jamaica hard, chiefly, but not exclusively, in making staves and headers for barrels sold in the West Indies. More like a feudal seigneur than the Enlightenment man he, in so many ways, certainly was, Dunbar whipped and confined his slaves for slackness, while grumbling at their lack of gratitude for good treatment.

The Revolution did not worsen the pitiful lot of slaves in the southern colonies, but it did dispossess many Scots. During its course the state of Georgia took the property of Loyalists. After its conclusion, the peace treaty of 1783 gave the Floridas back to Spain, and

FIG. 26
Bernard Romans, *A Concise Natural History of East and West Florida*, New York, 1775. Romans was extremely well informed about all aspects of the British colonies of the "deep" South, and a close associate of the Superintendent of Indian Affairs, the Scot John Stuart. (Cat. no. 27).

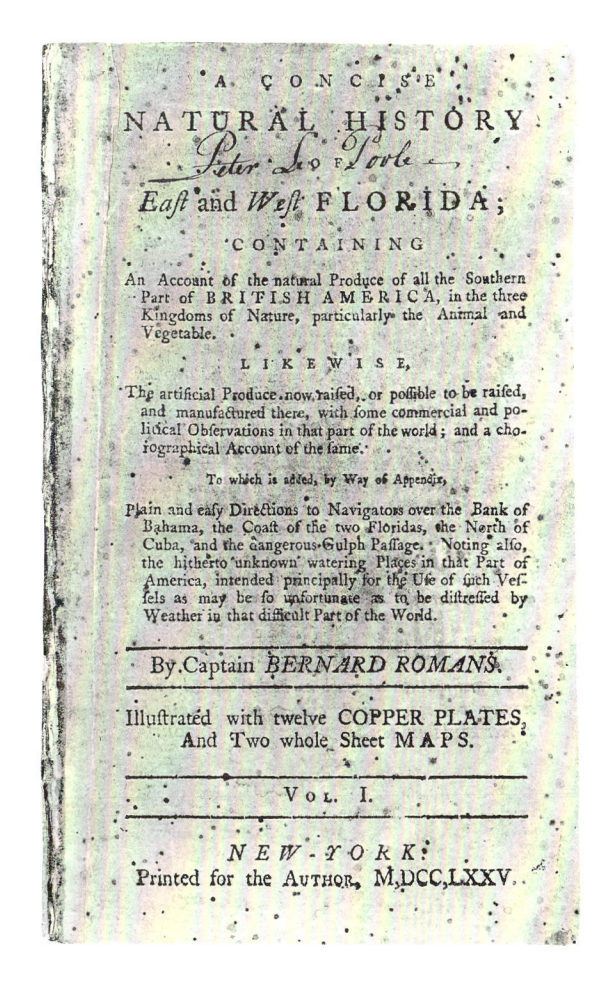

Extract of Col. Stephens journal

24 June 1741. Among other things sent me from Mr. Hopton by Penrose, I received the famous (or rather I should say infamous) Narrative of the State of Georgia, that had been so long expected, and advertised to be ready for publication, written by some of our acquaintance the Remnant of the Scotch Club; and which I had bespoke Mr. Hopton to get for me, as soon as it came abroad: and I hope he will also take care to send the same for the perusal of the Honble. Trustees. Such a heap of malicious calumny and vile falshoods, perhaps no instance can be found of, put together in the like compass. T'would be vain and silly in me to pretend here taking it to pieces, or to offer at answering any particulars, when I find almost as many lies as pages — possibly I may foul a little paper in making some attempt to expose a few of those falshoods in a true light, which with such unparalel'd impudence they have dared to assert as Facts, without any foundation.

If the honble. Trustees are contented to sit tame under such audacious Ribaldry as they will find in this Libel void of all shame and truth, then it may become me to be passive too, whom the World owes little or no regard to in comparison of those I serve: but I neither think they'l acquiesce patiently under such insults, nor leave me unprotected to the mercy of a wicked Crew, employ'd to worry my good name, which I must set at a very low value, if I did not esteem it a little more durable than the little remains of life yet left me.

Some passages will be found now in this journal, wch. I concieve will appear sufficient to draw conclusions what farther may be expected from a Band, whose rage and madness plainly means bringing all into confusion;

my

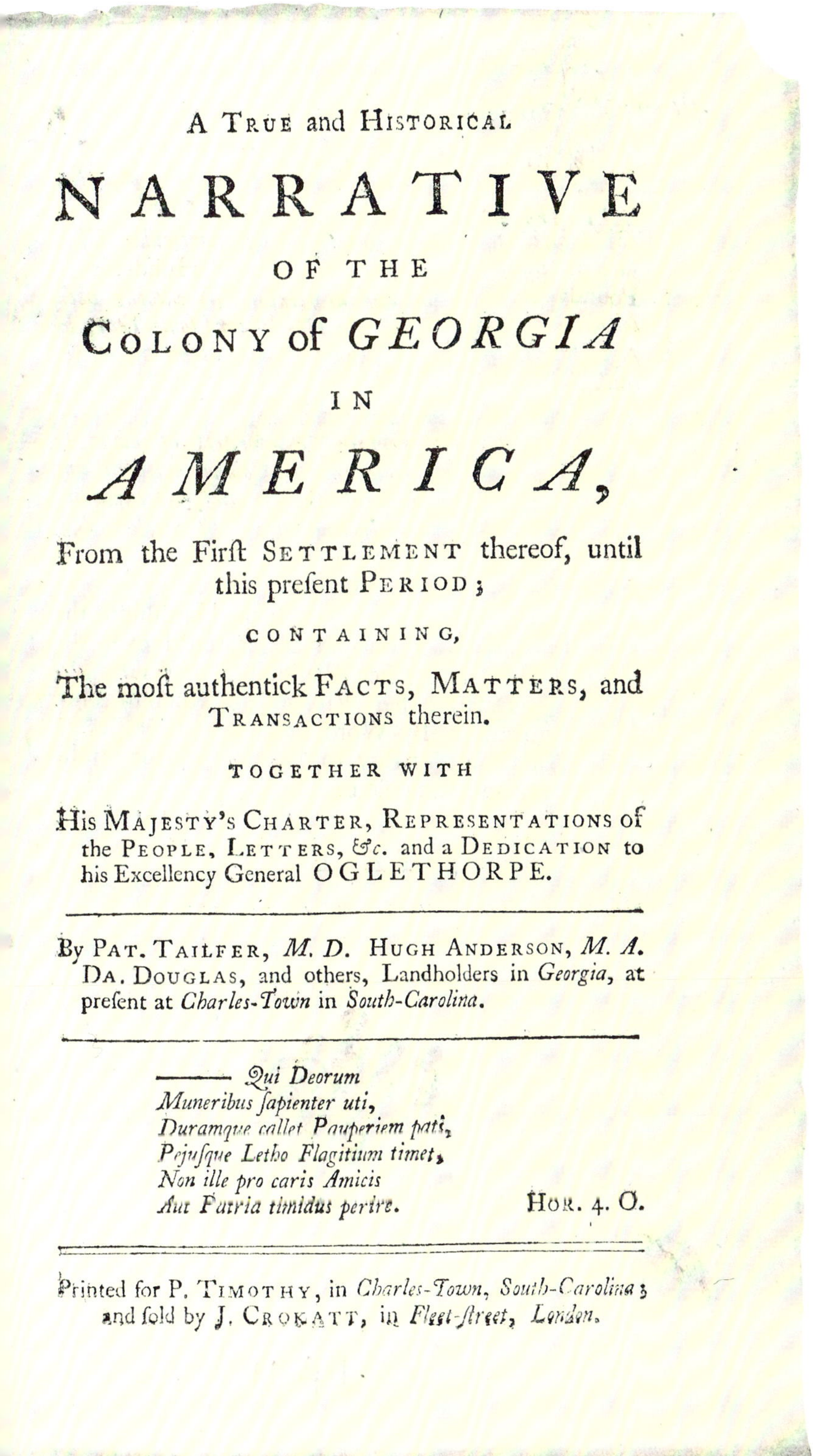

A True and Historical
NARRATIVE
OF THE
Colony of *GEORGIA*
IN
AMERICA,

From the First SETTLEMENT thereof, until this present PERIOD;

CONTAINING,

The most authentick FACTS, MATTERS, and TRANSACTIONS therein.

TOGETHER WITH

His MAJESTY's CHARTER, REPRESENTATIONS of the PEOPLE, LETTERS, &c. and a DEDICATION to his Excellency General OGLETHORPE.

By PAT. TAILFER, *M. D.* HUGH ANDERSON, *M. A.* DA. DOUGLAS, and others, Landholders in *Georgia*, at present at *Charles-Town* in *South-Carolina*.

———— *Qui Deorum*
Muneribus sapienter uti,
Duramque callet Pauperiem pati,
Pejusque Letho Flagitium timet,
Non ille pro caris Amicis
Aut Patria timidus perire. HOR. 4. O.

Printed for P. TIMOTHY, in *Charles-Town, South-Carolina*; and sold by J. CROKATT, in *Fleet-street, London*.

FIG. 27
Patrick Tailfer, *A True and Historical Narrative of the Colony of Georgia*, [London (?), 1741?]. This work, by a leader of the Scottish "Malcontents" in Georgia, is bitterly critical of the organization and management of the colony, which was in the hands of Trustees in Britain. The copy of the book shown here is a particularly valuable historical source because it contains a page-by-page handwritten rebuttal of Tailfer's charges, composed by John Perceval, Earl of Egmont, the leader of the Trustees. (Cat. no. 28).

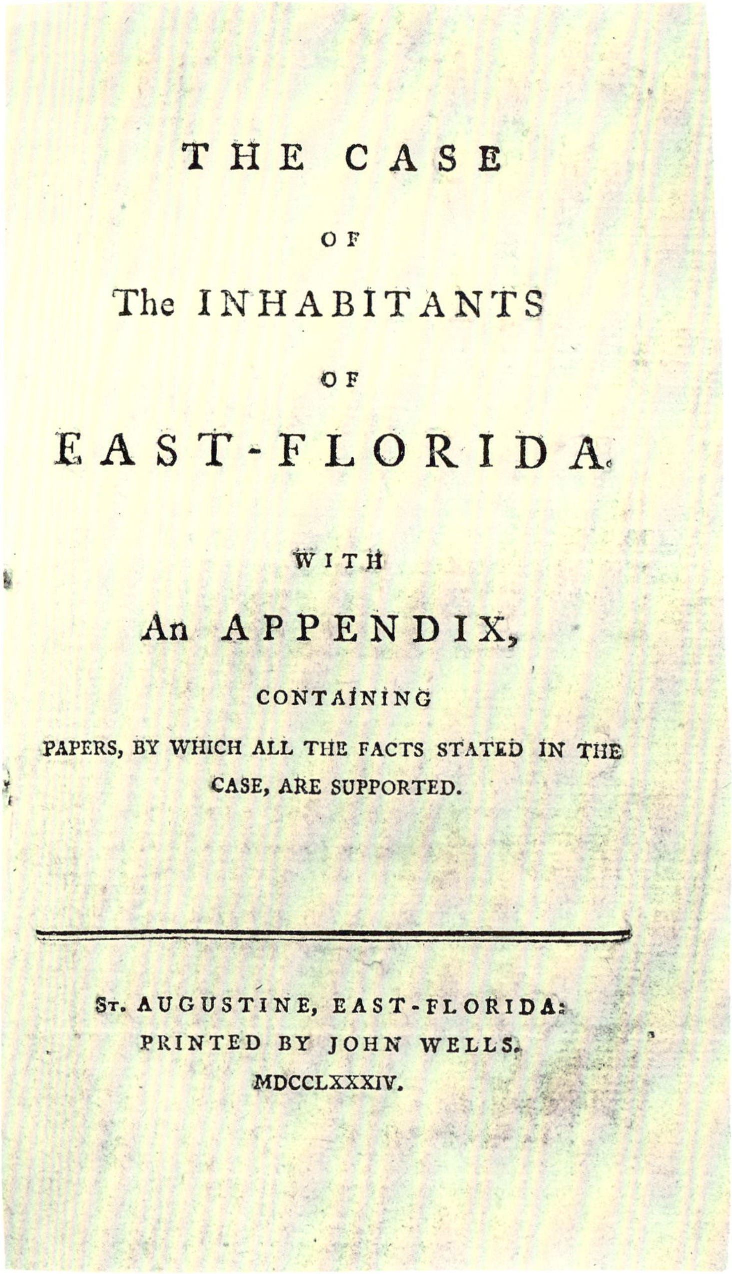

THE CASE

OF

The INHABITANTS

OF

EAST-FLORIDA.

WITH

An APPENDIX,

CONTAINING

PAPERS, BY WHICH ALL THE FACTS STATED IN THE CASE, ARE SUPPORTED.

St. AUGUSTINE, EAST-FLORIDA:
PRINTED BY JOHN WELLS.
MDCCLXXXIV.

FIG. 28
The Case of the Inhabitants of East-Florida, St. Augustine, 1784. When Florida was given back to the Spanish as part of the Peace of Paris of 1783, the British inhabitants, a good number of whom were Loyalist Scots, felt deeply aggrieved, as is stated in this pamphlet. They had kept East Florida from joining the Thirteen Colonies in the revolutionary movement, and at the peace table a few years later the British seemed to care little about this good service to the imperial cause. (Cat. no. 29).

the vast majority of their British inhabitants felt compelled to abandon their lands and emigrate again.

More cannily, five Scottish partners who were engaged in the Indian trade stayed on. William Panton, John Leslie, Thomas Forbes, Charles McLatchy, and William Alexander were all Loyalists who had fled to St. Augustine during the Revolution. So knowledgeable were they of the Indian trade, and so few were the Spaniards with comparable experience, that the Spanish authorities gave Panton, Leslie and Company a monopoly of the Floridian trade which would endure well into the nineteenth century.

Generalizing about Scots poses difficulties. In Scotland they had little homogeneity: there was a traditional antipathy between Highlanders and Lowlanders and clan rivalries were bitter. Immigration to America obscured but did not obliterate their differences. Through their St. Andrew's clubs, the Scots of Georgia seem to have formed more of a community than they did in the Floridas.

In West Florida, opponents' denunciation of Johnstone's "Scotch Party" was merely insubstantial rhetoric. Neither there nor in East Florida did the Scots form a distinctive community. Instead they were an enterprising, individualistic element in the frontier southern communities in which they found themselves. They were less noted for contributions to revolutionary ideology than as shrewd traders. Their most permanent effect probably, in the southernmost colonies at least, was on the Amerindians there.

23
James Adair.
The History of the American Indians: Particularly Those Nations Adjoining to the Mississippi, East and West Florida, Georgia, South and North Carolina and Virginia. London, 1775.

The author, James Adair, was an Irishman of Scottish descent. He left County Antrim for South Carolina while in his twenties. For the rest of his life—more than thirty years—he dwelt as a trader with Indians: Creeks, Cherokees, but chiefly Chickasaws. Although a salient purpose of his book is to assert the descent of the southern tribes from the lost tribes of Israel, Adair has also provided here accurate ethnic and historical information from the inside.

24
William Bartram.
Travels through North & South Carolina, Georgia, East and West Florida. Philadelphia, 1791.

Although Bartram was more interested in nature than he was in people, for an understanding of the southernmost American colonies, this is the most important, and a most beautiful, book to read. After wandering the region between 1773 and 1776, Bartram returned to convey, better than any other author, the atmosphere of the milieu in which backcountry Scots lived and traded.

25
Henry Fletcher.
MS Diary of an Officer of the 35th Regiment of Foot in America, 1757–1765.

This diary describes the activities of a regiment that had fought in most of the American campaigns of the Seven Years War. Sending it to unhealthy Pensacola at its conclusion was no way to encourage recuperation. The author has little to say about politics in West Florida except to note tersely that George Johnstone was "a bad man."

26
Peter Gordon.
A View of Savanah. London, 1734.

This engraving of Georgia's capital, where Gordon was first bailiff, in its very early days, accurately suggests the rigid planning that went into colonization of the province. (Fig. 25).

27
Bernard Romans.
A Concise Natural History of East and West Florida: Containing an Account of the Natural Produce of all the Southern Part of British America. New York, 1775.

This work of the versatile Dutch-born engineer and botanist resulted from his employment by the crown to survey the Floridas. Many unusual details, like sketches of representatives of the Indian peoples of the south and estimates of the expenses to be anticipated in emigrating there, distinguish this work from other travel books. (Fig. 26).

28
Patrick Tailfer.
A True and Historical Narrative of the Colony of Georgia.
[London(?), 1741?].

Tailfer was a physician, surgeon, and a leader of an immigration scheme for fellow Scots. On arrival in Georgia he felt swindled. Not only did his immigrants not receive promised provisions, tools, and weapons, but the land allocated to them at Sterling's Bluff was awkwardly remote from Savannah. Tailfer was a Malcontent leader but this work is valuable in giving both sides of the Malcontent controversy. (Fig. 27).

29
The Case of the Inhabitants of East-Florida.
St. Augustine, East Florida, 1784.

During the American Revolution Loyalists in some thousands had fled to East Florida and had begun a new life. They felt cheated when, in 1783, the British government ceded East Florida, which had remained unconquered during the Revolution, to Spain. In this pamphlet they argued that the crown owed them compensation for their losses. (Fig. 28).

FOR FURTHER READING

Bernard Bailyn, *Voyagers to the West: A Passage in the Peopling of America on the Eve of the Revolution* (New York, 1986). Essentially based on detailed emigration lists compiled by the British government between December 1773 and March 1776, this work analyzes who the emigrants were, where they came from, and how they fared after arrival in America.

Edward J. Cashin, *Lachlan McGillivray, Indian Trader: The Shaping of the Southern Colonial Frontier* (Athens, GA and London, 1992). The most influential, in his time, of many Scots pursuing similar careers, McGillivray linked the worlds of colonial Georgia and South Carolina with those of the Cherokees, Choctaws, and Chickasaws with whom he traded and, in the case of the Creeks, into which he also married.

Harold E. Davis, *The Fledgling Province: Social and Cultural Life in Colonial Georgia, 1733–1776* (Chapel Hill, 1976). This work is the best so far to detail the texture of life in Georgia in its earliest years. Davis gives due attention to Augusta, the center from which so many Scots traded with Amerindians.

Dorothy Downs, "British Influences on Creek and Seminole Men's Clothing, 1733-1858," *The Florida Anthropologist*, XXXIII, (1980), 46–65. The author goes into some detail, with suitable illustrations, to show how profoundly Scottish dress, in particular that of the Highlanders, affected the tribes of Georgia and the Floridas, an influence enduring long after the colonial period ended.

Ian C. G. Graham, *Colonists from Scotland: Emigration to North America, 1707–1783* (Ithaca, 1956). Graham is particularly good in analyzing the many forces underlying Scottish emigration to America. Although he takes notice of several prominent exceptions, he also insists that the Scots immigrants to America were predominantly Loyalists.

James Habersham, "Letters, 1756–1775," *Collections of the Georgia Historical Society*, VI (1904). Planter, merchant, president of the Georgia council and, finally, acting governor, Habersham was a society leader from 1738 until his death in 1775. His letters give unmatched information on social life and politics.

Grady McWhiney, *Cracker Culture: Celtic Ways in the Old South* (Tuscaloosa and London, 1988). Forrest McDonald wrote the prologue to this work. Both he and McWhiney are the main publicists for the theory that, above all other influences, it was the Celtic peoples, including the Irish as well as the Scots, who shaped the character and mores of southerners.

George C. Rogers, "The East Florida Society of London, 1766–1767," *The Florida Historical Quarterly*, LIV (1976), 479–496. Rogers discovered, in papers in Ballindalloch Castle, Banffshire, details of this speculative organization, which aimed to make huge profits from Britain's territorial gains in Florida. Its leaders were rich, aristocratic, and overwhelmingly Scottish.

Eron Dunbar Rowland, *Life, Letters, and Papers of William Dunbar* (Jackson, Miss., 1930). Dunbar created a civilized life-style to the benefit of himself and neighbors in West Florida's remotest region. He showed, what many contemporaries doubted, that planters could prosper in the frontier province.

Pierre Viaud, *Shipwreck and Adventures*. Orig. Bordeaux, 1768. Translated and edited by Robin F.A. Fabel. (Pensacola, 1990). This quasi-novel was based on the ordeal of a French naval officer whose survival, after being wrecked on the coast of East Florida, owed much to the kindness and generosity of Governor James Grant.

Abraham AN *Redwood*
APOLOGY
FOR THE
True Christian Divinity,

As the same is Held Forth, and Preached, by the People, called in Scorn,

QUAKERS:
BEING

A full Explanation and Vindication of their *Principles* and *Doctrines*, by many Arguments, deduced from *Scripture* and *Right Reason*, and the Testimonies of FAMOUS AUTHORS, both ancient and Modern: With a full Answer t͟o͟ ͟t͟h͟e͟ strongest Objections usually made against t͟h͟e͟m͟

Presented to the KING.

Written in *Latin* and *English*,

By ROBERT BARCLAY,

And since Translated into *High Dutch, Low Dutch,* and *French*, for the Information of Strangers.

THE SIXTH EDITION in *English.*

Acts 24. 14.——*After the Way which they call Heresy, so worship I the God of my Fathers, believing all things which are written in the Law and the Prophets.*
Titus 2. 11. *For the Grace of God, that bringeth Salvation, hath appeared to all Men.* Ver. 12 *Teaching us, that denying Ungodliness and worldly Lusts, we should live Soberly, Righteously, and Godly in this present World* Ver. 13. *Looking for that blessed Hope, and glorious Appearing of the Great God, and our Saviour Jesus Christ.* Ver. 14. *Who gave himself for us, that he might redeem us from all Iniquity, and purify unto himself a peculiar People, zealous of good Works*
1 Thess 5. 21. *Prove all things, hold fast that which is good.*

NEWPORT, *Rhode-Island*:
Printed by JAMES FRANKLIN. 1729.

CHAPTER FIVE: ## *Religion in the Affairs of Scotland and America*

ROBERT KENT DONOVAN AND
MICHAEL FRY

WHILE WE CANNOT GAINSAY the importance of Scots-American involvements in colonization, politics, trade, and education, religious associations, for their part, were manifold, powerful, and enduring. The clergy often shared or debated the same doctrines across the Atlantic, but religious ties and influences also entered the mundane world of trade, if only because so many Scottish or American clergy and merchants were kindred. Religion also operated very much in the realm of action, not just in that of thought and prayer. Action, furthermore, became institutionalized in various churches or denominations, and extra- or infra-denominational structures were in evidence on both sides of the Atlantic.

Once in America, as many have noted, some Scottish attitudes and customs disappeared within the dominant English or, perhaps, Spanish culture. But religious ideas and practices frequently escaped absorption and had considerable staying power. After all, the image of the Scot in the minds of others today still derives from identification with Calvinism, and American scholars studying in present-day Scotland will sooner or later encounter Americans—young men and, now women—studying divinity there. Influences moving either way across the Atlantic, of course, might pervade life so much as to be overlooked. American ideals and practices, for example, surely strengthened the protest against government interference in the Scots Kirk, just as the success of that effort may have encouraged Americans to avoid the pit of erastianism all the more. The readiness of churchmen here and in Scotland to judge and criticize civil government also comes partly from Calvinist views of the church set in judgment over against the state. (John Knox haranguing his lamentable queen presents a still vivid picture.)

Transatlantic influences frequently reflect the ideas or activities of a single individual, of course. The Scots Roman Catholic John Mair ("Johannes Major") at Paris published in 1519 reflections on American natives (who were "naturally" suited for slavery). The post-Reformation era saw Protestants figure more prominently than Catholics, of course. At the opening of the eighteenth century, correspondence sprang up, for example, between Cotton Mather, a great admirer of the Scots Kirk, and Principal Sterling of Glasgow and the historian Robert Woodrow. The Americans Thomas Prince, Sr., and Jonathan Edwards furnish a later illustration of this in exchanges with the eminent John M'Lauren of Glasgow and later still with John Erskine of Edinburgh, a spokesman of the Kirk's Popular party. Such correspondence was at least as brisk as much transatlantic scholarly communication today.

Clerics did not monopolize the correspondence either, given the family ties of Scottish ministers with pious merchants, sugar refiners,

FIG. 29
Robert Barclay, *Apology for the True Christian Divinity*, Newport, 1729. Barclay was a Scot, most famous for this book, first published in 1676 in Latin, which brought theological rigor to the beliefs of the Quakers. He was a great proponent of Scottish and Quaker emigration to America. (Cat. no. 30).

and ship-builders from Quebec to Demerara. Mercantile ties can be found among the American clergy, too. Among the busiest letter-writers were the Philadelphia physician, Benjamin Rush; the Edinburgh minister, John Erskine; and his cousin, the evangelical Earl of Buchan. They corresponded often on religion, among themselves and with many others in the era leading up to the American Revolution.

Books on divinity usually accompanied Erskine's letters. Some of them still repose in libraries in Philadelphia, Princeton, New Haven, Boston, and Cambridge. Other ministers exchanged books, too, and in addition to this sort of exchange (a reciprocal one), Scottish publishers reprinted American works as Americans published Scottish works of divinity. Writings of Hugh Blair, John Gillies, William Robertson, Henry Scougal, John Willison in the Establishment; the Presbyterian separatists Ebenezer and Ralph Erskine; the Glassite Robert Sandeman; and the Scots Quaker Robert Barclay were all reprinted here. Works by the Americans John Barnard, Joseph Bellamy, Charles Chauncy, Samuel Davies, Jonathan Dickinson, Jonathan Edwards, Samuel Hopkins, Increase and Cotton Mather, Thomas Prince, Thomas Shepherd—Calvinist luminaries all—came out in Scotland.

Such contacts customarily occurred within denominational bounds. By the mid-eighteenth century Scotland harbored a variety of churches, all conveyed to America by their adherents. Covenanting exiles in the seventeenth century brought presbyterian, as opposed to congregational, Calvinism to North America. In the next century their Presbyterian offspring gravitated into church parties similar to those in the Church of Scotland. For their part New England Puritans, perhaps surprisingly, viewed Presbyterianism as a sister communion, and an amicable sister at that. Scottish Presbyterian seceders from the Kirk also organized churches in far-scattered towns in Pennsylvania, New Hampshire, and Nova Scotia. Scots Glassites or Sandemanians came to Connecticut; Scottish Quakers settled in New Jersey; and Scottish Catholics in upper New York. Scottish Episcopalian clergy, dissenting and disadvantaged at home, seem to have migrated here in greater numbers than did the Kirk's more fortunate ministers. After independence, American Episcopalians had to validate their orders through the Scottish, rather than the English bishops.

A more dramatic endeavor than exporting churches was missionary action. Members of the Kirk by the close of the seventeenth century were aware of Anglican and also Catholic missions to America like that of Bartolomé de Las Casas. In 1709 they themselves established the Society in Scotland for the Propagation of Christian Knowledge in the Highlands and Islands and the Foreign Parts of the World, that last reference interpreted largely as meaning North America.

Several agencies profited from this attention, such as the Moors School at Lebanon, Connecticut, founded by the indefatigable missionary Eleazar Wheelock. His most celebrated convert, Samson Occom, a Monhegan preacher, raised funds in Britain, where he addressed the General Assembly of the Kirk. Scottish charity also extended to the Society for Propagating the Gospel among the Indians and Others in North America, established at Boston under S.S.P.C.K. aegis over strong, if clandestine, Anglican opposition, and re-established freely in 1787 under Massachusetts law, one of the early fruits of independence. Scottish involvement earlier was such that colonists often called it "the Honourable Scotch Commissioners." Colonial colleges, though not usually missionary institutions, also benefited from Scottish gifts of books and funds. Some of them attracted Scottish or Scots-Irish clergy, Presbyterian or Episcopalian, as their presidents.

How far missions influenced the astonishing evangelical revivals of the mid-eighteenth century awaits more study, but Scottish and North American Protestants of evangelical bent shared much in that burgeoning of fervor. The revival appeared to be international, including the English, the Scots and the Irish, the colonists, and even the Moravians in Saxony. The American "Great Awakening" and the Scottish "Cambuslang Wark," as they were called, made celebrities of some clergy

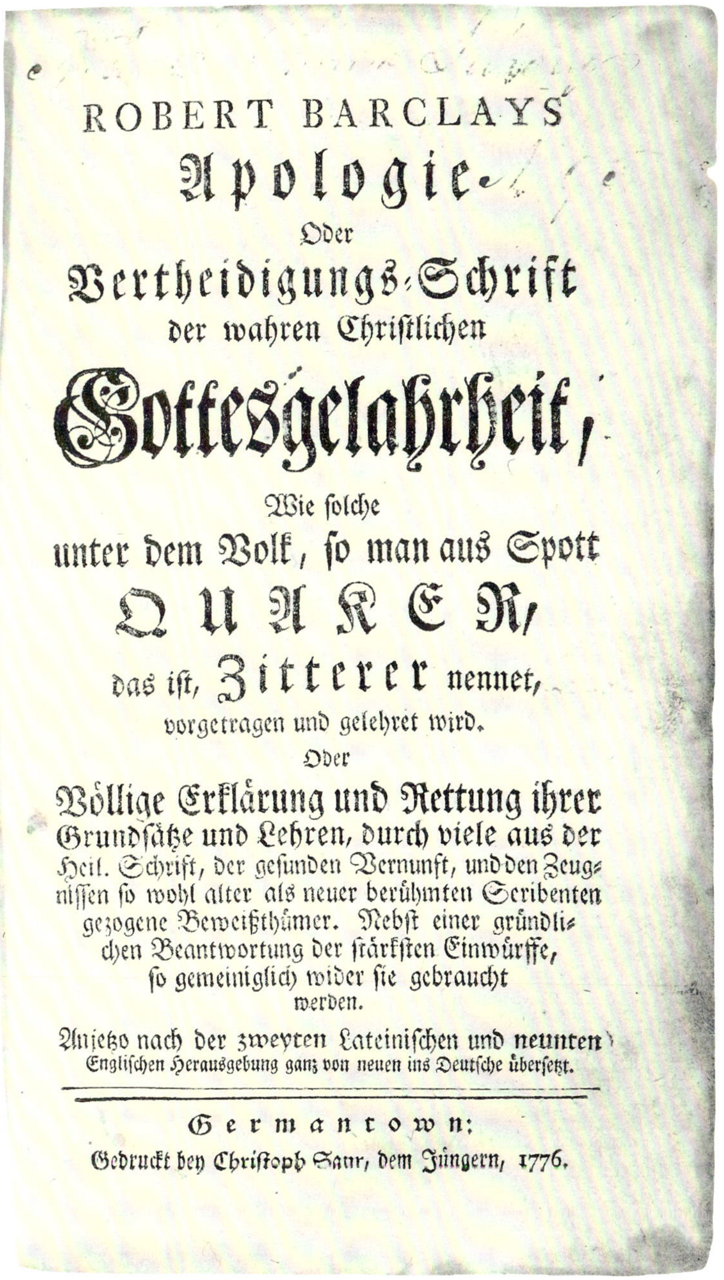

ROBERT BARCLAYS
Apologie.
Oder
Vertheidigungs-Schrift
der wahren Christlichen
Gottesgelahrheit,
Wie solche
unter dem Volk, so man aus Spott
QUAKER,
das ist, Zitterer nennet,
vorgetragen und gelehret wird.
Oder
Völlige Erklärung und Rettung ihrer
Grundsätze und Lehren, durch viele aus der
Heil. Schrift, der gesunden Vernunft, und den Zeugnissen so wohl alter als neuer berühmten Scribenten gezogene Beweißthümer. Nebst einer gründlichen Beantwortung der stärksten Einwürffe, so gemeiniglich wider sie gebraucht werden.

Anjetzo nach der zweyten Lateinischen und neunten Englischen Herausgebung ganz von neuen ins Deutsche übersetzt.

Germantown:
Gedruckt bey Christoph Saur, dem Jüngern, 1776.

FIG. 30
Apologie oder Vertheidigungs-Schrift der wahren christlichen Gottesgelahrheit, Germantown, 1776. A German edition of Barclay's *Apology* appeared as early as 1684. This edition was the first in the German language printed in America. (Cat. no. 31).

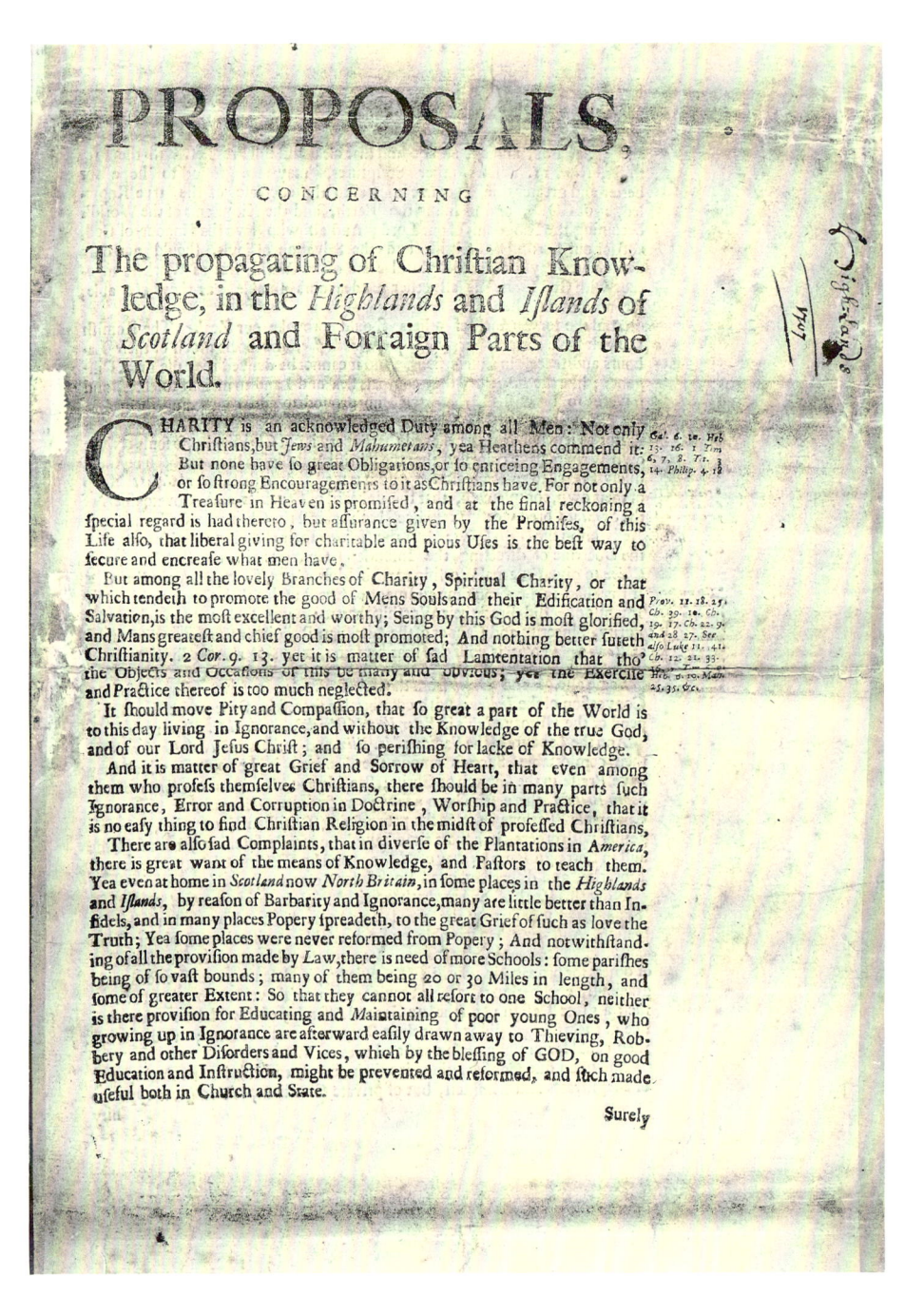

FIG. 31
[James Kirkwood?]
Proposals Concerning the Propagating of Christian Knowledge, [Edinburgh(?),1707?]. Calvinist Scots shared with many of the British in America an ardent wish to triumph over Roman Catholicism, exemplified by French and Spanish missionary work in the New World among the "heathen." "In many places Popery spreadeth, to the great Grief of such as love the Truth," it is remarked in this pamphlet, which has survived in only a few copies. (Cat. no. 32).

like the Anglican Calvinist George Whitefield, the Puritan theologian Jonathan Edwards, and to some extent the Scottish evangelicals John M'Lauren, John Gillies, and John Erskine. All became renowned, or notorious, depending on whose memoirs one reads.

In that evangelical era, such men viewed the ocean's vastness as naught. Their correspondence quickened, their exchange of books increased as did the publishing and republishing of their works reciprocally across the Atlantic. The parallel revivals in America and Scotland invigorated earlier associations and deepened Scottish interest in colonial religion. Scottish evangelicals closely followed the fortunes of Whitefield's Georgia orphanage, for example. More profound as a thinker, if less widely popular than Whitefield, was the masterful American theologian Jonathan Edwards, several of whose revival-inspired writings came off presses in America and Scotland alike. The vibrant *History of the Work of Redemption* (1774) was one of these. A mystical history of the church and a prophecy in apocalyptic terms of her future, its publication abroad long after the author's death shows the hold millennialism had over some of the best minds of Protestantism.

In the pre-industrial culture of these years, much more than today, religion pervaded most areas of life. Scottish clergy like John Witherspoon of Paisley, Charles Nisbet of Montrose, and William Thom of Govan promoted emigration for religious as well as economic reasons. Witherspoon and Nisbet themselves migrated to head Princeton and Dickinson Colleges, respectively. (Elsewhere Francis Alison, a Scots-Irish Presbyterian, came here and helped found the College of Philadelphia; and the Scots Episcopalian, James Blair, arrived to direct William and Mary.) Blair, the Bishop of London's Commissary in America, used his clerical and academic status to develop plans to reform Virginia Episcopalianism but also to bring down Governor Francis Nicholson's civil administration. Another Scottish Episcopal priest, William Gordon, involved himself similarly with the government of Barbados.

National and imperial politics always aroused clerical comment in America and Scotland alike. Benjamin Colman of Boston

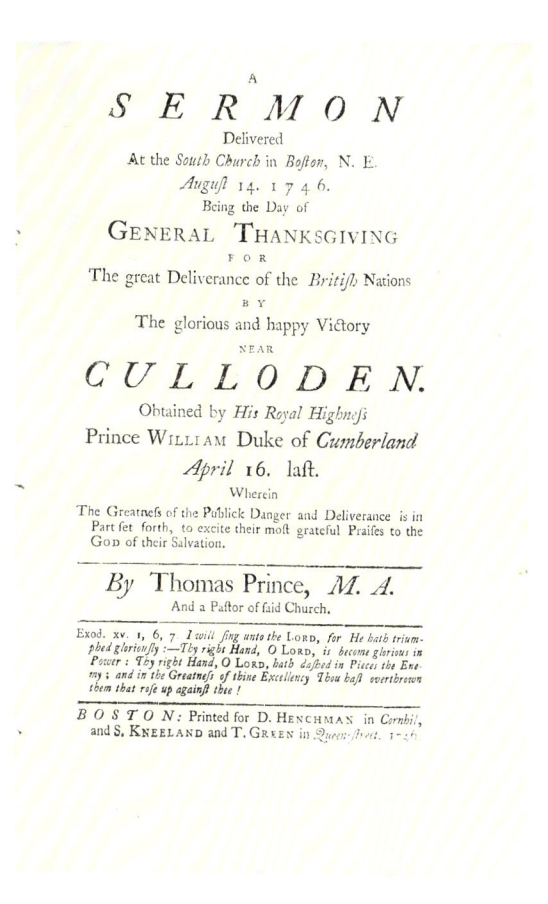

FIG. 32
Thomas Prince, *A Sermon Delivered at the South Church*, Boston, 1746. The victory at Culloden is interpreted by Prince for his fellow Bostonians as a spiritual victory over the evil forces of popery. (Cat. no. 33).

preached on the 1715 Jacobite rising in Scotland in the light of prophecy. The more serious rebellion in 1745 prompted sermons at Boston from Thomas Prince and Charles Chauncy and at Philadelphia from George Whitefield, and also from other, unpublished preachers. The clergy also preached on the victories of the Seven Years or French and Indian War finding the motion of the hand of God in all of them.

The last political problem of the imperial colonial era that attracted many churchmen saw some of them at their moral best. Efforts to end the African-American slave trade and slavery itself succeeded only after 1800 in the British Empire and the United States. Success, however, came from campaigns launched much earlier in Scotland, the colonies, and elsewhere. Many Scots abolitionists were churchmen, drawn from both the latitudinarian "Moderate" party and the evangelical Popular party. James Ramsay, a Royal Navy physician in Anglican orders and rector of West Indies parishes, like other clergy of his day, relished controversy and issued many abolition tracts. The diarist and Church of Scotland Moderate Thomas Soverville was so carried away by anti-slavery successes, that he published a thanksgiving sermon fourteen years before the trade ended.

30 and 31
Robert Barclay.
Apology for the True Christian Divinity. Newport, 1729.

Robert Barclay.
Robert Barclays Apologie oder Vertheidigungs-Schrift der wahren christlichen Gottesgelahrheit, wie solche unter dem Volk, so man aus Spott Quaker, das ist Zitterer nennet, vorgetragen und gelehret wird. Germantown, 1776.

Robert Barclay (1648–90) of Urie in Aberdeenshire systematized the theology of the Society of Friends. In his own country he is renowned for a second reason, as founder of the first Scottish colony in the area of the present United States, in East New Jersey, round the towns of Perth Amboy and Elizabeth. Since the Union of the Crowns in 1603, Scots had enjoyed the right to settle freely in English territory. A group of them did so in 1684 on land recently conquered from the Dutch. Though Barclay never visited America himself, he hoped to emulate the colony on the Delaware River of his co-religionist, William Penn. This one was meant partly as a refuge, for Quakers and for persecuted Presbyterians too, but perhaps more as a regular project of plantation, laid out on a plan of large estates like those common in the Northeast of Scotland whence many of the proprietors came. It thus never bore the same Quaker impress as Pennsylvania, though in 1693 one of the Scots, George Keith, wrote here the first protest against slavery to be published in America. Barclay's own greater contribution was his *Apology*, which also owed much to Keith. It was originally published in Amsterdam in 1676 in Latin, and quickly became the standard defence of the Friends' doctrines. The work was immensely popular; it was reprinted many times in English and translated into six other languages. (Fig. 29). The John Carter Brown Library owns editions in all of them except Arabic and Danish; the second volume exhibited was evidently aimed at the large German-speaking population of Pennsylvania. (Fig. 30).

32
[James Kirkwood?]
Proposals Concerning the Propagating of Christian Knowledge, in the Highlands and Islands of Scotland and Forraign Parts of the World. [Edinburgh(?), 1707?]

Scots shared the motives of other Europeans in their encounter with the outside world, not only to trade, but also to bring Christianity to the heathen. In America, they were aware of Anglican and Roman Catholic efforts to convert the Indians. Since they believed Pres-

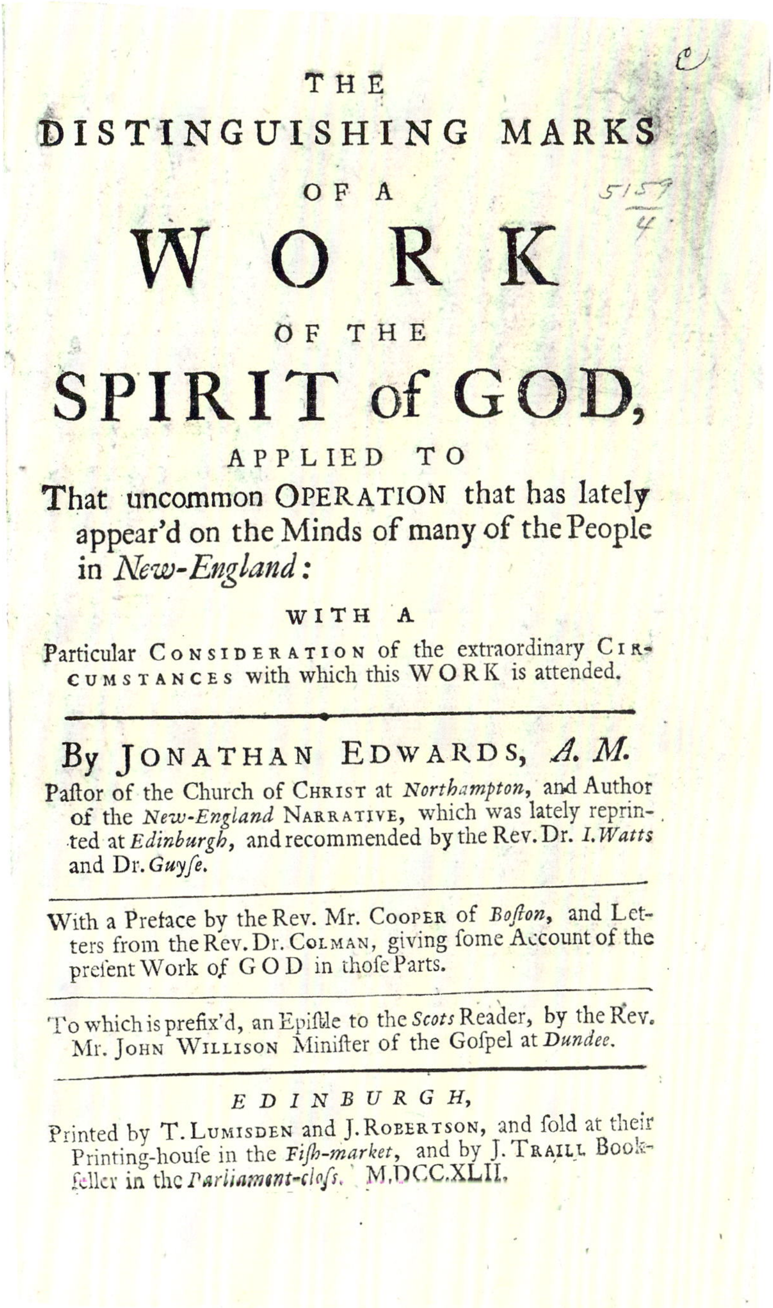

THE DISTINGUISHING MARKS

OF A

WORK

OF THE

SPIRIT of GOD,

APPLIED TO

That uncommon OPERATION that has lately appear'd on the Minds of many of the People in *New-England*:

WITH A

Particular CONSIDERATION of the extraordinary CIRCUMSTANCES with which this WORK is attended.

By JONATHAN EDWARDS, *A. M.*

Pastor of the Church of CHRIST at *Northampton*, and Author of the *New-England* NARRATIVE, which was lately reprinted at *Edinburgh*, and recommended by the Rev. Dr. *I. Watts* and Dr. *Guyse*.

With a Preface by the Rev. Mr. COOPER of *Boston*, and Letters from the Rev. Dr. COLMAN, giving some Account of the present Work of GOD in those Parts.

To which is prefix'd, an Epistle to the *Scots* Reader, by the Rev. Mr. JOHN WILLISON Minister of the Gospel at *Dundee*.

EDINBURGH,
Printed by T. LUMISDEN and J. ROBERTSON, and sold at their Printing-house in the *Fish-market*, and by J. TRAILL Bookseller in the *Parliament-closs.* M,DCC.XLII.

FIG. 33
Jonathan Edwards, *Distinguishing Marks of a Work of the Spirit of God*, Edinburgh, 1742. Originally published in Boston in 1741, this work, which had a major effect in justifying the evangelical fervor of the Great Awakening, was republished in Scotland just a year later, where religious enthusiasm akin to that in the American colonies was also burgeoning. (Cat. no. 35).

byterianism to represent the true Church, it became incumbent on them to undertake missions of their own. They felt especially called to this because they knew that beyond the pale of civilization in Scotland herself, in the Highlands and islands, there were still great numbers whom reformed religion had not reached. They thus saw missions to America and to the Highlands in the same light, as this document shows.

The putative author, James Kirkwood (1650?–1708), was chaplain to the Earl of Breadalbane, a chief of the Clan Campbell. Kirkwood visited his territory and was appalled at the ignorance of Scripture among its Gaelic-speaking people. He wrote for help to Robert Boyle, an Irish nobleman known for his generosity to evangelism, though better remembered today as a pioneer of chemistry and formulator of Boyle's Law. Boyle had seen in his own country the same problem, that the natives knew no English and could not read the Bible. To remedy this, he had it translated into Irish. Irish and Gaelic being mutually comprehensible, he presented Kirkwood with 200 copies of the translation and subscribed towards printing 3,000 more for distribution in Scotland.

Boyle was also governor of the Corporation for the Spread of the Gospel in New England, which translated the Scriptures into Indian languages. That may account for the terms of this four-page prospectus, smudged and foxed but still visually attractive, of the Society in Scotland for the Propagation of Christian Knowledge in the Highlands and Islands of Scotland and Forraign Parts of the World, which was to be established in 1709. The "foreign parts" meant primarily North America. (Fig. 31). The SSPCK would proselytize "the forlorn natives of that vast continent" and support "messengers of joy to the bewildered Indians." Reference is made to "Bishop Barthal Casas" (the Catholic missionary Bartolomé de las Casas) and his success in spreading popery, in an effort to shame Scots and goad them into action in the Protestant cause.

33
Thomas Prince.
A Sermon Delivered at the South Church in Boston, N.E....for...the Glorious and Happy Victory Near Culloden Obtained by His Royal Highness Prince William Duke of Cumberland. Boston, 1746.

In the Scotland and the America of the eighteenth century, sermons often dwelt on national or imperial politics, and often, at least till 1776, in remarkably similar terms. The John Carter Brown Library has many examples, from the Jacobite rising of 1715 to the Revolutionary War. The preachers usually saw God's hand at work in victories for the British monarch and constitution, which they praised accordingly. Among the most fulsomely loyal was Thomas Prince, minister at the South Church in Boston 1718–58, well-known in the Church of Scotland and among English dissenters, whom he had visited as a young man. His sizable collection of books, now in the Boston Public Library, has many works of Scottish divinity and historical treatises. His interest in history drew him to preach on the Hanoverian victory at Culloden over Prince Charles Edward Stuart. (Fig. 32). He examined the Jacobite menace at length, but its religious features preoccupied him. Culloden appears as not just a political or military, but a spiritual victory over the evil forces of the Pope and his conspiratorial Stuart minions. He points out that even Protestant Stuarts had Catholic wives and repeats the Whig canard that James VIII was a suppositious prince. He also voices the fear that, had the Jacobites won at Culloden, they would have handed back to popish France and Spain all the American territories taken from them by British arms or diplomacy. His sermon came out first in Boston, then in editions from Edinburgh and London. His correspondent in Edinburgh, John Erskine, published there the spiritual exercises of Prince's two daughters, as well as *Six Sermons* by the minister himself.

FIG. 31
James Robe, *Short Narrative of the Extraordinary Work at Cambuslang*, Boston, 1742. This work about the religious revival in the West of Scotland, was first published in Glasgow and is a Scottish counterpart to Edwards's *Distinguishing Marks of a Work of the Spirit of God*. (Cat. no. 36).

34
John Gillies.
Memoirs of the Life of...
George Whitefield.
New York, 1774.

The work of the great evangelist George Whitefield further illustrates how Calvinism could be a force for unity in the North Atlantic world of the mid-eighteenth century. He was himself an Englishman, brought up in the Anglican Church and intended for the priesthood. While at the University of Oxford he struck up a friendship with Charles Wesley. He finally passed over from Methodism, which was still compatible with Anglican orders, to rigid Calvinism, which was not. As an itinerant preacher, then, he made six tours of Scotland and crossed the ocean even more often to awaken America. He thus helped to strengthen the links between Scottish and American evangelicals, and allowed them to draw explicit parallels between the religious revivals which took place on both sides in the early 1740s. Printers in Boston and Philadelphia republished several of the sermons he had preached in Scotland. The first biography of him was written by John Gillies, minister of the College church in Glasgow and a member of Scotland's most influential group of evangelical clergymen, centered in that city.

35
Jonathan Edwards.
The Distinguishing Marks of a Work of the Spirit of God, Applied to that Uncommon Operation that Has Lately Appear'd on the Minds of Many of the People in New-England.
Edinburgh, 1742.

It struck the evangelicals forcefully that revivals took place at the same time in widely separated parts of the globe, in New England and in the West of Scotland. The numerous conversions and their rapid spread convinced sober witnesses that God alone could have instigated them. Evangelicals placed these events in their eschatology: converting the heathen, the lukewarm and the backsliders, no less than the Jews, not only spread the gospel but heralded the Second Coming. That, at any rate, was the conclusion drawn by the American theologian Jonathan Edwards. He rushed into print with an account of local events published in Boston in 1741. It was reprinted in Edinburgh the next year with a "Preface to the Scotch Reader" by John Willison, minister in Dundee, who had himself taken part in the Scottish revival at Cambuslang. (Fig. 33). Edwards's thinking, more profound if less accessible than Whitefield's, came to be highly regarded in Scotland. He and John M'Lauren, Gillies's father-in-law and leader of the Glaswegian evangelicals, formed the United Concert of Extraordinary Prayers (an institution revived by charismatics today to promote simultaneous universal prayer). Several of Edward's weightier theological works appeared posthumously in Scotland, edited by Erskine.

36
James Robe.
A Short Narrative of the Extraordinary Work at Cambuslang.
Boston, 1742.

Equally, Americans demanded accounts of what happened in Scotland at the "Cambuslang Wark." This description was promptly published in Boston, with 'Attestations' to the revival's authenticity by M'Lauren and others. (Fig. 34). The author, James Robe, was minister of Kilsyth, 15 miles north of Cambuslang. The revival immediately spread to his parish through the preaching of Willison. In reporting all this, the Scots clergymen had a serious message for their American brethren, that they should not rely on inchoate enthusiasm, but closely monitor the progress of converts and instill them with intellectual discipline through catechism and study of the Bible.

37
David Brainerd.
An Account of the Life of Mr. David Brainerd.
Edinburgh, 1798.

Committed to evangelism as the Church of Scotland was, it had before the nineteenth century neither the money nor the organization to send out regular missions. All it could do for the time being was appoint a young American, just licensed to preach, as agent of the Society in Scotland for Propagating Christian Knowledge. Brainerd, born in 1718 near Hartford, Connecticut, came from a puritan clerical family of English descent. He had some contact with Scots living in New York, who recommended him to the society in 1742. Two years later he was ordained in Newark by the presbytery of New Jersey. He then started ministering to the Indians in that colony and in Pennsylvania. But he always seems to have been sickly, and he died after only three years. Perhaps for this reason, his pious journals were greatly admired by religious readers. Jonathan Edwards first edited them for publication in Edinburgh in 1765 and, as this volume in the John Carter Brown Library shows, they were still in print more than 30 years later.

FOR FURTHER READING

B. S. Schlenter, "Scottish Influences, especially Religious, in Colonial America," *Records of the Scottish Church History Society*, XIX, 1976.

H. R. Sefton, "The Scotch Society in the American Colonies in the Eighteenth Century," *Records of the Scottish Church History Society*, XVII, 1971.

J. S. Moir, "Scottish Influences on Canadian Presbyterianism," *Scotia*, II, 1978.

L. J. Trinterud, *The Forming of an American Tradition* (Philadelphia, 1949).

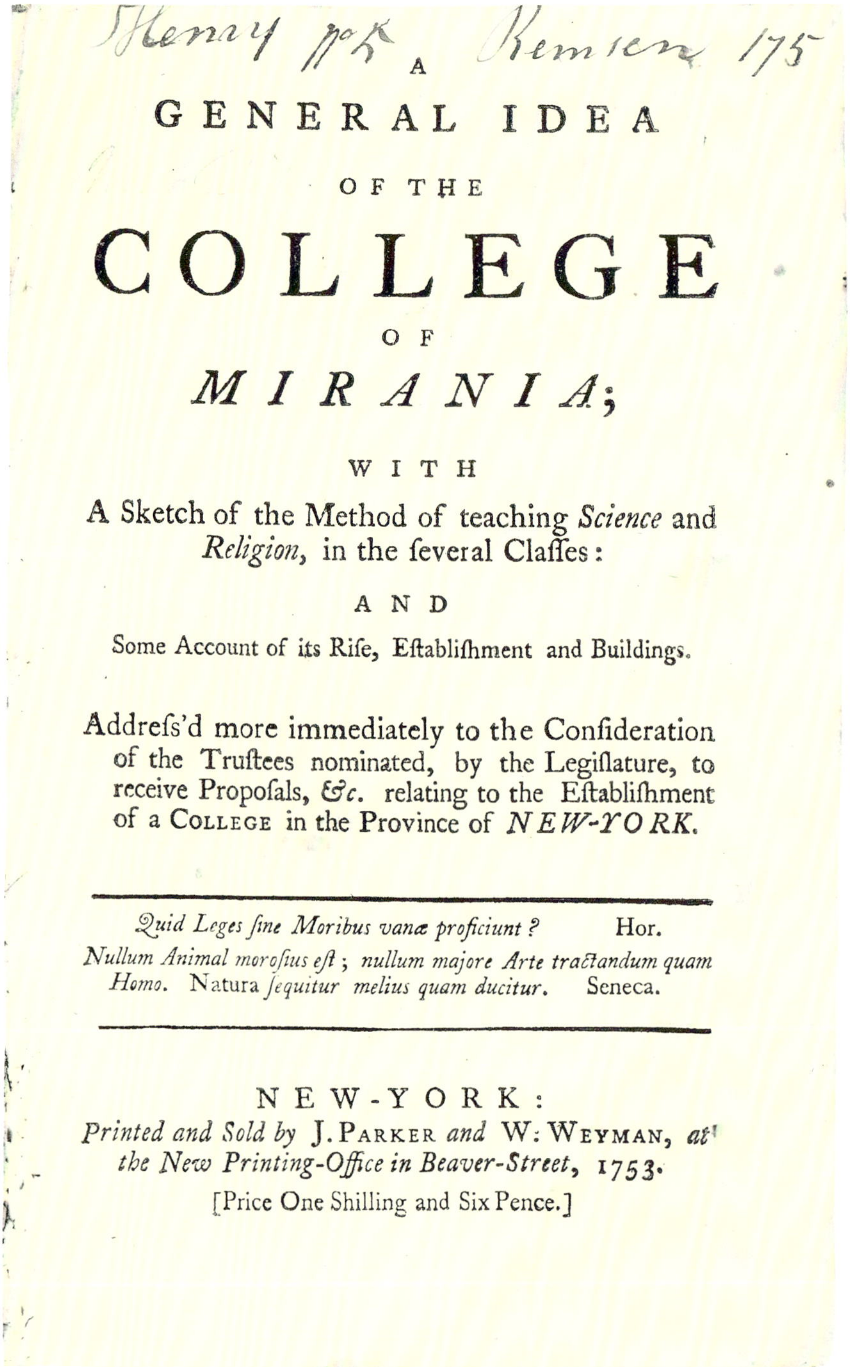

A
GENERAL IDEA
OF THE
COLLEGE
OF
MIRANIA;

WITH

A Sketch of the Method of teaching *Science* and *Religion*, in the several Classes:

AND

Some Account of its Rise, Establishment and Buildings.

Address'd more immediately to the Consideration of the Trustees nominated, by the Legislature, to receive Proposals, &c. relating to the Establishment of a COLLEGE in the Province of NEW-YORK.

Quid Leges sine Moribus vanæ proficiunt? Hor.
Nullum Animal morosius est; nullum majore Arte tractandum quam Homo. Natura sequitur melius quam ducitur. Seneca.

NEW-YORK:
Printed and Sold by J. PARKER and W. WEYMAN, at the New Printing-Office in Beaver-Street, 1753.
[Price One Shilling and Six Pence.]

FIG. 35
William Smith, *A General Idea of the College of Mirania*, New York, 1753. Smith emigrated from Scotland in 1751 and became a force in Philadelphia intellectual circles. His thinking about higher education, revealed in this theoretical work, led to his appointment as provost of the College of Philadelphia, later the University of Pennsylvania. (Cat. no. 38).

CHAPTER SIX: *Education*

JAMES MCLACHLAN

EDUCATION IS CONDUCTED through four main agencies: the family, the community, churches, and schools, both higher and lower. Of Scottish influences on education as practiced within families and communities we can say little, but in colonial America college and university-educated Scots played an influential role far disproportionate to their number in the higher schools and in certain churches.

At the basic level of direct institutional borrowings, Scottish influence on American higher education began with the founding of the first two American colleges, Harvard in 1636, and William and Mary in 1693. At early Harvard commencements, students—or the college authorities—printed and posted the philosophical and other theses that would be disputed in public by the degree candidates, a practice unknown at contemporary Cambridge and Oxford. The layout of the early Harvard commencement sheets virtually duplicates contemporary commencement sheets from the University of Edinburgh.

To Scotland, too, Americans would owe that distinctive mark of American undergraduate life, the organization of the student body into "classes". In Scotland each entering group of university students was placed in the charge of a single "regent," who instructed the group —or class—throughout its undergraduate years. (Professorships in single subjects were not introduced until much later.) Harvard, and later, Yale and other American colleges followed this practice. In America such instructors, usually recent graduates of the colleges themselves, were called tutors. Yet for all of these borrowings, we do not know who initiated these practices in New England. Only one alumnus of a Scottish university appears to have migrated there during the seventeenth century, and he in 1662.

To the south, the initial plans for the settlement of Virginia had called for the establishment of a college there. The plans were not fulfilled for many decades and for many reasons, perhaps chief among the latter the fearful mortality rate in the Chesapeake, where the population did not even begin to reproduce itself until the third quarter of the seventeenth century. A place with comparatively few children had little need for schools, let alone a college. But by the early 1690s the population had stabilized, and wealth had grown to the point where Virginians felt confident enough to establish the College of William and Mary. Chief among the promoters and long the College's president was a Scottish Episcopalian migrant of 1685, James Blair, a clergyman and graduate of Marischal College, Aberdeen, who had attended the University of Edinburgh as well. Blair served as the representative of the Bishop of London in the colony and was a powerful figure in Virginia politics. At least one scholar has claimed that William and Mary during Blair's regime was essentially a Scottish college. This is open to dispute, but it is certain that one of the College's earliest instructors, Mungo Ingles, an Edinburgh graduate, was styled "Professor of Humanity" in Virginia public records. This was a title unknown to the English universities, but common in Scotland, where it signified an instructor in Latin and Greek beyond the level of the grammar schools. What is certain is that in William and Mary's early decades it was suffused with a Scottish spirit and had some Scottish instructors.

Examples of other "borrowings" and Scottish influences on American colleges abound, and some are indicated elsewhere in this chapter. But if there was one pervasive and continuing Scottish "influence" on education in the mainland colonies, it came in the form of the actual migration to and presence in America of the products of Scottish higher education. There were five universities in Scotland in the seventeenth century: Edinburgh, Glasgow, St. Andrews, and two in Aberdeen—Marischal, and 'University and Kings'. (The Aberdeen colleges were combined into one institution in the nineteenth century.) Small institutions teaching a late-Medieval curriculum towards the end of the seventeenth century, a hundred years later they were among the centers of the European Enlightenment, leaders in science—especially medical science—philosophy, history, literature, and in those areas of intellectual inquiry known in the twentieth century as the social sciences. In a land poor in capital and natural resources, a university education provided thousands of youths with intellectual capital that was valuable, negotiable, and above all, portable. Over the course of this long process of institutional transformation, many of the graduates of these universities found their way to the American colonies. In the cases of their presence in the two main areas of early British colonization, New England and the Chesapeake (Virginia and Maryland), this "Scottish intellectual presence" can be described with some precision.

Between the initial settlement of Virginia and the year 1780 some 818 college or university educated men migrated from Britain and Europe to New England and the Chesapeake. About 26 per cent (213) went to New England, and about 74 per cent (605) to the Chesapeake. Of the total number of learned migrants, about one third (211) had been educated in one of the Scottish universities. The Scottish universities attracted many foreign students, both Presbyterian and Episcopalian, particularly from Ireland, and from England and Wales as well: of the 211, 48 were not native Scots.

The Scottish intellectual migration to the two regions was directed overwhelmingly to the Chesapeake: only 29 of the 211 went to New England, where their educational influence was virtually nil. Between 1640 and 1700 the ratio of learned men to the total population of New England had dropped by over 200 per cent; but after 1700 the shortage of learned men in New England was gradually repaired. There was no call for foreign assistance, Scottish or English. With the exception of a half-dozen Episcopalian ministers, the twenty-nine learned Scots who made their way to New England over the course of 130 years were mainly Presbyterian ministers who served the small number of Scotch-Irish settlements in New England. Harvard and Yale, and later the College of Rhode Island (now Brown), and Dartmouth, provided New England with all the intellectual workers that it could absorb —and then some. The region was an intellectually provincial backwater, where until the nineteenth century new people and new ideas arrived only at a trickle, a situation illustrated by the fact that in all of New England before 1780 only one university-trained Scot (Dr. William Douglass of Boston, educated at the universities of Edinburgh, Leyden, and Utrecht) is known to have practiced medicine.

If in New England the slide into intellectual degeneracy was arrested from within towards the turn of the seventeenth to the eighteenth century, such was not the case in the Chesapeake. There the ratio of the university-trained to the total population, never as high as New England's to begin with, declined by almost five-hundred per cent between 1630 and 1700. At one point in the middle of the seventeenth century the Virginia legislature was even reduced to offering ships' captains a bounty of £25 upon the delivery of a live minister, educational level not specified. Bacon's Rebellion in 1676 only accentuated the lack of educated civil and religious leadership in the colony. In neighboring Catholic Maryland, too, the growing numbers of Protestants lacked civil and religious leadership. (Throughout the colonial period the Maryland Catholics, on a per capita basis, were probably the most highly-educated group in the American colonies outside New England; mainly of English descent, they had little contact with Scottish Catholics.) Given that only a relatively small number of learned Englishmen could be attracted to the colonies, a turn to the products of the Scottish universities was perhaps inevitable.

Between 1681 and 1780 some 443 college or university educated men migrated to the Chesapeake. They were recruited from twenty-four institutions of higher education in Scotland, Ireland, England, and continental Europe. As a group, universities in Scotland, contributed the largest number, 171—58 from the university of Glasgow, the same number from Aberdeen, 51 from Edinburgh, and 4 from St. Andrew's. Universities in England sent 153—95 from Oxford and 58 from Cambridge. (The faculties of Philosophy and Theology maintained by the English Jesuits at Liège sent the next largest number [53], but only one learned Scottish Jesuit is known to have migrated to the Chesapeake, and he was educated at the Scots College in Rome.) Of the 171 trained in the Scottish universities three were involved with government (among them Virginia's Governor Robert Dinwiddie, an alumnus of Glasgow), seven were businessmen, sixteen were medical doctors (among them Dr. Alexander Hamilton, son of a principal of the University of Edinburgh and the center of a celebrated Annapolis literary group), six were involved with education (mostly at the College of William and Mary), the occupation of one is not known, and the overwhelming majority, 138, were clergymen—115 Episcopalians and 23 Presbyterians.

If in an absolute sense these numbers seem small, in the context of Chesapeake society and culture they loomed large, particularly the number of Scottish Episcopalian clergymen. (Use of the nineteenth-century word "Anglican" seems singularly inappropriate here.) Clergymen were the central cultural figures in their areas, the chief interpreters and expounders of first and last things, serving often as schoolmasters and medical practitioners as well. In the early eighteenth century a prominent Marylander was already complaining that it was difficult to hear a sermon "in my own language," while in Virginia, Commissary James Blair was constantly accused of stuffing Virginia parishes with his fellow Scots. One English clergyman even went so far as to complain of the ministers "from the Scotch Universitys, who usually come young, raw & undisciplin'd, tainted with Presbyterian principles, & no reall friends to our Episcopal Government." The accusation was not wholly accurate: the average age at migration of Scottish ministers was 28, of English ministers, 31. And only three of the 115 Scottish Episcopalian ministers were converts from Presbyterianism. Perhaps the English minister was simply jealous of the hardiness of the Scots: the average age at death of Scottish migrants to the Chesapeake after 1700 was 67, while the English died at an average age of 54.

Whether or not James Blair did any stuffing of pulpits, the proportion of Scots among the clergy of the established churches of Maryland and Virginia was extraordinarily high from the 1680s onwards and was sustained after his death in 1743 to the time of the American Revolution. For example, of all the university-educated Episcopalian clergymen throughout the Chesapeake in 1710 (and at any one moment in time most of the Episcopalian clergy in the Chesapeake were university-educated), the Scottish-educated comprised 44 percent of the total. Forty years later, their proportion had fallen to 31 percent, while the rest of the Episcopal clergy was 38 percent English-educated and 15 percent American-educated. By 1770, on the eve of the Revolution, the English-educated proportion of the Episcopalian clergy throughout the Chesapeake had fallen to 25 percent, the American-educated had risen to 39 percent, and the Scots had increased their share to 36 percent.

The reasons for the considerable number of highly-educated Scots in central positions in the Chesapeake are several and complex. They took shape in the 1670s and 1680s in bitter quarrels between some Scottish Episcopalians and the Stuarts, and in vicious conflicts between Scottish Presbyterians and Scottish Episcopalians for ecclesiastical dominance. In brief, the outcome of the several situations was that Scottish Episcopalians lost. Many university-educated clergy, like James Blair, sought preferment abroad, in England, the colonies, and elsewhere, and continued to do so throughout the eighteenth century. A second reason for the Scottish professional presence in the Chesapeake was Glasgow's rise in the early eighteenth century to predominance in the extremely lucrative international tobacco trade. In the eighteenth century seemingly every other navigable creek along the Chesapeake had its resident Scottish storekeeper or tobacco factor. These tradesmen, though seldom themselves university-educated, had brothers, cousins, and connections who were either university students or prospective clergymen. The printed records of the University of Glasgow are unusually revealing in this respect. A look at class lists quickly shows the presence together in the same class of students who later migrated to the Chesapeake with sons and connections of Glasgow's "tobacco lords." News of a potential opening in a Maryland or Virginia parish was quickly conveyed home to Scotland, and the wheels of ecclesiastical patronage were set in motion. As is so often the case, intellect followed commerce. Something of the same process must have occurred at the other Scottish universities, though routes between Scotland and the Chesapeake other than the tobacco trade existed.

The intellectual and personal links between learned Scotland and America were many and intricate. Consider the case of the sons of Andrew Rosse, Professor of Humanity at the University of Glasgow from 1706 to 1735. One of Rosse's sons, also Andrew, was a student of his father while at university, and later migrated to Virginia as a merchant. A second son, George, remained in Glasgow, where he succeeded his father as Professor of Humanity from 1735 to 1754. Among George's students was his younger brother, John, who migrated to Maryland where he was rector of All Hallow's Parish for over twenty years. Besides his brother, at least seven more of the second Professor Rosse's students migrated to the Chesapeake, four of them merchants and four (including his brother) Episcopalian clergymen. The Rosse link between Scotland and America did not end with Professor George's death in 1754, for from Maryland Reverend John Rosse sent his American-born son Andrew (doubtlessly named after his uncle and his professorial grandfather) to Scotland to be educated. There young Andrew matriculated at the University of Glasgow in 1774.

Andrew Rosse's enrollment at the University of Glasgow suggests another important educational link between America and Scotland: study by Americans at Scottish universities. During the whole colonial period only 321 Americans are known to have attended overseas colleges and universities as undergraduates. Another twenty-six, after finishing their undergraduate work at American colleges, traveled to Europe for graduate work. All but one of the latter group were medical students at the University of Edinburgh.

Of the 321 foreign-educated Americans, the largest group consisted of 132 American Catholics, mostly from Maryland, along with a handful from Pennsylvania. Forbidden to maintain institutions of their own in their homeland and denied admission to existing institutions, like their English co-religionists they were educated at the English Catholic colleges scattered across Europe and in European universities. Only one of them had any connection with Scotland. (This was Joseph Digges of Prince George's County, Maryland, who after attending the English Jesuit College of St. Omer's somehow received his M.D. from the University of Glasgow). Of the remaining 191 non-Catholic Americans, about 44 per cent (84) pursued their higher educations in Scotland—1 at St. Andrew's, 12 at Aberdeen, 26 at Edinburgh and 45 at the University of Glasgow. (By way of comparison, during the same period 44 Americans attended Oxford and 55 went to Cambridge.) Most of the American students in Scotland were drawn from the Chesapeake—22 from Maryland and 41 from Virginia. Of the remainder, Massachusetts sent 3, New York 2, Pennsylvania 3, South Carolina 6, and 8 came from places in America unknown. American patronage of Scottish institutions coincided mainly with the rise to international eminence—particularly excellence in medical science and instruction—of the Scots universities during the third quarter of the eighteenth century. Only a dozen American students are known to have attended a Scottish university before

1751, and all but two of these attended the University of Glasgow.

If we combine the group of American students in Scotland who had already completed their undergraduate studies in the colonies together with the Americans who between 1750 and 1780 pursued their higher studies solely in Scotland, we arrive at a number of 98 American colonials who attended Scottish universities in those three decades, 50 at Edinburgh, 37 at Glasgow, and 11 at Aberdeen. This eastward flow across the Atlantic in pursuit of higher education maintained the regional pattern of the movement of highly educated Scots westward to America: about 70 per cent (68) of the American students in Scotland were drawn from the Chesapeake, 19 from Maryland and 49 from Virginia. (New England sent three, the Middle Colonies 16, and the Lower South 5. Eight have not been traced.) Of the students who had already graduated from American colleges, 11 were educated at the College of William and Mary, 6 at the College of Philadelphia (later the University of Pennsylvania), 5 at the College of New Jersey (later Princeton University), and 4 at King's College (later Columbia University).

Some of these youths, like Andrew Rosse, were the sons of Scots resident in the colonies, or were of more distant Scottish or Scotch-Irish heritage. But many were not. Arthur Lee of Virginia was of English ancestry, John Morgan of Pennsylvania was of Welsh descent, and Benjamin Rush of Philadelphia kept the sword of his grandfather, an English Cromwellian soldier, displayed in his home. As the names Morgan and Rush might suggest to those familiar with American medical history, by a very large majority—61 of the 98 became medical doctors—these youths went to Scotland in pursuit of instruction in medicine, particularly to the University of Edinburgh, where John Black in chemistry, William Cullen in physiology, and several others had established international reputations. (To avoid double counting, the number given above for those who attended the University of Edinburgh necessarily masks the fact that many of the Edinburghians had first attended Glasgow as undergraduates. Many stayed in Glasgow for their full medical education.)

American students in Scotland absorbed much more than medical knowledge and skills in their stays in Scotland. They formed lifelong connections with learned Scots and with the broader achievements of the high Scottish Enlightenment. For example, while in Scotland Benjamin Rush, acting as agent for a group at home that included Scots, helped to persuade the eminent Presbyterian divine John Witherspoon to emigrate to America in order to assume the presidency of the College of New Jersey at Princeton. Rush wrote back to Philadelphia: "Methinks I see the place of my nativity becoming the Edinburgh of America." Once home in America Rush and several of his friends set about doing just that. On his return to America in 1765 Rush's friend John Morgan persuaded the trustees of the young College of Philadelphia to establish the first Medical Faculty in North America, on a plan that owed a good deal to the University of Edinburgh. Philadelphia in turn became a model for American medical study, moving it from instruction by apprenticeship towards location within an institution where rigorous scientific study might develop over time. If we can think of Harvard and its institutional progeny as England's enduring educational legacy to America, perhaps we can think of Pennsylvania's Medical School and its institutional progeny as Scotland's institutional legacy to America.

Given the considerable number of Americans from the Chesapeake who studied medicine within an institutional setting in Scotland one might have expected the center of medical education in British America to have been established there (say in Williamsburg), rather than in the Middle Colonies. And, in fact, James McClurg, a William and Mary alumnus who had studied in Edinburgh, was appointed professor of medicine at his alma mater. But the disruptions caused by the Revolution and the removal of Virginia's capitol from Williamsburg to Richmond (along with the removal of McClurg himself to Richmond) aborted a

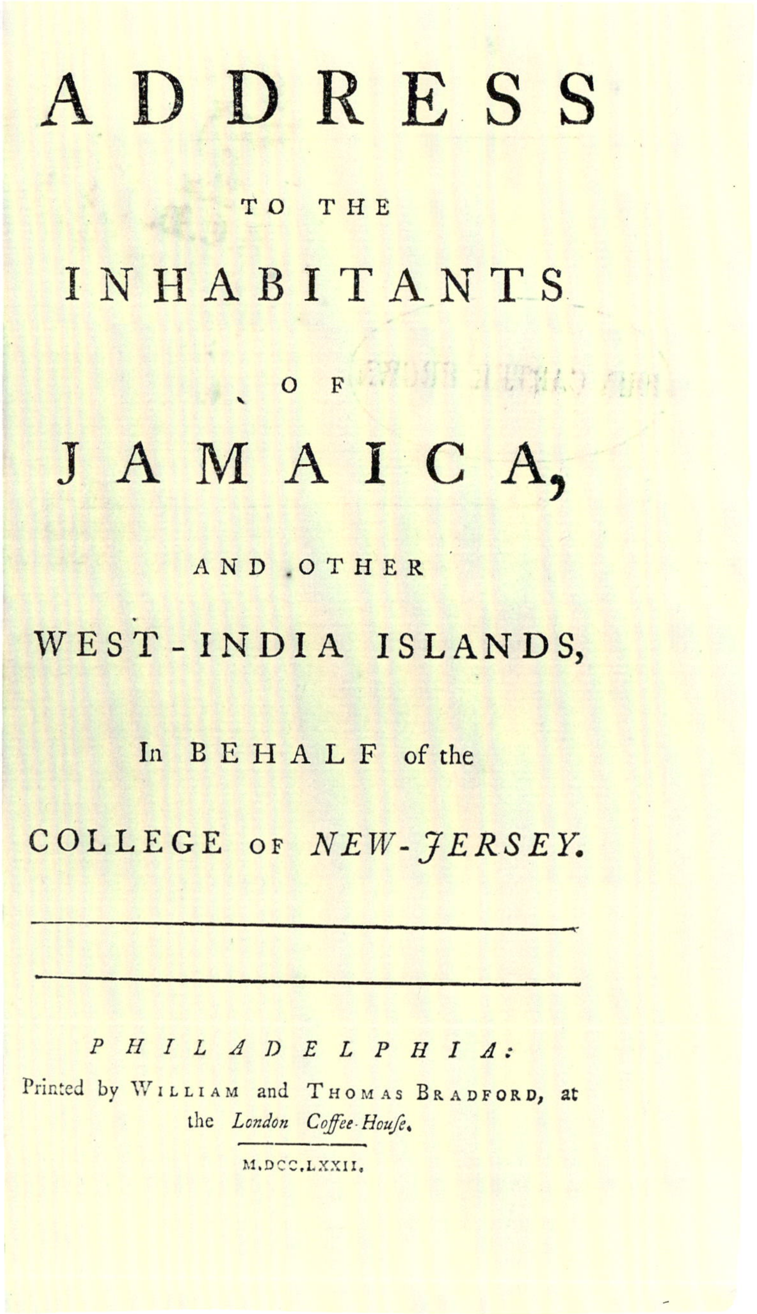

ADDRESS

TO THE

INHABITANTS

OF

JAMAICA,

AND OTHER

WEST-INDIA ISLANDS,

In BEHALF of the

COLLEGE OF *NEW-JERSEY.*

PHILADELPHIA:
Printed by W<small>ILLIAM</small> and T<small>HOMAS</small> B<small>RADFORD</small>, at the *London Coffee-House.*
M,DCC,LXXII.

FIG. 36
John Witherspoon, *Address to the Inhabitants of Jamaica*, Philadelphia, 1772. The Scottish-born Witherspoon was a Signer of the Declaration of Independence, the leading Presbyterian in America, and the principal fundraiser for the College of New Jersey (later Princeton), of which he was president. With this pamphlet he hoped to gain support for the College from wealthy merchants in the islands. (Cat. no. 39).

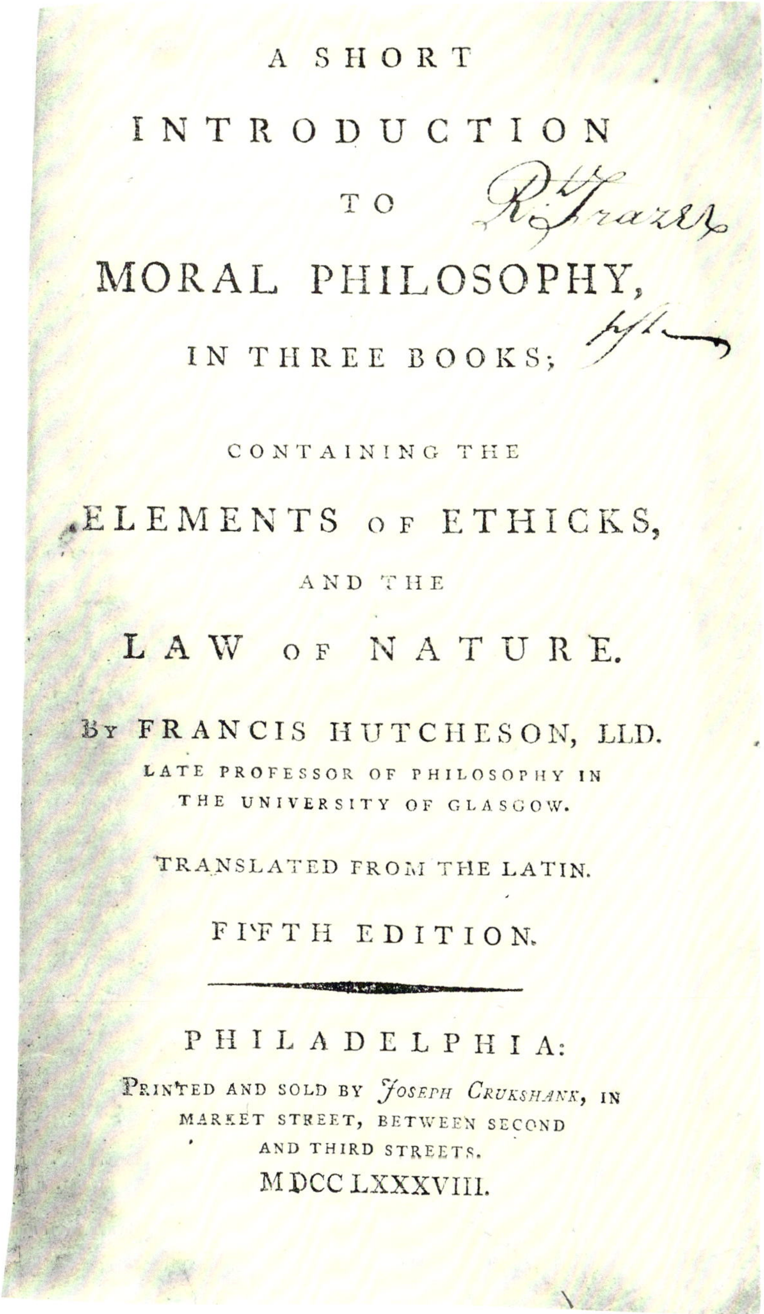

A SHORT

INTRODUCTION

TO

MORAL PHILOSOPHY,

IN THREE BOOKS;

CONTAINING THE

ELEMENTS OF ETHICKS,

AND THE

LAW OF NATURE.

By FRANCIS HUTCHESON, LL.D.

LATE PROFESSOR OF PHILOSOPHY IN
THE UNIVERSITY OF GLASGOW.

TRANSLATED FROM THE LATIN.

FIFTH EDITION.

PHILADELPHIA:

PRINTED AND SOLD BY *Joseph Crukshank*, IN
MARKET STREET, BETWEEN SECOND
AND THIRD STREETS.
MDCCLXXXVIII.

FIG. 37
Francis Hutcheson, *Short Introduction to Moral Philosophy*, Philadelphia, 1788. For more than a century, college education in America was heavily influenced above all by the writings of academics in Scotland, none more important in teaching and learning on these shores than those of Hutcheson. (Cat. no. 40).

nascent center of medical education in the Chesapeake. This raises some final reflections about the role of university-educated Scots in colonial America.

We mentioned earlier that New England had become "intellectually provincial" around 1700. There can be a considerable amount of cultural strength in provincialism. One gloss on the notion of provincialism is that an area may be at the same time not only inward-looking and out-of-touch with a center, but also self-sufficient and able to provide for itself without outside help. Comparatively few highly-educated Scots migrated to New England because New Englanders were able to create educational institutions that produced natives who met the area's needs. The consistent demand for highly-educated Scots and English in the Chesapeake suggests that American colonials there, despite the best efforts of the College of William and Mary, were unable to fulfill their own educational needs. The Chesapeake's educational dependency on the centers of the first British Empire left it for a time, after the links with Scotland and England were broken and the flow of highly-educated Scots and English into the region stopped, in a position of deeper intellectual provinciality (in the perjorative sense of the term) than New England had ever known.

38
William Smith.
A General Idea of the College of Mirania; with a Sketch of the Method of Teaching Science and Religion.
New York, 1753.

Smith (1727–1803), a Scottish Episcopalian minister, was one of two Scots responsible for reshaping Benjamin Franklin's Philadelphia Academy into the College of Philadelphia (later the University of Pennsylvania), the fifth college established in British North America. Educated at the University of Aberdeen's King's College, he emigrated to New York as a tutor for a wealthy family in 1751, aged twenty-four. The second of two pamphlets Smith published in New York, *Mirania* outlined in Utopian form a complete framework of education designed for the New World and for all classes of society. (Fig. 35). It caught the attention of Franklin, and Smith soon found himself in Philadelphia designing a curriculum for a college.

Smith's curriculum for the College of Philadelphia was modern, thorough, and detailed. Constructed on the principles of Scottish realism (a planned progression of studies moving from the particular to the general), it drew heavily on Smith's own educational background, recent reforms at Marischal College, Aberdeen, as well as other sources.

Smith served many years as provost of the College, and in concert with the Scottish Presbyterian educator Francis Alison, who had studied at the University of Glasgow, succeeded in maintaining a coherent educational program in the biggest and most multi-cultural city in British North America. Somewhat vain and a constant controversialist, Smith has not been treated kindly by historians. But his educational plans were sound, and his college, through its many transformations, became an important university and the earliest major center of medical education in North America.

39
John Witherspoon.
Address to the Inhabitants of Jamaica and other West-India Islands, in Behalf of the College of New-Jersey.
Philadelphia, 1772.

John Witherspoon (1723–1794) was the most distinguished of learned Scots to emigrate to America during the eighteenth century. A graduate of the University of Edinburgh, minister at Paisley, and with an already considerable reputation in Scotland and America as a forceful and effective polemicist for the conservative wing of the Presbyterian Church of Scotland, he was persuaded in 1768 to become, at the age of forty-eight, sixth president of the College of New Jersey at Princeton, the fourth college established in the Amer-

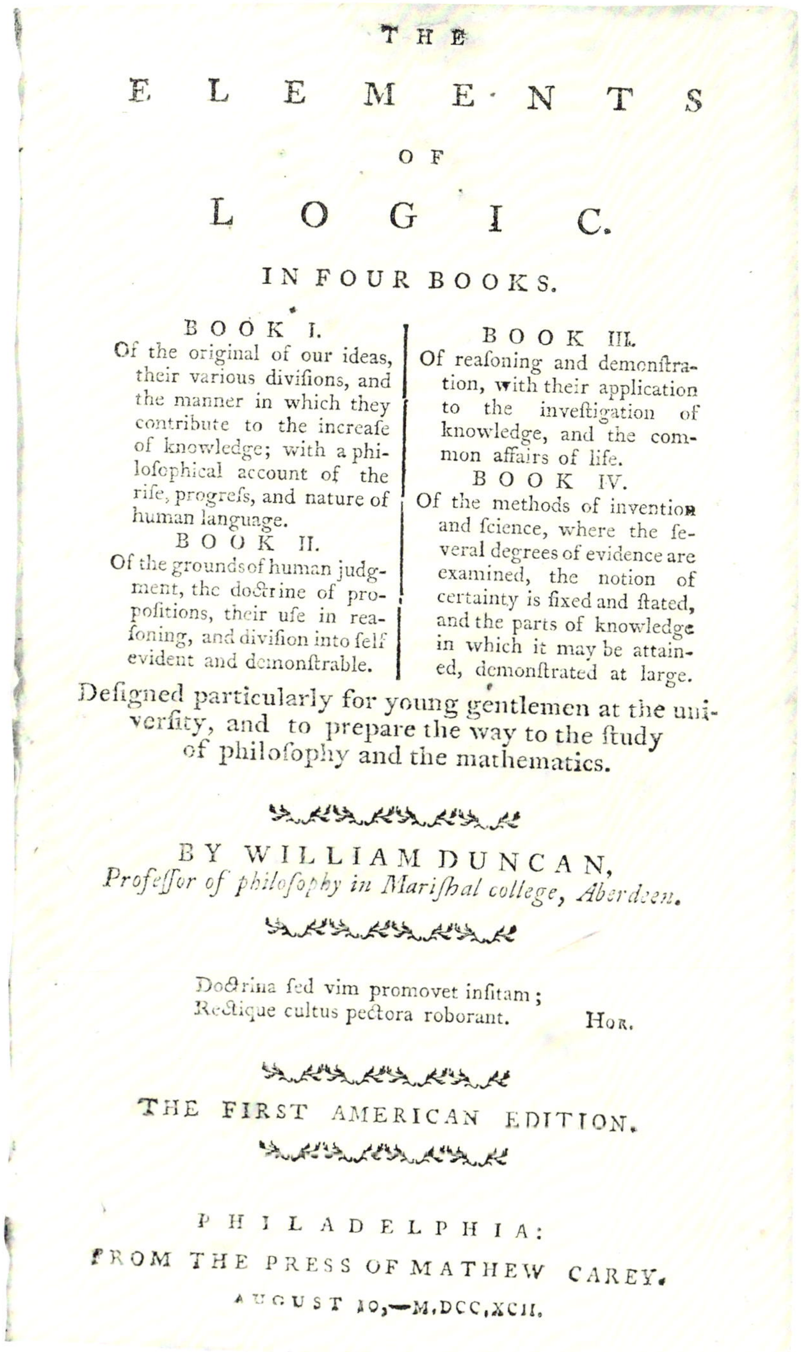

THE ELEMENTS OF LOGIC.

IN FOUR BOOKS.

BOOK I.
Of the original of our ideas, their various divisions, and the manner in which they contribute to the increase of knowledge; with a philosophical account of the rise, progress, and nature of human language.

BOOK II.
Of the grounds of human judgment, the doctrine of propositions, their use in reasoning, and division into self evident and demonstrable.

BOOK III.
Of reasoning and demonstration, with their application to the investigation of knowledge, and the common affairs of life.

BOOK IV.
Of the methods of invention and science, where the several degrees of evidence are examined, the notion of certainty is fixed and stated, and the parts of knowledge in which it may be attained, demonstrated at large.

Designed particularly for young gentlemen at the university, and to prepare the way to the study of philosophy and the mathematics.

BY WILLIAM DUNCAN,
Professor of philosophy in Marishal college, Aberdeen.

Doctrina sed vim promovet insitam;
Rectique cultus pectora roborant. HOR.

THE FIRST AMERICAN EDITION.

PHILADELPHIA:
FROM THE PRESS OF MATHEW CAREY.
AUGUST 10,—M.DCC.XCII.

FIG. 38
William Duncan, *Elements of Logic*, Philadelphia, 1792. Duncan was another Scottish academic whose work was so much in demand that an American edition made sense to a Philadelphia publisher, Matthew Carey. (Cat. no. 41).

ican colonies. He revivified Princeton, remodeled its curriculum along Scottish lines, and attracted a new clientele from the South. His address to the Jamaicans was a substitute for a fund-raising trip on behalf of Princeton to the island, where many Scots held prominent positions in business and government. (Fig. 36).

Witherspoon, highly respected among the Scotch-Irish and their offspring in America, was the only signer of the Declaration of Independence who was a clergyman. As a member of the Continental Congress he was an indefatigable and extraordinarily effective committeeman. Much of his effort in the postwar years was devoted, with equal success, to the organization of the Presbyterian church in America.

40
Francis Hutcheson.
A Short Introduction to Moral Philosophy.
Philadelphia, 1788.

Francis Hutcheson is often called the "father of Scottish 'Common Sense' philosophy," the form of philosophy that reigned supreme in many American colleges from the middle of the eighteenth century well into the Victorian era. Hutcheson was Professor of Moral Philosophy at the University of Glasgow from 1730 to 1746. The *Short Introduction* was first published in 1742 and went through many editions. (Fig. 37). Several of Hutcheson's students emigrated to North America, perhaps the best known being the Presbyterian minister Francis Alison, vice-provost at the College of Philadelphia, where he taught, among other things, logic and moral philosophy until he died in 1779. Alison's philosophical lectures were based squarely on Hutcheson's work, as were John Witherspoon's lectures on the same subject at Princeton. Generations of young Americans were trained to think in Hutcheson's categories. His thought provided a common ground of intellectual discourse for the educated classes of America during the late colonial and early national eras.

41
William Duncan.
The Elements of Logic.
Philadelphia, 1792.

This is the Scottish work that determined the form and progression of arguments that Thomas Jefferson used in composing the Declaration of Independence. Its author, William Duncan, was an alumnus of Marischal College, Aberdeen. The work first appeared, anonymously, as the section on logic in Robert Dodsley's *The Preceptor* (London, 1748), a compendium designed to introduce young people to knowledge. *The Preceptor* was widely circulated in North America and used heavily by students, tutors, and professors there. Duncan's section of the work was later published in a separate edition under his own name. (Fig. 38).

Duncan became a professor at Marischal College in 1753. Among his students was William Small, who in 1761 came to America to teach moral philosophy and logic at the College of William and Mary. Among Small's students in Williamsburg was Thomas Jefferson. Jefferson later declared that Small "probably fixed the destinies of my life." Small taught Duncan's method of logical argument, "one designed to create certainty and conviction among enlightened readers." The wide acceptance of the Declaration of Independence was not only a testimony to Jefferson's skill, but an indication that readers in every part of the colonies were already primed and receptive to arguments couched in the terms of Duncan's logic.

42
Papers Relating to an Affadavit Made by His Reverence James Blair, Clerk, Pretended President of William and Mary.
[London], 1727.

James Blair (1655–1743), a Scottish Episcopalian clergyman, was the first President of the College of William and Mary in Williamsburg, the second college established in the American colonies. Blair, an alumnus of Marischal College, Aberdeen, went out to Virginia as a missionary in 1685. He was shortly appointed commissary (representative of the Bishop of London, who had authority for church affairs in the colonies) for Virginia. Among the chief supporters of the founding of the College, he served as its president for fifty years. Blair was a major force in Virginia politics for the course of his long life and the bane of one royal governor after another. The "Affadavit" is a souvenir of Blair's violent disagreements with one of the unfortunate officials, Governor Francis Nicholson. A vivid outline of quarrels between powerful personalities confined to a small place, it reads somewhat like a supermarket tabloid.

FOR FURTHER READING

William R. and C. Helen Brock, *Scotus Americanus: A Survey of Links between Scotland and America in the Eighteenth Century* (Edinburgh, 1982).

Lawrence A. Cremin, *American Education: The Colonial Experience, 1607–1783* (New York, 1970).

Douglas M. Sloan, *The Scottish Enlightenment and the American College Ideal* (New York, 1971).

THE
SPANISH Empire
IN
AMERICA.

CONTAINING,

A succinct Relation of the Discovery and Settlement of its several Colonies; a View of their respective Situations, Extent, Commodities, Trade, &c.

AND

A full and clear Account of the Commerce with OLD SPAIN by the *Galleons, Flota, &c.*

ALSO

Of the Contraband Trade with the *English, Dutch, French, Danes,* and *Portuguese.* With an exact Description of *Paraguay.*

By an *ENGLISH* MERCHANT.

LONDON:
Printed for M. COOPER in *Pater-noster Row.* 1747.

CHAPTER SEVEN: *Colonial Warfare and Imperial Identity*

BRUCE P. LENMAN

BY THE TIME OF the Act of Union of 1707, the Scots had a history of unsuccessful colonial enterprises behind them. Article IV of the Treaty of Union provided:

"That all the Subjects of the United Kingdom of Great Britain shall from and after the Union have full Freedom and Intercourse of Trade and Navigation to and from any port or place within the said United Kingdom and the Dominions and Plantations thereunto belonging."

So the Scots, since 1660 excluded in theory from commercial intercourse with the English overseas empire, were at last free to trade with, settle in, and hold office in any part of that empire. In fact, they do not appear to have been very interested in this issue around 1707. Arguably, their attempts to establish their own colonies had been misguided. There was much more advantage for them in penetrating and trading with the long-established colonies of greater European powers. It was never illegal under Scots law for Scottish merchants to trade with English or Spanish America, and the English and Spanish metropolitan governments lacked the ability to stop their colonists from trading with interloping foreign merchants. Glasgow, already deeply involved in the Chesapeake Trade before 1707, was a center of opposition to the Act of Union, opposition carried to the point of riot.

However, once the political structure of the United Kingdom of Great Britain was in place, it was natural for ambitious Scots of non-Jacobite persuasion to regard its overseas empire as a potential field of profit and preferment. Alexander Spotswood, Governor (technically Lieutenant-Governor) of Virginia from 1710 to 1722 was an early figure in a long succession of Scots to govern eighteenth-century British colonies. Virginia alone was ruled by such Scots as Robert Dinwiddie, who governed in Williamsburg from 1751 to 1757, playing a key role in the early stages of the French and Indian War, and Lord Dunmore, the unpopular last royal Governor whose career showed that even ex-Jacobite families, like his own, were becoming pillars of the British Empire. By the 1720s Scottish writers of a Whig-Unionist disposition were actively promoting the creation and popularization of a new imperial British identity designed to supersede the narrower confines of English of Scottish nationality. It is no accident that during his London years, between 1725 and 1748, the Scots poet James Thomson not only wrote "Liberty", a lengthy poetical panegyric to Whig values, but also the lyric for "Rule Britannia."

The early writings of John Campbell, supporting a buccaneering assault of a neo-Elizabethan kind on the Spanish Empire in the Americas can therefore be seen as what one might expect from a London-Scot anxious to set the seal on British identity with a series of lucrative triumphs. Born into the family of Campbell of Glenlyon which was

FIG. 40
[John Campbell], *The Spanish Empire in America*, London, 1747. From their vantage point outside of the London establishment, and as a result of their particular historical experience, Scots were often shrewd strategic observers of the Atlantic world. Campbell, writing here under the guise of an "English Merchant," was among the best of them. (Cat. no. 45).

identified with the horrors of the 1692 Massacre of Glencoe, where Campbell of Glenlyon commanded the government troops. John Campbell was an ultra-Whig by heredity. He rode the rising current of enthusiasm for conflict with Spain which pushed Sir Robert Walpole reluctantly into war in 1739. Though he did his writing in London, fueling his muse with up to fifteen bottles of port a day, it is clear from other items published in Edinburgh that there was strong contemporary interest in Scotland in the details of the campaigns of this War of Jenkins' Ear, so called after the English captain used as a *casus belli*. It was alleged, dubiously, that Spanish *guardacostas* had cut off his ear.

This anti-Catholic and anti-Bourbon crusading mentality probably peaked amongst the Scottish ruling classes during the French and Indian War, in which the first shots were fired by troops commanded by the young George Washington, who had been sent to the Ohio Valley by Governor Dinwiddie. In Europe this conflict became the Seven Years War. Scottish troops, especially from the former Jacobite areas of the Highlands, played a prominent role in the conflict. It was a broadsword charge by Fraser's Highlanders which finished off Montcalm's already shattered army before the gates of Quebec.

Educated Scots hoped to do well out of an expanded British Empire. They did secure a disproportionate amount of the imperial patronage available after the triumphal Peace of Paris of 1763. Yet they had not inherited the commitment to the *Leyenda Negra*, that black legend of Spanish iniquity, especially in the Americas, which from the days of Drake had been an integral part of English identity. It has to be said that John Campbell, as well as urging war against metropolitan Spain, had conveyed a great deal of accurate and sympathetic material on Spanish America to his readers.

Of course, there was always a market for anti-Catholic views, especially among the commercial and manufacturing classes in the expanding Scottish towns, for they tended to embrace a seceding Presbyterianism of a notably evangelical kind, but the men of the Scottish Enlightenment distrusted "enthusiasm" in religion. Principal Robertson, himself the much-published leader of the moderate literati of Edinburgh, belonged to the politically very conservative elite of the high Enlightenment. His political sympathies lay with George III, and his own patron Lord Bute, a fellow-Scot hounded out of high office by the scurrilous abuse of English populists. His ideal British empire was to acquire some of the reverence for metropolitan authority which characterized the Bourbon Empires. It was to live in liberal, Christian harmony with them. Understandably, Robertson set out to stamp out the appeal of the *Leyenda Negra*. His widely-praised *History of America* was very rapidly translated into nearly all the major European languages. Despite its affectation of serene detachment (much reinforced by beautifully balanced sentences), it was in fact a highly partisan performance. It was a paen of praise to metropolitan rule, with no great enthusiasm for white settlers, and a vision of Amerindians, both in North and in South America, as living barbarically as "savages" before European contact. It is ironic that Robertson's conservative Scottish vision of an imperial British Atlantic community should have been destroyed by those recalcitrant provincial Englishmen in Virginia and Massachusetts who led the revolt which created a separate American identity.

43
A New Plan of the Harbour, City, & Forts of Cartagena. [Edinburgh, 1741.]

This small but accurate situation map published in Edinburgh shows how closely Scottish opinion followed the fate of Admiral Vernon's attack on the Spanish Caribbean. (Fig. 39). The Anglo-Spanish War of 1739 was one which Prime Minister Sir Robert Walpole deeply disliked and had tried to avoid.

At first all went well. Admiral Vernon captured Porto Bello in November 1739. The

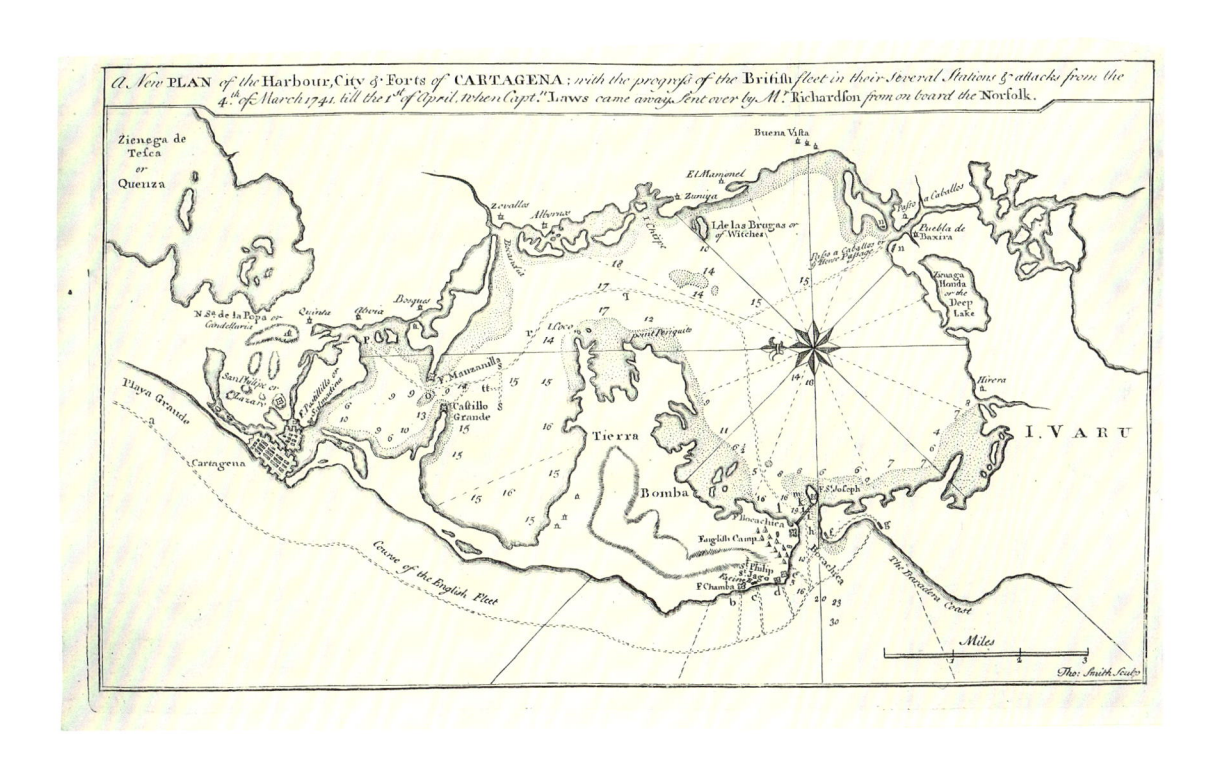

FIG. 39
A New Plan of the Harbour, City, & Forts of Cartagena, [Edinburgh, 1741]. The War of Jenkins' Ear, a four-year struggle between Spain and England, broke out in 1739. Most of the battles took place in Florida, Georgia, and the Caribbean basin, areas where many Scottish interests were concentrated. Admiral Vernon quickly captured Puerto Bello at Panama, but was disastrously defeated at Cartagena. (Cat. no. 43).

theatre of operations was close to the Gulf of Darien, which carried the memories of the Scots colony suppressed by Spanish power. The 1741 attack on Cartagena failed. Vernon retained his popularity, but triumphalism and expectation of quick, cheap victory faded. By 1742 Walpole had been made the scape-goat for failure and hounded out of office. The Washington family home on the Potomac, Mount Vernon, was so called for Admiral Vernon. One of Vernon's old seamen settled down on the coast of the Firth of Forth near Edinburgh, and eventually gave the name Porto Bello to the suburb which developed there. Few today understand its origin in the war-craze of 1739–41.

44
John Campbell.
Lives of the Admirals and Other Eminent British Seamen.
London, 1742–44.

The first two volumes of this collection appeared in 1742, the remaining two in 1744. Campbell had already established a reputation as an historical author. He read extensively in foreign languages for his many contributions to both the ancient and the modern *Universal History*. The *Lives of the Admirals*, though occasionally marred by Campbell's lack of a practical seaman's knowledge, was a success

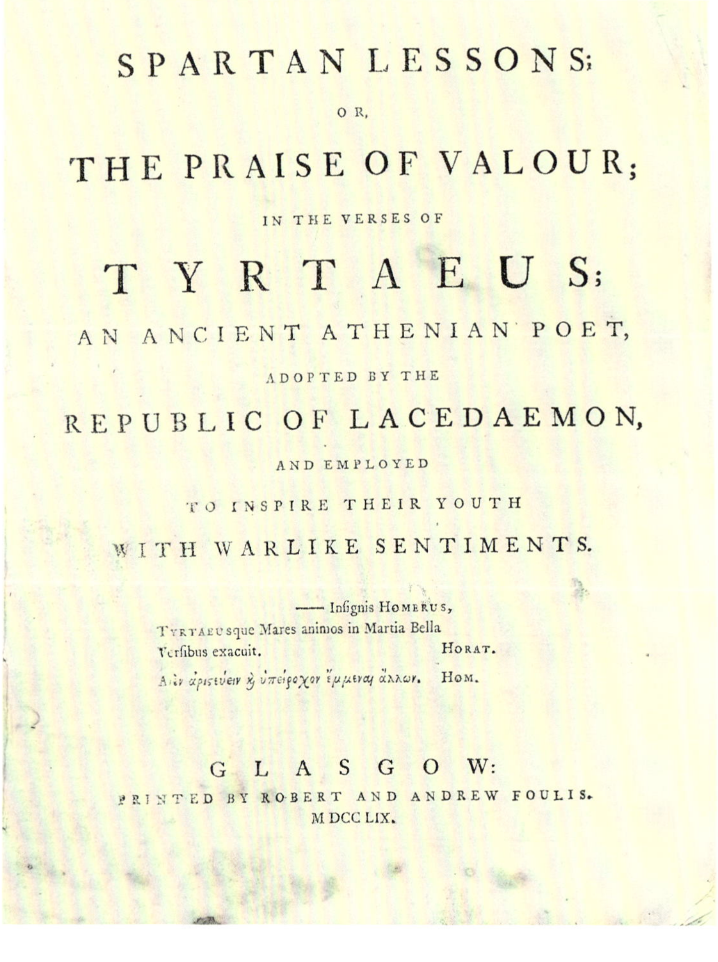
SPARTAN LESSONS;
OR,
THE PRAISE OF VALOUR;
IN THE VERSES OF
TYRTAEUS;
AN ANCIENT ATHENIAN POET,
ADOPTED BY THE
REPUBLIC OF LACEDAEMON,
AND EMPLOYED
TO INSPIRE THEIR YOUTH
WITH WARLIKE SENTIMENTS.

—— Insignis HOMERUS,
TYRTAEUSque Mares animos in Martia Bella
Versibus exacuit. HORAT.
Αἰὲν ἀριστεύειν καὶ ὑπείροχον ἔμμεναι ἄλλων. HOM.

GLASGOW:
PRINTED BY ROBERT AND ANDREW FOULIS.
M DCC LIX.

FIG. 41
Tyrtaeus, *Spartan Lessons; or, The Praise of Valour*, Glasgow, 1759. Scotland specialized in exporting people, and many of those were tough soldiers recruited to fight in American wars. This work was intended to sustain the martial spirit among Scottish youth. (Cat. no. 46).

commercially, being translated into German and achieving three editions in Campbell's lifetime, as well as many later ones. It provided a continuous narrative from the days of the Ancient Britons up to the date of publication. It set naval events in their wider politico-economic context, and represented massive reading. Campbell emphasized particularly his use of French and Dutch materials.

Cosmopolitan sources did not imply lack of patriotic purpose, for Campbell was anxious to blend English, Welsh, and Scottish traditions to support the greatness of a British Empire based on the maritime might of "this happy isle." Naval history was valuable because it taught lessons for the future. In the Preface to Volume I he says: "For to know, and in Consequence thereof to assert our Country's Rights, is in this World the great Business of a Briton."

Hence, Campbell's account of a medieval Welsh discovery of America, placing prior right of discovery and therefore title to America in the hands of the Tudor dynasty rather than the Spanish. Hence also his stress on the fact that the Treaty of London of 1604, whereby James I put an end to the Elizabethan war with Spain, was reasonable and did not represent a betrayal of English interests by the new Scots king. Campbell's volume IV opens with the statement that after 1707: "I propose to make the Union of the two Kingdoms the great Event from whence, in this Volume, I shall deduce our Naval History to the present Times."

Campbell could see that many Scots opposed the 1707 Union for patriotic reasons, but was himself a passionate supporter, for he saw it as "a mortal blow to the French." The preface to volume four was published as Britain entered a general war against the Bourbon powers. Campbell refers to the threat to British naval superiority openly mounted by France. He says that "I hope to add a Fifth Volume to this Work, containing our Triumphs over the common Enemy, and the establishing our just Rights of all kinds, by a safe, honourable, and solid Peace; and then my Book, and the public Happiness, will be equally complete." Significantly, volume five never appeared.

45
John Campbell.
The Spanish Empire in America.
London, 1747.

First published in 1741 when Admiral Vernon seemed poised to devastate the Spanish Caribbean, this edition came out towards the end of a disappointing war. The Edinburgh-born Campbell wrote as "an English Merchant." The war had started in 1739 as the purely Anglo-Spanish War of Jenkins' Ear but by 1744 had become an Anglo-French war as well. When this book was published the combatants were exhausted. Peace came in the next year. (Fig. 40).

Much of Campbell's success as a man of letters in London depended on catching current popular obsessions. In 1739 English chauvinists had embarked on an aggressive neo-Elizabethan war against Spain, in the hope both of looting the treasures of Spanish America and of forcing their way into Spanish imperial markets. Campbell is very clear in Chapter III of the Third Book that the attempt by the Spanish crown to prevent their American colonists from trading with other European nations for goods which Spain itself was incapable of supplying was a tyrannical infringement of the colonists' "Natural Rights." From this typical Enlightenment argument Campbell deduces the inevitability of widespread contraband trade by the English, Dutch, and French, condoned by Spanish colonists, if not by their royal masters.

However, Campbell does not envisage dismantling the Spanish Empire. The filibustering attacks on Spanish America, like the attack on Cartagena in which George Washington's beloved half-brother Lawrence Washington had participated, had failed. Campbell argues that if the Spanish crown would adopt more enlightened trade policies, the result would be a stronger, not a weaker Spanish Empire, and that it would be far better if Britain and Spain were allies because: "As an Ally, we are more concerned than any other to protect and promote their Interests, because they never can interfere with ours;

and in respect of Commerce, we can supply their Wants cheaper and more effectually than any other Nation and also take more of their Goods in Return."

46
Tyrtaeus.
Spartan Lessons; or, the Praise of Valour; in the Verses of Tyrtaeus; an Ancient Athenian Poet, Adopted by the Republic of Lacedaemon, and Employed to Inspire Their Youth with Warlike Sentiments.
Glasgow, 1759.

This short publication by the Foulis brothers of Glasgow is at first glance typical of their list. They were notable publishers of "immaculate" editions of classical Roman and Greek authors. Here we have an edition of the Greek text of poems in praise of war by the Greek poet who, next to Homer and Hesiod, was the earliest classical poet known. (Fig. 41). According to Sir Isaac Newton, he lived a hundred years after Lycurgus laid down the severe laws that ensured the essentially military spirit of Spartan society. Tyrtaeus was an Athenian, naturalized a Spartan, and both poet and general. It was he who led Sparta to final victory in the long and difficult Second Messenian War.

The contemporary relevance of the book is obvious from the Dedication which is to "The Young Gentlemen; lately bred at the University of Glasgow; at present serving their country as officers of the Highland Battalions now in America!"

The years 1754–58 had seen many British defeats at French hands. They also saw the elder Pitt recruit troops from former Jacobite clans to spearhead his campaigns in North America. The young Glasgow alums leading those troops are urged to cultivate the Spartan virtues of sacrifice, discipline, and persistence in the face of defeat. The text stresses that as paladins of a united Hanoverian Britain they fight for their birth-right of Liberty against French tyranny. They are reminded that: "where there is no Liberty, there can be no real birth-right." A Latin translation helps mobilize Scottish classical culture for anti-Bourbon war.

47
A Plan of the City and Harbour of Louisbourg. [Edinburgh, 1762.]

This small situation map, with a theatre map inset, is a cartographic curiosity. Like the 1741 map of Cartagena, it is clearly a *pièce d'occasion* from the periodical press. In this case the source is identified on the map by means of a reference to the *Scots Magazine* of Edinburgh.

By 1762 Louisbourg had been in British hands for four years since its capture by an expedition commanded by General Jeffery Amherst and Admiral Boscawen in 1758. It was a center of the cod fishery, and it was a strategic key to Quebec's supply lines. Despite heavy fortification, it had been captured by a New England force under General Pepperell in 1745. That victory and the evangelical zeal of the contemporary Great Awakening confirmed the New Englanders' view that they were truly a Chosen People, but the Peace of Aix la Chapelle returned Louisbourg to France in exchange for Madras, captured by the French in India.

After the 1758 capture the fortress was surrendered by France in 1763. Yet this is a map of Pepperell's campaign, showing the dispositions of the New England army in 1745. Presumably it was easier and cheaper to pull old *Scots Magazine* material, even if obsolete, than to pay for up-to-date cartography.

48
John Campbell.
An Account of the Spanish Settlements in America.
Edinburgh, 1762.

Campbell's preface stresses the way the current war has focused attention on America: "by far the largest of the four grand divisions of the world, and is now become of the great-

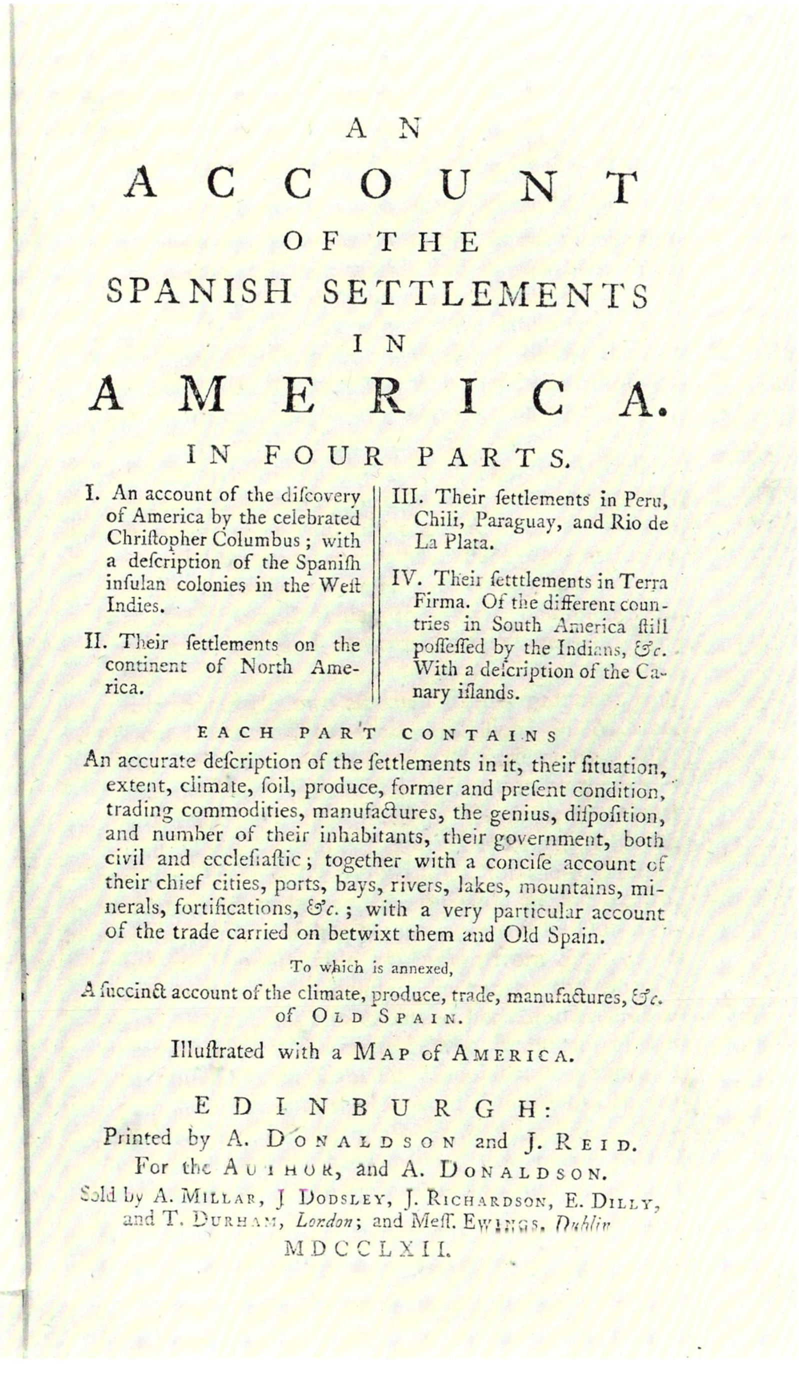

AN
ACCOUNT
OF THE
SPANISH SETTLEMENTS
IN
AMERICA.

IN FOUR PARTS.

I. An account of the discovery of America by the celebrated Christopher Columbus; with a description of the Spanish insular colonies in the West Indies.

II. Their settlements on the continent of North America.

III. Their settlements in Peru, Chili, Paraguay, and Rio de La Plata.

IV. Their setttlements in Terra Firma. Of the different countries in South America still possessed by the Indians, &c. With a description of the Canary islands.

EACH PART CONTAINS

An accurate description of the settlements in it, their situation, extent, climate, soil, produce, former and present condition, trading commodities, manufactures, the genius, disposition, and number of their inhabitants, their government, both civil and ecclesiastic; together with a concise account of their chief cities, ports, bays, rivers, lakes, mountains, minerals, fortifications, &c.; with a very particular account of the trade carried on betwixt them and Old Spain.

To which is annexed,

A succinct account of the climate, produce, trade, manufactures, &c. of OLD SPAIN.

Illustrated with a MAP of AMERICA.

EDINBURGH:
Printed by A. DONALDSON and J. REID.
For the AUTHOR, and A. DONALDSON.
Sold by A. MILLAR, J DODSLEY, J. RICHARDSON, E. DILLY, and T. DURHAM, *London*; and Mess. EWINGS, *Dublin*
MDCCLXII.

FIG. 42
John Campbell, *An Account of the Spanish Settlements in America*, Edinburgh, 1762. An expansion of Campbell's earlier work on the Spanish empire in America, where the author saw many opportunities for British commercial incursions and about which he wrote with an authority that few in Britain could match. (Cat. no. 48).

est importance to the maritime powers of Europe."

Spain had been drawn into the final stages of the Anglo-French conflict in support of France, and the ensuing "bloody war" created a popular demand for information about the Spanish Empire. Correctly, Campbell states that there is no up-to-date literature in English on the topic.

His own text is a development of the 1747 *Account*, updated by his own vast reading in many languages. His erudition had earned him an honorary doctorate from Glasgow University in 1754. This book is hostile to the metropolitan government of the Spanish Empire, seen as a treacherous opponent of Britain, and as holding down the native-born Spanish Americans by means of metropolitan bureaucrats. (Fig. 42). The native Indian peoples are depicted as victims of rapine and exploitation. Campbell stresses that only the warlike natives of southern Chile have truly benefitted from contact with the Spaniards, for they have retained their independence whilst acquiring European domestic animals and artifacts. The colonial church is depicted as excessively rich, lax, superstitious, and intolerant.

He ends on a triumphalist note with a detailed account, buttressed by reprinted official correspondence, of the successful British assault on Havana in the summer of 1762. A fortune in bullion was captured, but Campbell is more interested in the fact that this seemed to lay most of the Spanish Main (the Caribbean region) open to British assault. In fact,

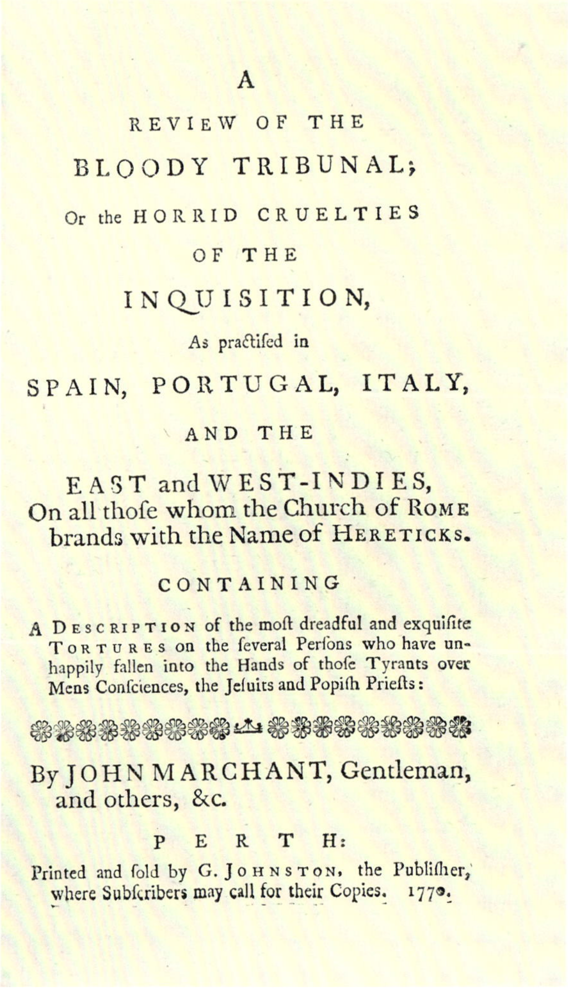

FIG. 43
John Marchant, *A Review of the Bloody Tribunal*, Perth, 1770. In contrast to Scots like John Campbell and William Robertson, who had complex views about the Spanish empire in America, seeing opportunities for both accommodation and battle, the simplistic Black Legend lived on in some circles in Scotland, as illustrated by this book. (Cat. no. 49).

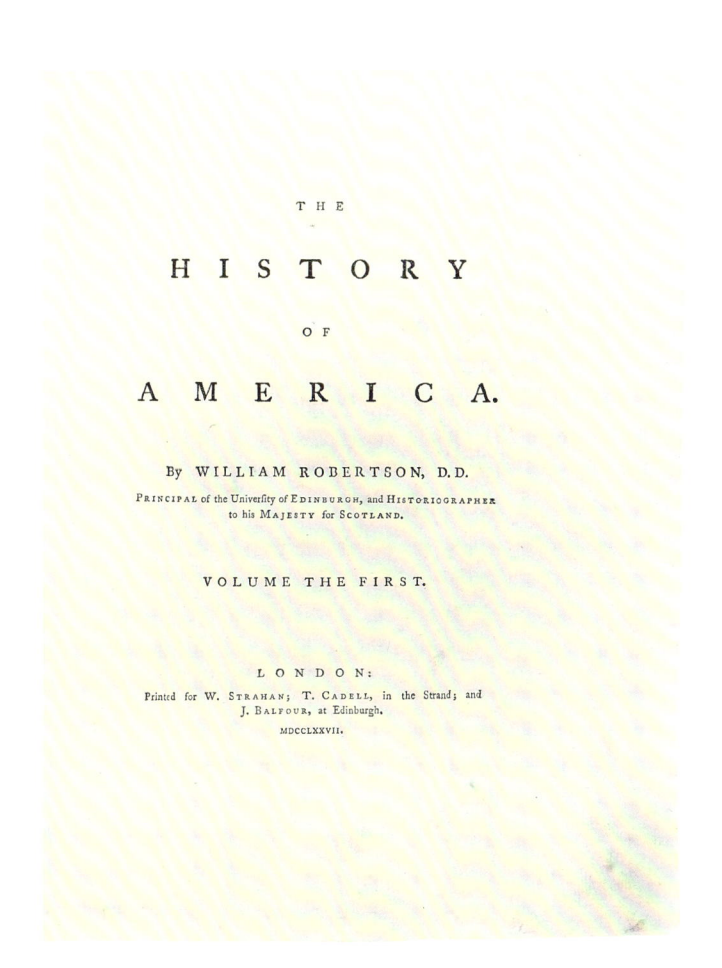

FIG. 44
William Robertson, *The History of America*, London and Edinburgh, 1777. One of the great products of Enlightenment Scotland, Robertson's sympathetic history had an important influence on Anglo-American attitudes toward Spanish culture. (Cat. no. 50).

financial pressures made the British government anxious for an early peace. The quality and precision of Campbell's regional material gave the book enduring value and secured its translation into other European languages such as Dutch.

49
John Marchant.
A Review of the Bloody Tribunal; Or the Horrid Cruelties of the Inquisition as Practised in Spain, Portugal, Italy, and the East and West-Indies, on All Those Whom the Church of Rome Brands with the Name of Hereticks.
Perth, 1770.

This book is an interesting example of the kind of consciousness that Principal Robertson was anxious to play down in the public culture of Protestant English-speaking lands. It was originally published in London in 1756 under the title *The Bloody Tribunal, or, An Antidote against Popery*. Though fighting had been going on between France and England in North America since 1754, the year 1756 saw the formal outbreak of a declared war in Europe whose duration was to give it the name of the Seven Years War. For Englishmen, it was primarily a crusade against Catholic France, but the material in this book is drawn mainly from Portugal, Spain, and Italy. One of the emotional triggers for this sort of writing was the mistreatment of English Protestant merchants by the Inquisition in Spain, and Chapter IV of the book is dominated by an account of one such, Isaac Martin, arrested by the Inquisition in Malaga in Andalusia in Spain in 1714 and eventually released only by the personal intervention of King George I.

Like all similar works of propaganda, this text trawls evidence from a vast sweep of time, treating it all as if it were contemporary. However, it would be quite wrong to say that the text is dominated by ignorance. It is notably well-informed about the legal niceties of the position of the Inquisition in the Post-Tridentine Roman Catholic Church. If it is itself a reflection of contemporary Protestant obsessions, it catches rather well the mirror-image of those obsessions in the contemporary Catholic mind. (Fig. 43).

The preface, which dedicates this edition to the Provost, Treasurer, and Town Council of Perth, is striking evidence of the regional vigor of Enlightenment Scotland. It makes the point that Perth, which had an expanding linen industry, was also a town on the Highland frontier. It does not fail to note the valor of the Highland regiments which had played a key role in the imperial triumphs of the years 1759–63. Perth was a town with strong Evangelical traditions. George Johnston, the publisher, opened his printing business partly to exploit a new local paper manufacture and partly to encourage "the Northern and surrounding Geniuses to bring their literary productions to light." He saw himself as a responsible, conservative publisher not "fomenting discord in a civilized country" like the mercenary hacks of London's Grub Street.

50
William Robertson.
The History of America.
London and Edinburgh, 1777.

Robertson's *History* was undoubtedly the most important and influential history of America published in the English-speaking world before 1800. More than that, however, it was a book that had a profound impact throughout the world of the Enlightenment, from Philadelphia to St. Petersburg. Translations into other European languages came rapidly with French, German, and Italian versions, but by the 1790s it could be read also in Swedish and in Greek. The first American edition was published in New York in 1798. In the formation of Enlightenment consciousness about European colonization and empire in the Americas, it ranks with the abbé Raynal's *Histoire philosophique et politique des établissemens et du commerce des Européens dans les deux Indes*, first published in Amsterdam in 1770, and frequently reprinted and translated thereafter.

Robertson's *America*, however, has a complex structure, as well as a curious publishing history, and its ideological thrust was entirely different from Raynal's. Whereas the latter was a bitter critic of European imperialism, Robertson wrote to encourage reconciliation between traditionally rival European imperialisms, all of which he saw as ultimately justified, because they were part of the working of Divine Providence. Taking the Scottish Enlightenment's theory of a four-stage progression of human society from savagery to polite commercial society, Robertson fitted European imperialism into it primarily as God's way of accelerating Progress in the Americas. It followed that the Spanish Empire was not the monstrous aberration of the *Leyenda Negra*, but another European civilizing mission, no doubt too authoritarian in its political structure and certainly too exclusive in its commercial policies originally, but improving steadily in the later eighteenth century.

What Robertson published in his own lifetime was only Books I–VIII of the work, devoted to Luso-Hispanic, and more especially, Spanish America. (Fig. 44). His researches in Spanish and other European libraries for early printed and manuscript sources were unprecedented. Fittingly, the book enabled him to add membership in the Royal Academy of History at Madrid to his roll of honors, which already included a Chaplaincy to the King, the Principalship of Edinburgh University, and the post of Historiographer Royal in Scotland.

Like Campbell, Robertson does not support the idea of destabilizing the Spanish Empire. On the contrary, he argues that Spanish imperialism was becoming more tolerant in religion, less authoritarian in politics (at least to Robertson's ultra-conservative eye), and more inclined towards freer or even free trade policies (as was indeed the case under the later Bourbons). Unlike Campbell, Robertson champions metropolitan Spanish imperialism against *criollo* settlers. When his son and namesake published the suppressed books IX and X in the posthumous 1796 edition, it was possible to see where Robertson placed North American Indians in his scheme of Progress. They fitted in only at the lowest stage of savagery.

The second impression and the 1778 second edition are graced with four commissioned maps of Luso-Hispanic America by Thomas Kitchin, Senior "Hydrographer to his Majesty". The map of "Mexico or New Spain" in the second volume of the quarto edition retains "New Albion" as the name for California, not to mention "Harbour of Sir Francis Drake" for San Francisco Bay. The latter must have been Kitchin's doing. Robertson was no neo-Elizabethan Englishman. He was a Scot who wanted to kill the *Leyenda Negra*.

FOR FURTHER READING

Linda Colley, *Britons: Forging the Nation 1707–1837* (New Haven and London: Yale University Press, 1992).

John V. Howard and William Jacks, eds. *The Celebrated Doctor Robertson* (Edinburgh: Edinburgh University Library, 1993).

Bruce P. Lenman, "Alexander Spotswood and the Business of Empire", in *Colonial Williamsburg*, Fall 1990.

Bruce P. Lenman, *Integration, Enlightenment, and Industrialization: Scotland 1746–1832* (Edinburgh: Edinburgh University Press, 1992).

Bruce P. Lenman, "The Old Imperialist and the Young Soldier: Dinwiddie and Washington," *Colonial Williamsburg*, Spring 1994.

Mary Jane W. Scott, *James Thomson, Anglo-Scot* (Athens and London: University of Georgia Press, 1988).

The SCOTCH BUTCHERY, Boston. 1775.

1 — B——
2 — M—— } Super Intendants of the Butchery, from the two great Slaughter Houses.
3 — Col. F——
4 — W—— } Deputies to the above.

5 — Scotch Butchers.
6 — English Soldiers struck with Horror, & dropping their Arms.
7 — The English Fleet with Scotch Commanders.
8 — Boston.

Pub.d According to Act of Parl.t 1775.

CHAPTER EIGHT: *Scotland and the American Revolution*

MICHAEL FRY

THE SCOTS AND THE AMERICANS spent nearly three-quarters of a century together as members of the British Empire, from the Union of 1707 to the Revolutionary War. They had much in common as imperial provinces trying to define their relationship to the English metropolis. Nevertheless their experience produced opposite results. Though most Scots originally opposed the Union, they became steadily more attached to it, especially to the economic system in which it placed them. The Americans, while they long shared a pride in British expansion, grew away from the mother country till they decided to sever their connection with it. It is in the light of this paradox that Scottish reactions to the American Revolution must be judged.

In both provinces, dependent status helped to foster an Enlightenment. Adjustment to expanding imperial power loosened the hold of traditions and habits on the provincial, in both America and Scotland, and opened his mind to fresh thinking and different ways of regarding his inheritance. In Scotland the intellectual ferment arrived by the last quarter of the century at a new and mature consensus on modern political economy, that it should combine economic freedom with respect for the legitimate political authority guaranteeing an ordered society. For various reasons, important groups of Americans took a more radical view.

A few Scots agreed with them. One was a leading minister in the Church of Scotland, John Erskine. He represented a circle of evangelical Presbyterians who had long maintained friendly relations with men of like mind across the Atlantic, and readily understood that strain of revolutionary thinking owed to the puritan legacy. In private, the two leading philosophers, David Hume and Adam Smith, sympathized with American grievances, too. To Hume it was clear that the colonies had since their foundation developed into moral communities, bound to take a course of their own no longer amenable to control from England. The best thing was to accept this reality. He accordingly declared in a letter to a friend: "I am American in my principles." Smith was never so forthright, but made his position clear enough when the crisis in Anglo-American relations broke just as he was about to bring out his great work, *The Wealth of Nations*, in 1776. He said there that the Americans ought either to be fully integrated into the British political system with representation in Parliament, in which case the seat of the Empire might in time be transferred across the Atlantic, or else they should be set free.

For all the cogency of these arguments, not many other Scots were willing to accept them. They believed that the Americans were in the wrong, and that the British government should coerce them till they again submitted to legitimate authority. The belief was shared at all levels of society, by other enlightened figures, especially those with experience

FIG. 47
The Scotch Butchery, Boston, 1775, [London], 1775. A symbolical representation of the political situation in Massachusetts in 1775. American revolutionaries generally associated Scotland with imperial power and Loyalism. (Cat. no. 54).

of America, such as Adam Ferguson and James Macpherson, by the practical men conducting Scottish affairs, Henry Dundas and the rest of the political establishment, by the people at large. In the winter of 1775–6, while rebellion spread, more than 70 petitions were sent up to London from the citizens of Scottish counties and burghs urging the Government to suppress it by force—as many as came from the whole of England, with five times the population. After war broke out, Scots remained notably hawkish, and not a single petition was ever sent up in favor of peace. It is striking, too, how this sentiment was shared by Scotsmen on both sides of the ocean.

The near unanimity of the reaction has been something of a historical puzzle. Since Scotland and America had a good deal in common, why could they not make common cause? Contemporary literature, much of it represented in the John Carter Brown Library, allows us to attempt some answers. At a certain level, there was sheer material calculation. America, along with India, was one of the two great fields of commercial enterprise opened up to Scots since 1707. They made a particular success of exploiting the tobacco grown in Virginia and the Carolinas and came largely to dominate its distribution in Great Britain and Europe. In the process the little market town of Glasgow developed into a major emporium, and started accumulating the capital to embark on its headlong industrial evolution during the next century. Tobacco was Scotland's first taste of big business, and Scots were naturally reluctant to lose it. Since it was channelled into the colonial system, regulated by the English Navigation Acts, they had an interest in maintenance of the political structure underpinning it. The Virginians, at any rate, quickly identified the many Scots agents and merchants in the ports of the Chesapeake and in the back-country as enemies. Most did indeed remain staunchly loyalist, to the point of losing their property and livelihoods, when the fortunes of war turned in favor of the Americans.

Since these Scots were in general only temporary residents, sojourners operating an imperial trade, their attitude is not surprising. But the same attitude could be observed among many who had chosen the New World as their permanent home. This proved especially true where they concentrated in blocs of settlement, as a result of projects of emigration relieving the pressure of population at home. While some were to be found in the northern colonies, most lay south of the Mason-Dixon line, the largest probably in North Carolina, along the Cape Fear River. Here the emigrants were Highlanders, and this gives a clue to their loyalism. Highland society was changing its old tribal, martial character, under intensifying economic pressure. With less and less room for more and more people, the chieftains of the clans turned into commercial landlords. Still, tradition died hard. When the Highlanders found that their ancient home could no longer offer them a living, they preferred if possible to leave in a body, often led by some kinsman of their chief (very seldom by the chiefs themselves, who were now looking to be absorbed into the upper ranks of society in Edinburgh, or even in London). This was how, for example, the Jacobite heroine Flora Macdonald, and her husband Alan Macdonald of Kingsburgh, migrated to the settlement now known as Fayetteville, North Carolina.

They came to the New World not to find a new way of life, to cast off the shackles of the Old World, as so many millions have done in their time and since. On the contrary, they came because they wanted to preserve their old way of life in a more hospitable setting. Loyalty formed an essential element of that way of life: loyalty to fellow clansmen, loyalty even to chieftains who scarcely deserved it, loyalty to established authority, loyalty above all to the king, the person at the summit of the social edifice who held it all together, without whom it would descend into anarchy. It made no difference that they or their fathers had regarded George III's title as usurped, and fought against it in the Jacobite rebellions. He had by now established his right, as a plain reality or as a matter of divine judgment. In any event they accepted it. That meant in turn that they had to fight against the Revolution. Those clansmen of

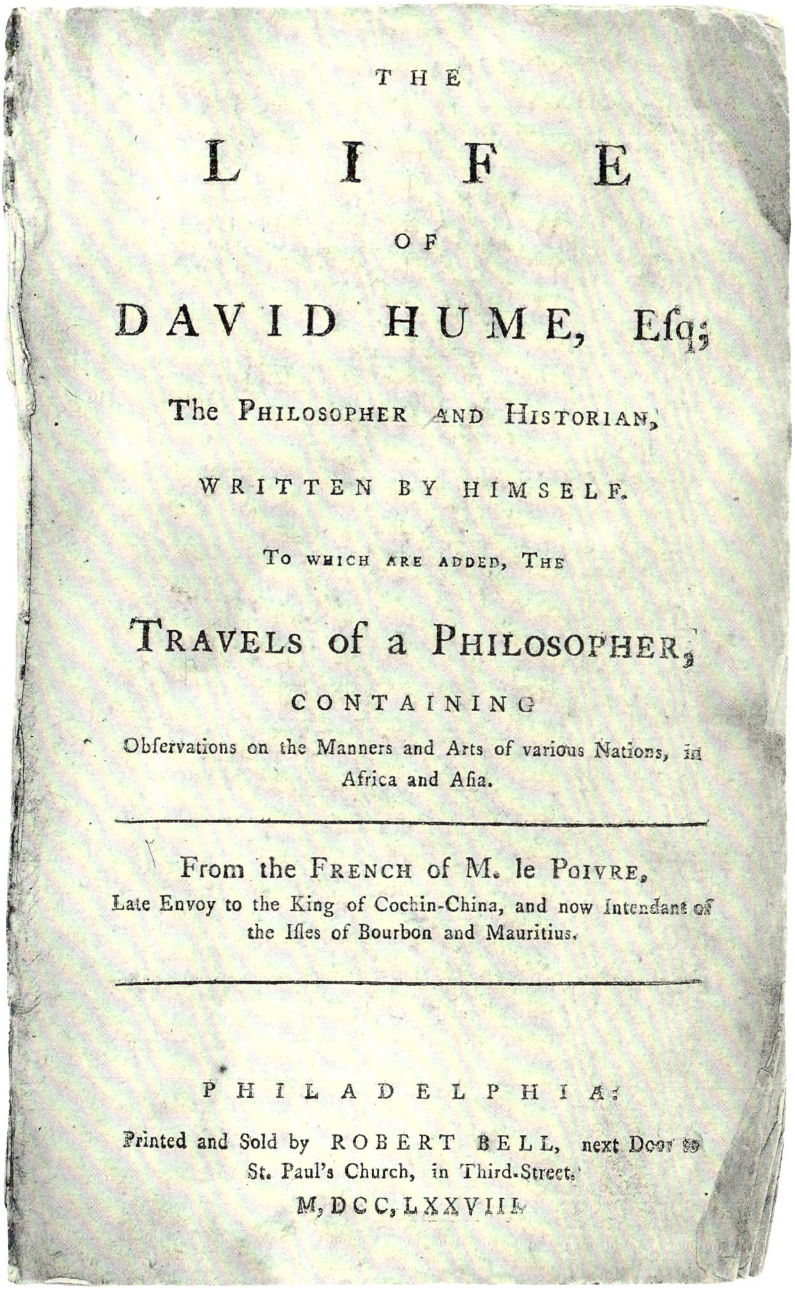

THE

LIFE

OF

DAVID HUME, Efq;

The PHILOSOPHER AND HISTORIAN,

WRITTEN BY HIMSELF.

TO WHICH ARE ADDED, THE

TRAVELS of a PHILOSOPHER,

CONTAINING

Obfervations on the Manners and Arts of various Nations, in Africa and Afia.

From the FRENCH of M. le POIVRE,
Late Envoy to the King of Cochin-China, and now Intendant of the Ifles of Bourbon and Mauritius.

PHILADELPHIA:

Printed and Sold by ROBERT BELL, next Door to St. Paul's Church, in Third-Street.
M,DCC,LXXVIII.

FIG. 45
The Life of David Hume, Philadelphia, 1778. The publication of a work about David Hume in Philadelphia in 1778 probably had more to do with Hume's fame as a historian, essayist, and economist than with his achievements as an analytical philosopher with few equals in all of Western thought. (Cat. no. 51).

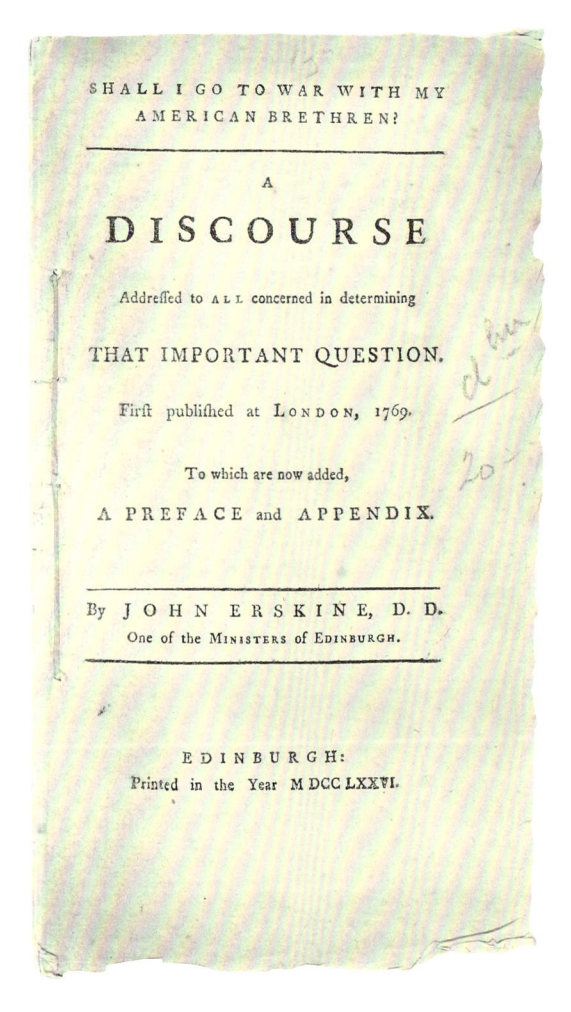

FIG. 46
John Erskine, *Shall I Go to War with My American Brethren?*, Edinburgh, 1776. Erskine's sympathies with the American cause were based mostly on his correspondence with American Presbyterians and other Calvinist clergymen. (Cat. no. 53).

North Carolina sprang to the king's standard, and were among the first to raise a force in his name on American soil. They fought and were beaten at the Battle of Moore's Creek Bridge early in 1776 while marching down to relieve Wilmington from the patriots. The officers, including Macdonald, were captured, imprisoned, and eventually expelled, some making their way to Canada, others returning to Scotland. Their men, deprived of social leadership, simply returned to their farms and caused the revolutionaries no more trouble. Their descendants live to this day in the counties they settled.

That brings us to a third and different Scottish reaction to the Revolution, from those Scots who shared the motives of the millions who have come to the New World, wanting truly to build a new life for themselves and shake the dust of the Old World off their feet. Faced by a conflict of values they ceased to be Scots, and became Americans. Most were anonymous, ordinary citizens who, having made their choice had no trouble in merging their identity into that of the young republic.

It is worth picking out a couple of cases where the transition in mentality emerges more explicitly, the cases of the two Scots who signed the Declaration of Independence. One was the Reverend John Witherspoon, principal of the College of New Jersey, now Princeton University, to which he had somewhat reluctantly accepted a call from his previous charge as minister of Paisley, near Glasgow. He carried in his baggage Scottish philosophy as well as Scottish religion, and his message to America was that enlightened principles pointed the way not just to political liberty but also to moral regeneration, an enduring element in American ideology. The second Scottish signatory was James Wilson who, together with James Madison, received the commission of the Philadelphia Convention of 1787 to draw up the Constitution of the United States. Wilson was a lawyer, educated at the university of St. Andrews, and he brought to America a Scottish concept of the central importance of law to the well-being of society.

To him is attributed the great innovation of a Supreme Court, a distant analogy of the Court of Session in its role as an interpreter of legislation in the Scotland of the eighteenth century. In America, however, he had the chance to entrench this institution amid a logically rigorous system of separated powers, in a way that his Scottish peers could only have admired.

By now, of course, Great Britain had recognized American independence. With the courage of their convictions, many Scots on both sides of the Atlantic had resisted doing so right till the end of the war. But since their Enlightenment also taught realism, they at last accepted that if America could not be held, then America must be let go. They hastened to point out that intercourse among the world's peoples proceeds primarily from their natural and mutual interests. This deduction from enlightened principles has been amply vindicated by two further centuries of friendly relations between Scotland and America.

51
David Hume.
The Life of David Hume, Esq. The Philosopher and Historian, Written by Himself....
Philadelphia, 1778.

David Hume (1711–1776), a leader of the Scottish Enlightenment and acknowledged as one of the greatest European philosophers, had a paradoxical relationship with the American colonies. On the one hand, he was a supporter of their independence as early as 1768, before most Americans, and did not deviate from that position. His political essays had an enormous influence on major theorists among the Founding Fathers, especially James Madison, who incorporated principles drawn from Hume in the Constitution of the United States and in the Federalist Papers by which he defended it. On the other hand, he was not at all sympathetic to the abstract American political arguments of the Jeffersonian ideol-

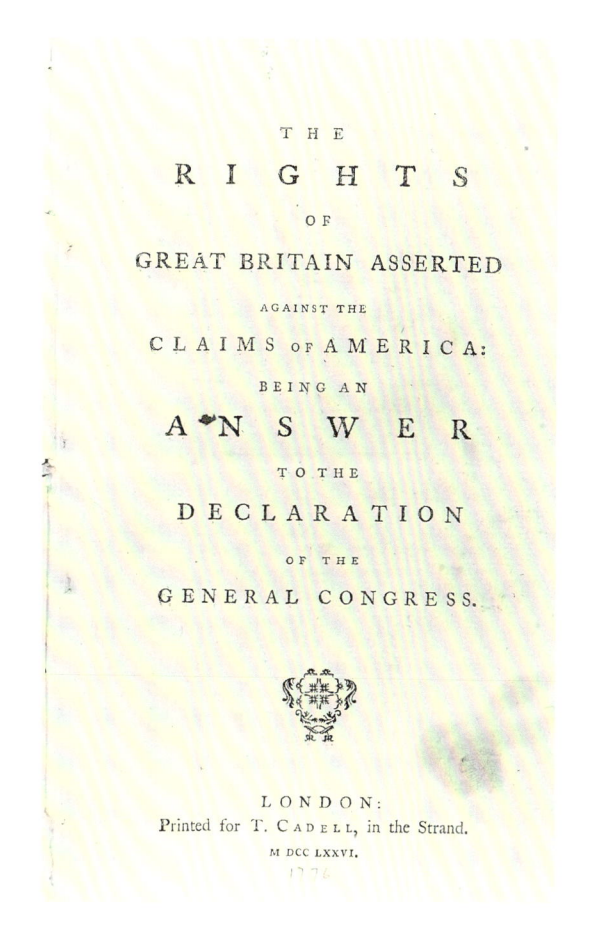

FIG. 48
James MacPherson, *The Rights of Great Britain Asserted*, London, 1776. Most Scots wished to see the American Revolution quashed by Great Britain. The justification for repression of the Revolution is set forth here. (Cat. no. 55).

ogy. He died just as war between Great Britain and the colonies was breaking out. This brief autobiographical sketch, posthumously published by his close friend, Adam Smith, contains the latter's eulogy: "Upon the whole, I have always considered him ... as approaching as nearly to the idea of a perfectly wise and virtuous man, as perhaps the frailty of human nature will admit." (Fig. 45).

52
Adam Smith.
An Inquiry into the Nature and Causes of the Wealth of Nations.
London, 1776.

The John Carter Brown Library owns a first edition of Smith's book, the foundation of the modern science of economics. In order to show the direct relevance of his work to the situation in 1776, he held up publication so that he could add his comments on it. Here, on the final pages, is a call to face reality, and apply economic principles to what was being taken in London as primarily a political problem. In the body of his argument, Smith had set out the damaging results of the illiberal trading regulations imposed by Britain on America, and built a cast-iron case against the colonial system. Now he also derived political proposals from his economics, commercial equality and American representation at Westminster. It did not surprise him that they hardly appealed even to those of his compatriots who at once caught on to his general theory. He well understood that particular national communities were unlikely to take measures they considered harmful to themselves for the general benefit of mankind. Indeed he too, in a manner typical of the Scottish philosophers, advocated balance among the claims of politics and economics, of authority and freedom, and he could appreciate how others might reach a different judgment of the right balance for given circumstances. By the same token, he accepted the case for American independence.

53
John Erskine.
Shall I Go to War with My American Brethren....
Edinburgh, 1776.

Erskine was the most prominent Scotsman to give open support to the Americans once war broke out. A leader of the Popular or evangelical party in the Church of Scotland, he shared the charge of Old Greyfriars in Edinburgh with William Robertson, principal of the university, whose views were diametrically opposed to his own. Erskine's stance was grounded on both political and religious principles. He believed there had been a steady encroachment of executive power on fundamental British liberties. To him this was clear enough in Scotland, especially as it affected the rights of the Presbyterian Kirk. But it had taken a far more blatant form in America, especially since George III came to the throne. The colonists were therefore right to resist. His sympathy was strengthened by his wide personal contact among clergymen on the other side of the Atlantic, his understanding of the way American religion was developing, and his approval of it. It seemed to him to be realizing, if not always by means of the same ecclesiastical structure, the ultimate Presbyterian ideal of a Christian community. For all these reasons the Americans were his "brethren," against whom he could not in conscience fight. (Fig. 46).

54
The Scotch Butchery. Boston, 1775.
[London,] 1775.

This cartoon follows a view common in English radical circles during the American War of Independence. It was essentially the idea that the Scots, lackeys of arbitrary executive power, were engaged in a plot to suppress the Anglo-Saxon liberties that the colonists had taken from the mother country

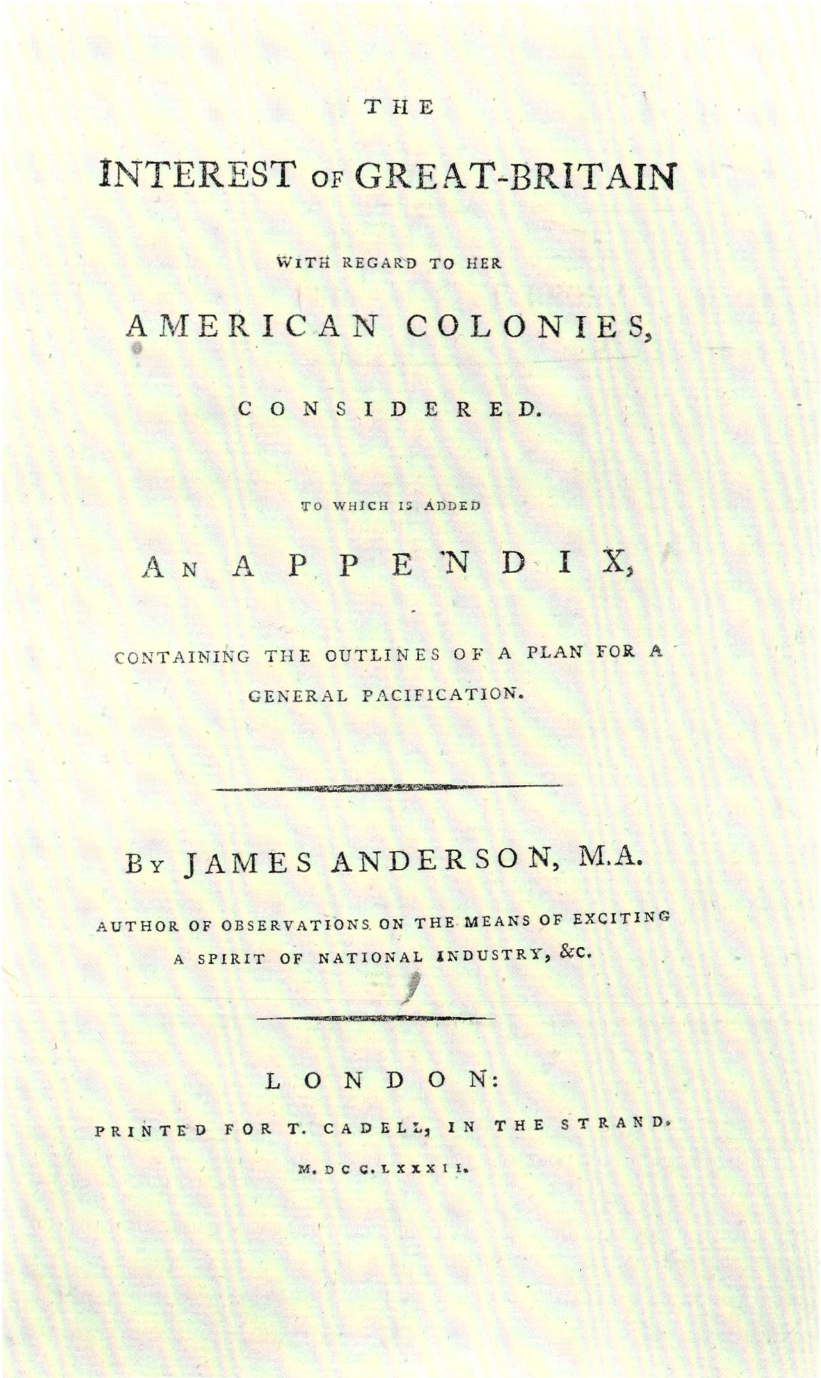

THE
INTEREST OF GREAT-BRITAIN

WITH REGARD TO HER

AMERICAN COLONIES,

CONSIDERED.

TO WHICH IS ADDED

AN APPENDIX,

CONTAINING THE OUTLINES OF A PLAN FOR A
GENERAL PACIFICATION.

By JAMES ANDERSON, M.A.

AUTHOR OF OBSERVATIONS ON THE MEANS OF EXCITING
A SPIRIT OF NATIONAL INDUSTRY, &c.

LONDON:
PRINTED FOR T. CADELL, IN THE STRAND.
M.DCC.LXXXII.

FIG. 49
James Anderson, *The Interest of Great-Britain with Regard to Her American Colonies*, London, 1782. Written after the war for American independence had been lost by Great Britain, Anderson, a Scottish economist of note, correctly argued that in the end commerce across the Atlantic beneficial to Britain would not thereby diminish. (Cat. no. 57).

to the New World. The evidence presented here is that Scottish regiments and Scottish generals figured prominently among the troops sent to quell the first outbreak of rebellion in Boston. (Fig. 47). In the right center, two Scottish politicians, the former Prime Minister, Lord Bute (who had in fact been in retirement for 12 years), and the Lord Chief Justice, Lord Mansfield, direct operations. Further off stand Simon Fraser, the former Jacobite rebel leader later reconciled to the King, bearing the pardon he won for gallantry at the capture of Quebec (1759); and Alexander Wedderburn, the Scots-born Attorney-General of England. They are evidently inciting Highland soldiers to deeds too dirty for the English troops. In the background, the "Scotch commanders" of the fleet, curiously nameless, have already opened fire on the civilian population. The cartoon distorts the facts to make its point, but it does correctly identify the hostility of Scots to the American patriots.

55
James Macpherson.
The Rights of Great Britain Asserted Against the Claims of America.... London, [1776, i.e. 1775]

Macpherson (1736–1796) may be taken as representative of Scottish opinion during the American War of Independence. He was one of the most celebrated literary characters of his age, as publisher of the *Works of Ossian*, which he claimed were authentic translations of Gaelic poems by a bard of the third century A.D. In Scotland and in much of Europe, his claim was accepted at face-value. To nationalist Scots, it proved that they had a corpus of ancient poetry as rich as any other and, more to the point, older than English literature. To Europeans it revealed an unsuspected, elemental substratum of Western culture and gave a vital stimulus to the birth of the romantic movement. The poems made Macpherson famous, but not as rich as he had hoped. In 1764 he became secretary to Governor Johnstone of West Florida, and settled at Pensacola. He travelled among the Indians, but could find little to admire, and advocated armed force to subdue them. After only two years, however, he quarrelled with his employer and returned to Britain. Still in need of money when the American Revolution erupted, he was one of several writers employed by Lord North's Ministry to churn out propaganda to rebut the rebels' case. This pamphlet is an example of such hack-work. It takes to task the ideas behind the Declaration of Independence, and asserts instead a legitimist view of the foundations of liberty. (Fig. 48).

56
Allan Ramsay.
Letters on the Present Disturbances in Great Britain and Her American Provinces. London, [i.e. Rome] reprinted [1782]

A still more striking example of how the Scottish cultural elite sprang to the defence of Britain's cause is that of Allan Ramsay. He is remembered today as a painter, especially for his delicate portraits of women. One formative influence on him was nationalist: his father, also Allan, set out to preserve in his poetry the heritage of the Scots language threatened after the Union. Another was cosmopolitan: he befriended Hume, Voltaire, and Rousseau, matured his artistic technique during residence in Italy, and assimilated the homely British style of portraiture to the grander one of Europe. Yet the American revolt brought out in him what can only be called a streak of bloodcurdling chauvinism. He went into print, apparently at his own expense, with pamphlets such as this one asserting that the colonists had by their insolence forfeited all their rights. Britain should occupy certain strongholds along the Atlantic seaboard—New York, Charleston and others —from which to visit a policy of scorched earth on the surrounding countryside, making clear that only abject submission by the rebels will bring any relief.

57
James Anderson.
The Interest of Great-Britain with Regard to Her American Colonies. London, 1782.

James Anderson (1739–1808) was a leading Scottish political economist who came to his discipline from a background in practical agricultural improvement. His approach to economics was almost opposite to that of his more famous contemporary, Adam Smith, who derived his own theories from moral philosophy. Yet the two often reached similar conclusions. In particular, they agreed that the independence of America would not damage the prosperity of the mother country. This commentary was written at a time when Britain had clearly lost the war, and negotiation of the peace was well under way. Demonstrative loyalty had dominated debate among Scots while the fighting went on, but now Anderson had the chance to show where their true interest lies. (Fig. 49). He pointed out that the old colonial system had held back economic development on the other side of the Atlantic. The colonists would therefore never have been able to pay for their own government and defence, which would have remained a charge on Britain. It was better to accept the separation and use the savings to benefit the domestic economy. As America flourished in her new freedom, trade with Britain was bound to revive.

FOR FURTHER READING

Bailyn, B. & Clive, J., "England's Cultural Provinces, Scotland and America," *William & Mary Quarterly*, XI, 1954.

Brown, W., *The Good Americans, the Loyalists in the American Revolution* (New York, 1969).

Devine, T. M., *The Tobacco Lords* (Edinburgh, 1975).

Howe, D. W., "Why the Scottish Enlightenment was Useful to the Framers of the American Constitution," *Comparative Studies in Society and History*, XXXI, 1989.

Nelson, W. H., *The American Tory* (Oxford, 1961).

Shepperson, G., "The American Revolution and Scotland," *Scotia*, I, 1977.

About the Authors

DAVID ARMITAGE is a professor of history at Columbia University. He is the author of "The Scottish Vision of Empire: Intellectual Origins of the Darien Venture," in John Robertson, ed., *A Union for Empire: Political Thought and the British Union of 1707* (Cambridge, 1995) and co-editor, with Armand Himy and Quentin Skinner, of *Milton and Republicanism* (Cambridge, 1995).

ROBERT KENT DONOVAN is a professor of history at Kansas State University. He is the author of *No Popery & Radicalism: Opposition to Roman Catholic Relief in Scotland 1778–1782* (New York: Garland Publishing Company, 1987).

ROBIN FABEL is a professor of history at Auburn University in Alabama. He is the author of *Bombast and Broadsides: The Lives of George Johnstone* (Tuscaloosa, 1987), and editor and translator of *Shipwreck and Adventures of Monsieur Pierre Viaud* (Pensacola, 1990).

MICHAEL FRY is an independent scholar living in Edinburgh, Scotland. He is the author of *Patronage and Principle, a Political History of Modern Scotland* (Aberdeen, 1987) and *The Dundas Despotism* (Edinburgh, 1993). He is at present working on a full-scale study of the Scottish Empire.

DAVID HANCOCK is a professor of history at Harvard University. He is the author of *Citizens of the World: London Merchants and the Integration of the British Atlantic Community, 1735–1785* (Cambridge: Cambridge University Press, 1995).

NED C. LANDSMAN is a professor of history at the State University of New York at Stony Brook. He is the author of *Scotland and Its First American Colony, 1683–1765* (Princeton, 1985).

JAMES MCLACHLAN is an independent scholar living in Princeton, New Jersey. He is the author of *American Boarding Schools: A Historical Study*, (New York, 1970), and *Princetonians, 1748–1760: A Biographical Dictionary* (Princeton, 1976).

BRUCE LENMAN is a professor of history at St. Andrews University in Scotland. He is the author of *The Jacobite Risings in Britain, 1689–1746* (London, 1984), and *The Jacobite Clans of the Great Glen, 1650–1784* (London, 1984). He is currently sponsored by the British Academy to write a history of British colonial wars, 1558–1776.

Appendix

Burton Van Name Edwards

Preface

A DEFINITIVE BIBLIOGRAPHY of printed works pertinent to the relationship between Scotland and the Americas in the seventeenth and eighteenth centuries would be a valuable and desirable tool for further research in this field. Such a work would complement William and Helen Brock's *Scotus Americanus* (Edinburgh: 1982), which focused on manuscript material and limited its investigations to the eighteenth century. The creation of such a bibliography would not be without difficulty, for the field of Scottish-American relations is quite wide-ranging, containing many imprints whose relevance, while significant, is nevertheless somewhat tangential, forcing the bibliographer to spend much time making difficult judgments about the inclusion of such works.

The goals of the bibliographical Appendix that follows are much more modest. First, complete bibliographic descriptions are provided for the 57 works selected by the authors of the preceding essays. This section comprises the section "Bibliographical Supplement" in what follows. Second, briefer descriptions of more than 90 monographs are added in the section "Selected Additional Resources." The net effect of this bibliographical sketch is not only to demonstrate the wealth and range of printed material available for research into the relationship between Scotland and the Americas, but also to suggest that the John Carter Brown Library would be the best place to pursue such research, since the library owns all of these works and may very well possess the highest concentration of imprints relevant to Scottish-American studies.

It cannot be emphasized too strongly that the following list is enormously incomplete, being only a partial listing of the John Carter Brown Library's holdings relevant to Scotland and the Americas. The point of departure for this bibliographic essay was a list of some 160 titles compiled a few years ago by R. Kent Donovan of Kansas State University. Divided into sections covering the American Revolution, education, exploration, emigration, settlement, historiography, medicine, military affairs, philosophy, literature, humanities, political affairs, religion, science, slave trade and abolition, social life and trade, Professor Donovan's list demonstrates the breadth of Scottish influence on American affairs. While a number of titles have been added or subtracted from the original list, this brief bibliography preserves the framework and range of Professor Donovan's original list.

Turning to John Scott's bibliography of the Darien expedition, the insufficiency of the present bibliography as well as the richness of the John Carter Brown Library collection becomes immediately apparent. While this bibliographical sketch contains only 12 items included in Scott's bibliography, the John Carter Brown Library obtained 79 Darien items in 1906 when Scott's library came up for public sale. Thanks to later acquisitions, the JCB now owns almost half of the several hundred items listed in Scott's Darien bibliography.

Finally, a glance at the relative strength of other North American libraries, as reflected in the number of titles in the Bibliographical Supplement held by them, proves that the John Carter Brown Library possesses the strongest collection of imprint material relevant to Scottish-American relations. Nevertheless, those libraries with significant holdings, such as New York Public (31), the Library of Congress (28), Yale (25), Harvard (23) and the William L. Clements (23) must also be considered as important resources in the field of Scottish-American studies.

List of References

ADAMS, T. R. Amer. pamphlets
Adams, Thomas Randolph. American independence: the growth of an idea, a bibliographical study of the American political pamphlets printed between 1764 and 1776 dealing with the dispute between Great Britain and her colonies. Providence: Brown University Press, 1965.

ADAMS, T. R. Brit. pamphlets
Adams, Thomas Randolph. The American controversy: a bibliographical study of the British pamphlets about the American disputes, 1764–1783. Providence: Brown University Press; New York: Bibliographical Society, 1980.

ALDEN, J. E. Rhode Island
Alden, John Eliot. Rhode Island imprints, 1727–1800. New York, Published for the Bibliographical Society of America [by] Bowker, 1949 [i.e. 1950]

ALDEN-LANDIS. European Americana
European Americana: a chronological guide to works printed in Europe relating to the Americas, 1493–1776. Ed. by John Alden, with the assistance of Dennis C. Landis. New York: Readex Books, 1980–.

ALDIS, H. G. Scotland
Aldis, Harry Gidney. A list of books printed in Scotland before 1700. Edinburgh: Edinburgh Bibliographical Society, 1904. Reprint. Edinburgh: National Library of Scotland, 1970.

AUSTIN, R. B. Early Amer. medical imprints
United States. National Library of Medicine. Early American medical imprints: a guide to works printed in the United States, 1668–1820, by Robert B. Austin. Washington: U.S. Dept. of Health, Education, and Welfare, Public Health Service, 1961.

BAER, E. 17th cent. Maryland
Baer, Elizabeth. Seventeenth century Maryland: a bibliography. Baltimore: John Work Garrett Library, 1949.

BM (compact ed.)
British Museum. Dept. of Printed Books. General catalogue of printed books to 1955. Compact ed. New York: Readex Microprint Corp., 1967–.

BRISTOL
Bristol, Roger Pattrell. Supplement to Charles Evans' American bibliography. Charlottesville: Published for the Bibliographical Society of America and the Bibliographical Society of the University of Virginia [by] University Press of Virginia, [1970]

BROWN, J. C. Cat., 1493–1800
Brown, John Carter. Bibliotheca Americana: a catalogue of books relating to North and South America in the library of John Carter Brown of Providence, R.I. Providence: Printed by H. O. Houghton & Co., Cambridge, 1865–1871.

BROWN, J. C. Cat., 1482–1700
Brown, John Carter. Bibliotheca Americana: a catalogue of books relating to North and South America in the library of the late John Carter Brown of Providence, R.I. Providence: Printed by H. O. Houghton & Co., Cambridge, 1875–1882.

CHURCH, E. D. Discovery
Church, Elihu Dwight. A catalogue of books relating to the discovery and early history of North and South America forming a part of the library of E. D. Church. Comp. and annotated by George Watson Cole. New York: Dodd, Mead & Co.; Cambridge: University Press, 1907.

CLARK, T. D. Old South
Clark, Thomas Dionysius. Travels in the Old South: a bibliography. Norman: University of Oklahoma Press, 1956–59.

DE RENNE, W. J. Cat. of the Georgia Lib.
Wymberley Jones De Renne Georgia Library, Wormsloe. Catalogue of the Wymberley Jones De Renne Library at Wormsloe, Isle of Hope near Savannah, Georgia.... Wormsloe: Privately Printed, 1931.

DIPPEL, H. Americana Germanica
Dippel, Horst. Americana Germanica: 1770–1800: Bibliographie deutscher Amerikaliteratur. Stuttgart: J. B. Metzler, 1976.

ESTC
Eighteenth-Century Short-Title Catalogue. Datebase available through the Research Libraries Information Network.

EVANS
Evans, Charles. American bibliography: a chronological dictionary of all books, pamphlets, and periodical publications printed in the United States of America from the genesis of printing in 1639 down to and including the year 1820. Chicago: Prv. print. for the author by the Blakely Press, 1903–59. Reprint. New York: P. Smith, 1941–59.

FIELD, T.W. Indian bib.
Field, Thomas Warren. An essay towards an Indian bibliography: being a catalogue of books relating to the history, antiquities, languages, customs, religion, wars, literature, and origin of the American Indians, in the library of Thomas W. Field. New York: Scribner, Armstrong, and Co., 1873. Reprint. Detroit: Gale Research Co., 1967.

FOXON
Foxon, David Fairweather. English verse 1701–1750: a catalogue of separately printed poems with notes on contemporary collected editions. London and New York: Cambridge University Press, 1975.

GASKELL, P. Foulis
Gaskell, Philip. A bibliography of the Foulis Press. 2nd ed. Winchester: St. Paul's Bibliographies, 1986.

GEORGE
British Museum. Dept. of Prints and Drawings. Catalogue of prints and drawings in the British Museum: Division I, political and personal satires. Vols. 1–4 prepared by F. G. Stephens; v. 5–11 by M. D. George. London: Printed by order of the Trustees, 1870–1954.

GOLDSMITHS' LIB. cat.
London. University. Goldsmiths' Company's Library of Economic Literature. Catalogue of the Goldsmiths' Library of Economic Literature. Comp. by Margaret Canney and David Knott. London: Cambridge University Press, 1970–.

GOULD & MORGAN. South Carolina
Gould, Christopher and Morgan, Richard Parker. South Carolina imprints, 1731–1800: a descriptive bibliography. Santa Barbara, Calif.: ABC-Clio Information Servies, c1985.

GUERRA, F. Amer. medical bib.
Guerra, Francisco. American medical bibliography, 1639–1783. New York: L. C. Harper, 1962.

HALKETT & LAING (2nd ed.)
Halkett, Samuel, and Laing, John. Dictionary of anonymous and pseudonymous English literature. 2nd ed. Edinburgh: Oliver and Boyd, 1926–[62].

HANDLER, J. S. Barbados
Handler, Jerome S. A guide to source materials for the study of Barbadoes history, 1627–1834. Carbondale: Southern Illinois University Press, [c1971].

HANSON
Hanson, Laurence William. Contemporary printed sources for British and Irish economic history, 1702–1750. Cambridge: University Press, 1963.

HIGGS, H. Bib. of economics, 1751–1775
Bibliography of economics...prepared for the British Academy.... Cambridge: The University Press, 1935–; vol. 1, 1751–1775, by Henry Higgs.

HILDEBURN, C. R. Pennsylvania
Hildeburn, Charles Swift Riché. A century of printing. The issues of the press in Pennsylvania, 1685–1784. Philadelphia: [Press of Matlack & Harvey], 1885–86.

HILL, F. P. Amer. plays
Hill, Frank Pierce. American plays printed 1714–1830: a bibliographical record. Stanford University: Stanford University Press; London: H. Milford, Oxford University Press, 1934. reprint?

HOGG, P. C. African Slave trade
Hogg, Peter C. The African slave trade and its suppression, a classified and annotated bibliography of books, pamphlets and periodical articles. London: Frank Cass, [1973]

HOLMES, T. J. Cotton Mather
Holmes, Thomas James. Cotton Mather, a bibliography of his works. Cambridge, Mass.: Harvard University Press, 1940.

HOWES, W. U.S.iana (2nd ed.)
Howes, Wright. U.S.iana, 1650–1950: a selective bibliography in which are described 11,620 uncommon and significant books relating to the continental portion of the United States. Rev. and enl. [i.e. 2nd] ed. New York: Bowker for the Newberry Library, 1962. Reprint. New York: Bowker, 1978.

JCB LIB. cat., pre–1675
Brown University. John Carter Brown Library. Bibliotheca Americana: catalogue of the John Carter Brown Library in Brown University, Providence, Rhode Island. Providence: The Library, 1919–1931.

JCB LIB. cat., 1675–1700
Brown University. John Carter Brown Library. Bibliotheca Americana: catalogue of the John Carter Brown Library in Brown University, books printed 1675–1700. Providence: Brown University Press, 1973.

JOHNSON, H. A. New London
Johnson, Hazel A. A checklist of New London, Connecticut, imprints, 1709–1800. Charlottesville: Published for the Bibliographical Society of America [by] University Press of Virginia, 1978.

JOHNSON, T. H. Edwards
Johnson, Thomas Herbert. The printed writings of Jonathan Edwards, 1703–1758: a bibliography. Princeton: Princeton University Press; London: H. Milford, Oxford University Press, 1940.

KAPP, K. S. Early Maps of Columbia
Kapp, Kit S. The early maps of Columbia up to 1850. London: Map Collectors' Circle, 1971.

KNUTTEL
Hague. Koninklijke Bibliotheek. Catalogus van de pamfletten-verzameling berustende in de Koninklijke Bibliotheek. Bewerkt door Dr. W.P.C. Knuttel. 's Gravenhage: Algemeene Landsdrukkerij, 1889–1919.

KRESS LIB.
Harvard University. Graduate School of Business Administration. Baker Library. Kress Library of Business and Economics. Catalogue: with data upon cognate items in other Harvard libraries. Boston: Baker Library, Harvard Graduate School of Business Administration, 1940–67.

MCMURTRIE, D. C. Florida
McMurtrie, Douglas C. A preliminary short-title check list of books, pamphlets and broadsides printed in Florida, 1784–1860. Jacksonville: Historical records survey, 1937.

MILLER, C. W. Franklin
Miller, Clarence William. Benjamin Franklin's Philadelphia printing, 1728–1766: a descriptive bibliography. Philadelphia: American Philosophical Society, 1974.

NCBEL
New Cambridge bibliography of English literature. Ed. by George Watson. Cambridge: University Press, 1969–77.

PALAU Y DULCET (2nd ed.)
Palau y Dulcet, Antonio. Manual del librero hispano-americano; bibliografía general española e hispano-americana desde la invención de la imprenta hasta nuestros tiempos, con el valor comercial de los impresos descritos. 2. ed. corr. y aumentada por el autor. Barcelona: A. Palau, 1948–1977.

PHILLIPS
U.S. Library of Congress. Map Division. A list of geographical atlases in the Library of Congress, with bibliographical notes. Washington: Govt. Print. Off., 1909–1974.

PILLING, J. C. Proof-sheets of a bib. of the languages of the North Amer. Indians
Pilling, James Constantine. Proof-sheets of a bibliography of the languages of the North American Indians. Washington: Government Printing Office, 1885.

RAGATZ, L. J. British Caribbean
Ragatz, Lowell Joseph. A guide for the study of British Caribbean history, 1763–1834, including the abolition and emancipation movements. Washington: United States Government Printing Office, 1932.

SABIN
Sabin, Joseph. Bibliotheca Americana, a dictionary of books relating to America from its discovery to the present time. New York: Sabin, 1868–1892; Bibliographical Society of America, 1928–1936. Reprint. Amsterdam: N. Israel, 1961–1962.

SCOTT, J. Darien Company
Scott, John. A bibliography of printed documents and books relating to the Darien Company. Edinburgh: Privately printed, 1904.
———. With additions and corrections by George P. Johnston. Edinburgh: Privately printed, 1906.

SEIDENSTICKER, O. German Printing.
Seidensticker, Oswald. The first century of German printing in America, 1728–1830. Philadelphia: Schaefer & Koradi, 1893.

SHIPTON & MOONEY
Shipton, Clifford Kenyon and Mooney, James E. National index of American imprints through 1800; the short-title Evans. [Worcester, Mass.]: American Antiquarian Society, 1969.

SMITH, J. Friends' books
Smith, Joseph, bookseller. A descriptive catalogue of Friends' books, or books written by members of the Society of Friends, commonly called Quakers, from their first rise to the present time, interspersed with critical remarks and...biographical notices. London: J. Smith, 1867.
——— Supplement. London: E. Hicks, 1893.

STAUFFER, D. M. American engravers
Stauffer, David McNeely. American engravers upon copper and steel. New York: The Grolier Club of the city of New York, 1907.

STOKES-HASKELL. Amer. hist. prints
New York Public Library. American historical prints, early views of American cities, etc., from the Phelps Stokes and other collections, by I.N. Phelps Stokes and Daniel C. Haskell.... New York: The New York Public Library, 1932.

STC (2nd ed.)
Pollard, Alfred William, and Redgrave, G. R. A short-title catalogue of books printed in England, Scotland & Ireland and of English books printed abroad, 1475–1640. 2nd ed., rev. & enl. London: Bibliographical Society, 1976–91.

TORONTO PUBLIC LIBRARY. Canadiana
Toronto. Public Libraries. A bibliography of Canadiana; being items in the Public Library of

Toronto, Canada, relating to the early history and development of Canada. Toronto: Public Library, 1934.

TREMAINE
Tremaine, Marie. A bibliography of Canadian imprints, 1751–1800. Toronto: University of Toronto Press, 1952.

TRINTERUD, L. J. Amer. Presbyterianism
Trinterud, Leonard J. A bibliography of American Presbyterianism during the colonial period. Philadelphia: Presbyterian Historical Society, 1968.

TRUMBULL, J. H. Connecticut
Trumbull, James Hammond. List of books printed in Connecticut, 1769–1800. [Hartford, Conn.: Hartford press, the Case Lockwood & Brainard company], 1904.

VAIL, R. W. G. Old frontier
Vail, Robert William Glenroie. The voice of the old frontier. Philadelphia: University of Pennsylvania Press, 1949.

WARING, E. J. Bib. therapeutica
Waring, Edward John. Bibliotheca therapeutica; or, Bibliography of therapeutics, chiefly in reference to articles of the materia medica, with numerous critical, historical, and therapeutical annotations, and an appendix containing the bibliography of British mineral waters. London: The New Sydenham Society, 1878–79.

WATT, R. Bib. Britannica
Watt, Robert. Bibliotheca britannica; or, A general index to British and foreign literature. Edinburgh: Printed for A. Constable and Company, 1824.

WING (2nd ed.)
Wing, Donald Goddard. Short-title catalogue of books printed in England, Scotland, Ireland, Wales, and British America, and of English books printed in other countries, 1641–1700. 2nd ed., rev. and enl. New York: Index Committee of the Modern Language Association of America, 1972–1983.

Key to Location Symbols

Note: The numbers in parentheses following the names of the individual libraries represent the number of titles in the Bibliographical Supplement owned by that library.

CALIFORNIA

CLU	University of California, Los Angeles. (4)
CSmH	Henry E. Huntington Library, San Marino. (17)
CSt	Stanford University, Palo Alto. (7)
CU	University of California, Berkeley. (4)

CONNECTICUT

CtHt	Trinity College, Hartford. (4)
CtY	Yale University, New Haven. (25)

DISTRICT OF COLUMBIA

DFo	Folger Shakespeare Library. (4)
DLC	U.S. Library of Congress. (28)

FLORIDA

FMU	University of Miami, Coral Gables. (5)
FTaSU	Florida State University, Tallahassee. (4)
FU	University of Florida, Gainesville. (3)

GEORGIA

GU	University of Georgia, Athens. (2)
GU-De	University of Georgia, DeRenne Georgia Library. (3)

ILLINOIS

ICN	Newberry Library, Chicago. (20)
ICU	University of Chicago. (6)
IU	University of Illinois, Urbana. (6)

INDIANA

InU	Indiana University, Bloomington. (18)

IOWA

IaU	University of Iowa, Iowa City. (1)

LOUISIANA

LNT	Tulane University, New Orleans. (4)
LU	Louisiana State University, Baton Rouge. (4)

MARYLAND

- MdBJ — Johns Hopkins University, Baltimore. (9)
- MdBP — Peabody Institute, Baltimore. (6)

MASSACHUSETTS

- MB — Boston Public Library. (16)
- MBAt — Boston Athenaeum, Boston. (8)
- MH — Harvard University, Cambridge. (23)
- MH-AH — Harvard University, Andover-Harvard Theological Library. (1)
- MH-BA — Harvard University, Graduate School of Business Administration, Baker Library, Boston. (10)
- MHi — Massachusetts Historical Society, Boston. (7)
- MShM — Mount Holyoke College, South Hadley. (3)
- MWA — American Antiquarian Society, Worcester. (12)
- MWiW-C — Williams College, Chapin Library. (3)

MICHIGAN

- MiU — University of Michigan, Ann Arbor. (5)
- MiU-C — University of Michigan, William L. Clements Library. (23)

MINNESOTA

- MnU — University of Minnesota, Minneapolis. (9)

MISSOURI

- MoU — University of Missouri, Columbia. (4)

NEW JERSEY

- NjP — Princeton University Library. (13)
- NjR — Rutgers – The State University, New Brunswick. (5)

NEW YORK

- N — New York State Library, Albany. (4)
- NHi — New York Historical Society, New York. (6)
- NN — New York Public Library. (31)
- NIC — Cornell University, Ithaca. (14)
- NNC — Columbia University, New York. (14)
- NNUT — Union Theological Seminary, New York. (3)
- NSyU — Syracuse University. (3)

NORTH CAROLINA

- NcD — Duke University, Durham. (7)
- NcU — University of North Carolina, Chapel Hill. (5)

OHIO

- OCl — Cleveland Public Library. (5)
- OClWHi — Western Reserve Historical Society, Cleveland. (4)

PENNSYLVANIA

- PHi — Historical Society of Pennsylvania, Philadelphia. (17)
- PPAmP — American Philosophical Society, Philadelphia. (9)
- PPL — Library Company of Philadelphia. (16)
- PPPrHi — Presbyterian Historical Society, Philadelphia. (4)
- PPRF — Rosenbach Foundation, Philadelphia. (4)
- PU — University of Pennsylvania, Philadelphia. (11)

RHODE ISLAND

- RPB — Brown University, Providence. (3)
- RPJCB — John Carter Brown Library, Providence. (52)

TEXAS

- TxDaM — Southern Methodist University, Dallas. (1)
- TxU — University of Texas, Austin. (7)

UTAH

- UU — University of Utah, Salt Lake City. (2)

VIRGINIA

- ViU — University of Virginia, Charlottesville. (11)
- ViW — College of William and Mary, Williamsburg. (4)
- ViWC — Colonial Williamsburg, Inc. (2)

Canada

BRITISH COLUMBIA

- CaBVaU — University of British Columbia, Vancouver. (3)

ONTARIO

- CaOHM — McMaster University, Hamilton. (3)
- CaOTU — University of Toronto. (6)

Bibliographical Supplement

ADAIR, JAMES, ca. 1709–1783.

The history of the American Indians; particularly those nations adjoining to the Mississippi [sic], East and West Florida, Georgia, South and North Carolina, and Virginia: containing an account of their origin, language, manners, religious and civil customs, laws, form of government, punishments, conduct in war and domestic life, their habits, diet, agriculture, manufactures, diseases and method of cure, and other particulars, sufficient to render it a complete Indian system. With observations on former historians, the conduct of our colony governors, superintendents, missionaries, &c. Also an appendix, containing a description of the Floridas, and the Missisippi [sic] lands, with their productions—the benefits of colonising Georgiana, and civilizing the Indians—and the way to make all the colonies more valuable to the mother country. With a new map of the country referred to in the history. By James Adair, esquire, a trader with the Indians, and resident in their country for forty years.

London: Printed for Edward and Charles Dilly, in the Poultry, MDCCLXXV. [1775]

Collation: 30 cm. (4to): pi² A-3N⁴. [12], 464 p., [1] folded leaf of plates: map.

Notes: Page 101 misnumbered 102. "Contains terms in Cheerokee, Choktah, Chikkasah, and Muskohge"; cf. Pilling.

References: Brown, J. C. Lib. cat., 1493–1800, III: 2013; Sabin 155; Vail, R. W. G. Old frontier, 643; Field, T. W. Indian bib., 11; Pilling, J. C. Proof-sheets of a bib. of the languages of the North Amer. Indians, 18; De Renne, W. J. Cat. of the Georgia Lib., I, p. 208.

JCB Library Copy: Acquired before 1859.

Locations: CaBVaU DLC FMU GU-De InU MB MHi MWA MdBP MiU-C NIC NN NcD NjP OCl PHi PPL PPRF PU RPJCB ViU ViW.

ANDERSON, JAMES, 1739–1808.

The interest of Great-Britain with regard to her American colonies, considered. To which is added an appendix, containing the outlines of a plan for a general pacification. By James Anderson, M. A. author of Observations on the means of exciting a spirit of national industry, &c.

London: Printed for T. Cadell, in the Strand. M.DCC.LXXXII. [1782]

Collation: 21 cm. (8vo): [A]⁴ B-S⁴ a-d⁴ e². vii, [1], 136, 36 p.

References: Brown, J. C. Cat., 1493–1800, III: 2746; Sabin 1400; Adams, T. R. Brit. pamphlets, 82–7.

JCB Library Copy: With: A letter to Henry Laurens, Esq. [London? : s.n., 1782?]; acquired before 1870.

Locations: CSmH CtY DLC FTaSU ICN InU LNT MB MH MWA MShM MiU-C NIC NN NNC PHi PPAmP RPJCB ViU.

BARCLAY, ROBERT, 1648–1690.

[Theologiae verè Christianae apologia. English]
An apology for the true Christian divinity, as the same is held forth, and preached, by the people, called in scorn, Quakers: being a full explanation and vindication of their principles and doctrines, by many arguments, deduced from Scripture and right reason, and the testimonies of famous authors, both ancient and modern: with a full answer to the strongest objections usually made against them. Presented to the King. Written in Latin and English, by Robert Barclay, and since translated into High Dutch, Low Dutch, and French, for the information of strangers.

The sixth edition in English.

Newport, Rhode Island: Printed by James Franklin. 1729.

Collation: 20 cm. (8vo): A⁸ (-A1, -A2) B-2O⁸ ²P-²Q⁸ (A1, A2, ²Q8 blank). [16], 524 [i.e. 574], [34] p.

Notes: Translation of: Theologiae verè christianae apologia. Page 574 misnumbered 524. There are two states of gathering F: one has catchwords: p. 65 "to"; p. 68 "among"; p. 78 "that". The other has catchwords: p. 65 "and"; p. 68 "both"; p. 78 "we". Includes index.

References: Sabin 3364; Evans 3129; Smith, J. Friends' books, supplement, p. 36; Alden, J. E. Rhode Island, 11.

JCB Library Copy: This copy has catchwords: p. 65 "to"; p. 68 "among"; p. 78 "that". Imperfect: p. [1]-[4] (preliminary blank leaves) and p. [33]-[34] at the end (final blank leaf) wanting. Bound in contemporary calf. Binding attributed to Francis Skinner. Acquired in 1907 from Brown University Library. Provenance: Redwood, Abraham, 1710-1788: autograph.

Locations: CLU CSmH CSt CtY DLC MB MH MWA MiU-C NN NjR OClWHi PPAmP PPL RPJCB.

BARCLAY, ROBERT, 1648–1690.
[Theologiae verè Christianae apologia. German] Robert Barclays Apologie oder Vertheidigungs-Schrift der wahren christlichen Gottesgelahrheit, wie solche unter dem Volk, so man aus Spott Quaker, das ist, Zitterer nennet, vorgetragen und gelehret wird. Oder völlige Erklärung und Rettung ihrer Grundsätze und Lehren, durch viele aus der Heil. Schrift, der gesunden Vernunft, und den Zeugnissen so wohl alter als neuer berühmten Scribenten gezogene Beweissthümer. Nebst einer gründlichen Beantwortung der stärksten Einwürffe, so gemeiniglich wider sie gebraucht werden. Anjetzo nach der zweyten lateinischen und neunten englischen Herausgebung ganz von neuen ins Deutsche übersetzt.

Germantown: Gedruckt bey Christoph Saur, dem Jüngern, 1776.

Collation: 20 cm. (8ᵛᵒ): A-C⁸ D-5H⁴ (leaf A1, 5E3 and 5H4 versos blank). 797, [27] p.

Notes: Translation of: Theologiae verè christianae apologia. First German edition: Eine Apologie oder Vertheidigungs, Schrifft der Recht Christlichen...1684.

References: Sabin 3365; Smith, J. Friends' books, I, p. 183; Evans 14659; Hildeburn, C. R. Pennsylvania, 3333; Seidensticker, O. German Printing, 93.

JCB Library Copy: Acquired in 1906. Bound in contemporary calf. Provenance: E.W. Harlan, fl. 1863: autograph presentation to L. Beckhasett, L., fl. 1863.

Locations: CSt CtHT CtY DLC ICN MH MWA MiU-C N NN NNUT NjP OClWHi PHi PPL RPJCB ViU ViW.

BARTRAM, WILLIAM, 1739–1823.
Travels through North & South Carolina, Georgia, East & West Florida, the Cherokee country, the extensive territories of the Muscogulges, or Creek Confederacy, and the country of the Chactaws; containing an account of the soil and natural productions of those regions; together with observations on the manners of the Indians. Embellished with copper-plates. By William Bartram.

Philadelphia: Printed by James & Johnson. M,DCC,XCI. [1791]

Collation: 21 cm. (8ᵛᵒ): a⁴ b-d⁴ e² B-3U⁴ 3X1 (leaf e2 blank; gathering 3Q unsigned). [2], xxiv, [2], 522 p., [9] leaves of plates (some folded): ill., 1 map, 1 port.

Notes: Running title: Bartram's travels. Copyright notice on verso of title page. Errors in paging: p. 294 and 312 misnumbered 492 and 212; page numbers 265–266 omitted and 289–290 repeated. Frontispiece portrait of Mico Chlucco drawn by the author and engraved by James Trenchard. "An account of the persons, manners, customs and government of the Muscogulges, or Creeks, Cherokees, Chactaws. &c. Aborigines of the continent of North America. By William Bartram." —p. [481]–522, with separate title page.

References: Sabin 3870; Evans 23159; De Renne, W. J. Cat. of the Georgia Lib., I, p. 250; Clark, T. D. Old South, I, 197; Vail, R. W. G. Old frontier, 849.

JCB Library Copy: Bound in contemporary calf; acquired with the assistance of the JCB Library Associates.

Locations: CtY DLC FMU FTaSU MBAt MdBJ MH MHi MiU MiU-C MWA NcU NN OClWHi PPRF PPL PU RPJCB.

BELHAVEN, JOHN HAMILTON, BARON, 1656–1708.
A defence of the Scots settlement at Darien. With an answer to the Spanish memorial against it. And arguments to prove that it is the interest of England to join with the Scots, and protect it. To which is added, a description of the country, and a particular account of the Scots colony.

Edinburgh, Printed in the year M. DC. XC.IX.

Collation: 18 cm. (8ᵛᵒ): A-M⁴ (leaf M4 blank). [8], 86, [2] p.

Notes: First published the same year in quarto. Also published the same year as octavo in whole sheets. This issue published as octavo in half sheets. Variously attributed to Belhaven, Andrew Fletcher, Archibald Foyer, and George Ridpath. W. C. Mackenzie, Andrew Fletcher of Saltoun, Edinburgh, 1935, p. 314–323, argues for Belhaven. Dedication signed (p. [8] (1st count)); Philo-Caledon. Errata: p. [2] (1st group).

References: Sabin 18549; Brown, J. C. Cat., 1482–1700, II: 1560; Scott, J. Darien Company, 67; Wing (2nd ed.) F2047B.

JCB Library Copy: Leaf H[1] is a cancel. Acquired in 1910.

Locations (all issues): CU CtY DFo DLC FU LNT MB MH-BA MWA MiU-C NIC NN NjP PHi RPJCB TxU.

BRAINERD, DAVID, 1718–1747.
An account of the life of Mr. David Brainerd, missionary from the Society for Propagating Christian Knowledge, & pastor of a church of

BIBLIOGRAPHICAL SUPPLEMENT 111

Christian Indians in New-Jersey. Published by Jonathan Edwards, A. M.; with Mr. Brainerd's public journal. To this edition is added, Mr. Beatty's mission to the westward of the Allegheny Mountains.

Edinburgh: Printed by T. Maccliesh and Co. for J. Ogle, Parliament Square, and M. Ogle, Glasgow. 1798.

Collation: 22 cm. (8vo): pi1 A-4A^4, ^{2}[A]^4 ^{2}B-G^4 (pi1 and ^{2}[A]1 versos blank). [2], 560, 56 p.

Notes: First published: Boston, 1749, under title: An account of the life of the late Rev. Mr. David Brainerd…. Brainerd's journal (p. [357]–487) is in two parts, with separate title pages, as follows: [pt. 1] Mirabilia Dei inter indicos. The rise & progress of a remarkable work of grace amongst a number of the Indians in New Jersey and Pensylvania…. [pt. 2] Divine grace displayed; or, The continuance & progress of a remarkable work of grace among some of the Indians in New-Jersey and Pensylvania…. Following Brainerd's journal, p. [525]–560, with separate title page: A sermon preached in Newark, June 12, 1744, at the ordination of Mr. David Brainerd, missionary among the Indians. By E. Pemberton. With an appendix touching the Indian affairs. Edinburgh, 1798. Beatty's journal (56 p. at end) has separate title page, pagination and register: The journal of a two-months tour; with a view of promoting religion among the frontier inhabitants of Pensylvania, and of introducing Christianity among the Indians to the westward of the Alegh-geny Mountains. By Charles Beatty. Edinburgh, Printed by and for T. Maccliesh and Co. for J. Ogle, 1798.

References: Sabin 21928; Sabin 4149.

JCB Library Copy: Page 56 (3rd count) appears as '50'.

Locations: CSmH CtY DLC ICN MBAt NN NjP NjR PPPrHi RPJCB ViU.

BURNS, ROBERT, 1759–1796.
Poems, chiefly in the Scottish dialect. By Robert Burns.

Philadelphia: Printed for, and sold by Peter Stewart and George Hyde, the west side of Second-Street, the ninth door above Chesnut-Street.,|cM,DCC,LXXXVIII. [1788]

Collation: 16 cm. (12mo): A^4 B-2B^6 2C^4. viii, [1], 10-304 p.

Notes: Author's preface dated: Edinburgh, April 4, 1787. The first American edition. Probably printed by David C. Claypoole and John Dunlap. Cf. Painter, Anna M. "American editions of the Poems of Burns before 1800." The Library, 4th ser., v. 12 (1931–1932): 434–456. "Glossary."— p. 279-304.

References: Evans 20991.

JCB Library Copy: Bound in contemporary sheep. Provenance: Louis Howard Aricson: bookplate. Acquired in 1994 with the assistance of the Bloomingdale and Wormser Funds.

Locations: CSmH CtY DLC MWA MWiW-C MiU-C NN NjP PPL PPRF PU.

THE CALEDONIAN MERCURY. Num 5051. Edinburgh, Tuesday, September 4, 1753.

Edinburgh: Printed for and by Thomas and Walter Ruddimans, and sold at their printing-house in the Parliament-close; where advertisements and subscriptions are taken in. [1753]

Collation: 38 cm. (4to). [4] p.

Notes: Place of publication and publishers' names from colophon. "Plantation News. Newport, Rhode Island, June 29." (p. [1]-[2]); "For Kingston in Jamaica, The Sloop Dolphin" (p. [4]).

JCB Library Copy: Gift in 1979 of Stan and Barbara Miller.

Locations: InU NcU PHi PPAmP RPJCB.

CAMPBELL, JOHN, 1708–1775.
Candid and impartial considerations on the nature of the sugar trade; the comparative importance of the British and French islands in the West-Indies: with the value and consequence of St. Lucia and Granada, truly stated. Illustrated with copper-plates.

London: Printed for R. Baldwin in Pater-noster Row., MDCCLXIII. [1763]

Collation: 21 cm. (8vo): [A]^2 B-P^8 Q^2. [4], 228 p., [3] folded leaves of plates: maps, plan.

Notes: Attributed to Campbell by Higgs and Kress Cat.

References: Brown, J.C. Cat., 1493–1800, III: 1378; Sabin 10231; Goldsmiths' Lib. cat., 9862; Kress Lib., 6081; Higgs, H. Bib. of economics, 1751–1775, 2926.

JCB Library Copy: Bound in contemporary calf. Acquired before 1859.

Locations: CaOTU CSmH CtY CU DFo DLC FMU InU ICN IU LNT LU MB MH MH-BA MHi MdBP MiU-C MnU MShM N NIC NN NNC NcD NjP PPAmP PPL PU RPJCB ViU ViWC.

CAMPBELL, JOHN, 1708–1775.
[Concise history of the Spanish America]

The Spanish empire in America. Containing a succinct relation of the discovery and settlement of its several colonies; a view of their respective situations, extent, commodities, trade, &c. And a full and clear account of the commerce with Old Spain by the galleons, flota, &c. Also of the contraband trade with the English, Dutch, French, Danes, and Portuguese. With an exact description of Paraguay. By an English merchant.

London: Printed for M. Cooper in Pater-noster Row. 1747.

Collation: 21 cm. (8vo): pi^6 (± pi1) A-U^8 X^4 chi^2 (pi1 verso blank). viii, [4], 330, [2] p.

Notes: Authorship from Halkett & Laing, Sabin, Howes and Alden-Landis. Third issue of this work; only the title page differs from the first edition, published under title: A concise history of the Spanish America. London, 1741. Second issue has title: A compleat history of Spanish America. London, 1742. One of two states: Title vignette depicts a vase with flowers flanked on each side by an eagle. The other state has a vignette with a bust on a pedestal. *Contents:* Book I. Containing the Spanish discoveries and conquests in America (p. [1]–73). —Book II. Comprehending a description of the Spanish settlements (p. 74–278). —Book III. Treating of the commerce of America (p. 279–319). —The appendix (p. 320–330). "Memoir concerning the settlements of the Jesuits in Paraguay." (p. 321–330; written by a French officer, translated into English). "Books printed for J. Stagg in Westminster Hall, and Daniel Browne at the Black Swan without Temple-Bar." (p. [1]–[2] at end).

References: Alden-Landis. European Americana, 747/28; Sabin 10240; Halkett & Laing (2nd ed.), 1: p. 396; Howes, W. U.S.iana (2nd ed.), C93; ESTC T155373.

JCB Library Copy: Bound in contemporary calf. Acquired in 1919.

Locations: CLU CaBVaU CaOHM CtY DLC ICN MH NN PU RPJCB.

CAMPBELL, JOHN, 1708–1775.
[Concise history of Spanish America]

An account of the Spanish settlements in America. In four parts. I. .... Each part contains an accurate description of the settlements in it, their situation, extent, climate, soil, produce, former and present condition, trading commodities, manufactures, the genius, disposition, and number of their inhabitants, their government, both civil and ecclesiastic; together with a concise account of their chief cities, ports, bays, rivers, lakes, mountains, minerals, fortifications, &c.; with a very particular account of the trade carried on betwixt them and Old Spain. To which is annexed, a succinct account of the climate, produce, trade, manufactures, &c. of Old Spain. Illustrated with a map of America.

Edinburgh: Printed by A. Donaldson and J. Reid. For the author, and A. Donaldson. Sold by A. Millar, J. Dodsley, J. Richardson, E. Dilly, and T. Durham, London; and Mess. Ewings, Dublin. MDCCLXII. [1762]

Collation: 21 cm. (8vo): a-b^4 A-3S^4 (a1 verso blank). xvi, 512 p., [1] folded leaf of plates: ill., map.

Notes: Authorship from Howes and ESTC. An extended edition, predominantly based on the author's earlier original edition: A concise history of the Spanish America. London, 1741. Plate (map) unnumbered, with bottom left insert: illustration of Havana. Errata: p. xvi. *Contents:* (from title page): I. An account of the discovery of America by the celebrated Christopher Columbus; with a description of the Spanish insulan colonies in the West Indies. II. Their settlements of the continent of North America. III. Their settlements in Peru, Chili, Paraguay, and Rio de La Plata. IV. Their settlements in Terra Firma. Of the different countries in South America still possessed by the Indians, &c. With a description of the Canary Islands.

References: Brown, J.C. Cat., 1493–1800, III: 1312; Sabin 102; Howes, W. U.S.iana (2nd ed.), C93; ESTC T045468.

JCB Library Copy: Provenance: Benjamin Butler, Painswick: bookplate. Bound in contemporary calf. Acquired before 1870.

Locations: DLC InU OCl PPL RPJCB.

CAMPBELL, JOHN, 1708–1775.
Lives of the admirals, and other eminent British seamen. Containing their personal histories, and a detail of all their public services. Including a new and accurate naval history from the earliest account of time; and, clearly proving by a continued series of facts, our uninterrupted claim to, and enjoyment of the dominion of our seas. Interspersed with many curious passages relating to our discoveries, plantations, and commerce. The whole supported throughout by proper authorities. By John Campbell, Esq;

London: Printed by John Applebee, for J. and H. Pemberton, in Fleet Street, and T. Waller, in the Temple. M,DCC,XLII–M,DCC,XLIV. [1742–1744]

Collation: 21 cm. (8vo): v. 1: A-2K^8 2L^4 2M^2; v. 2: A^4 B-2I^8 2K^4 2L^2 (-2L2); v. 3: A^4 B-2K^8; v. 4: A^4 B-2K^8 2L^4. 4 v.

Notes: Imprint varies: v. 3 and 4 dated 1744. Pagination: v. 1: [16], 496, [28] p.; v. 2: [8], 480, [26] p.; v.3: [8], 480, [32] p.; v. 4: [8], 496, [24] p. Bookseller's advertisements: v. 1, p. [16] (1st count); v. 3, p. [30]–[32] at the end; v. 4, p. [23]–[24] at the end. Later published under title: Lives of the British admirals. A "continuation" in a fifth volume issued in 1781. Includes bibliographical references and index in each volume.

References: Cf. Sabin 10236.

JCB Library Copy: Provenance: J. Boelen: stamp. This copy bound in contemporary mottled calf.

Locations: CSmH CSt CaOTU DFo ICN IU InU MoU NIC NN OCl RPB RPJCB.

THE CASE OF THE INHABITANTS of East-Florida. With an appendix, containing papers, by which all the facts stated in the case, are supported.

St. Augustine, East-Florida: Printed by John Wells. MDCCLXXXIV. [1784]

Collation: 20 cm. (8vo): pi^2 A-G^4 chi1. iv, 57, [1] p.

Notes: A protest of the cession of Florida to Spain in 1783. Errata: p. [1] at the end.

References: Evans 18392; McMurtrie, D. C. Florida, T1.

JCB Library Copy: Acquired in 1891.

Locations: MiU-C RPJCB.

CLERK, JOHN, SIR, 1676-1755.
An essay upon the xv. article of the Treaty of Union, wherein the difficulties that arise upon the equivalents, are fully cleared and explained.

[Edinburgh?: s.n.], Printed in the year M. DCC. VI. [1706]

Collation: 19 cm. (4to): A-C^4 D^2 (A1 verso blank). 28 p.

Notes: Authorship based on Alden-Landis. Place of imprint taken from Alden-Landis. Errata: p. 28.

References: Alden-Landis. European Americana, 706/47; Scott, J. Darien Company, 187; Hanson 639; Goldsmiths' Lib. cat., 4299.

JCB Library Copy: Bound in tooled calf decorated with gold leaf and signed McKelvie & Sons, Binders, Greenock. Acquired in 1906.

Locations: CLU CSmH ICN IU InU MB MH-BA MnU NIC NNC RPJCB TxU.

DUNCAN, WILLIAM, 1717-1760.
The elements of logic. In four books.... Designed particularly for young gentlemen at the university, and to prepare the way to the study of philosophy and the mathematics. By William Duncan, professor of philosophy in Marishal College, Aberdeen.

The first American edition.

Philadelphia: From the press of Mathew Carey., August 10,—M,DCC,XCII. [1792]

Collation: 18 cm. (12mo): [A]^2 B-V^6 X^4. 4, [1], vi-xii, [1], 14-239, [1] p.

Notes: First published: London, 1748. Bookseller's advertisements: p. [1] at the end.

References: Evans 24280.

JCB Library Copy: Bound in contemporary calf; acquired in 1912.

Locations: CSmH CtHT CtY DLC IU InU MH MdBP MiU-C NN NcD NjP PHi PU RPJCB ViW.

EDWARDS, JONATHAN, 1703-1758.
The distinguishing marks of a work of the spirit of God, applied to that uncommon operation that has lately appear'd on the minds of many of the people in New-England: with a particular consideration of the extraordinary circumstances with which this work is attended. By Jonathan Edwards.... With a preface by the Rev. Mr. Cooper of Boston, and letters from the Rev. Dr. Colman, giving some account of the present work of God in those parts. To which is prefix'd, an epistle to the Scots reader, by the Rev. Mr. John Willison minister of the Gospel at Dundee.

Edinburgh, Printed by T. Lumisden and J. Robertson, and sold at their printing-house in the Fish-market, and by J. Traill bookseller in the Parliament-closs. M.DCC.XLII. [1742]

Collation: 19 cm. (8vo): A-K^4 (A1 verso blank). xvi, 17-80 p.

Notes: Running title: The marks of a work of the true spirit. Originally published: Boston, 1741. Letter from J. Parsons to B. Colman: p. 77-80.

References: Brown, J. C. Cat., 1493-1800, III: 705. Alden-Landis. European Americana, 742/69. Johnson, T. H. Edwards, 54.

JCB Library Copy: Acquired in 1868.

Locations: MH RPJCB TxDaM.

ERSKINE, JOHN, 1721-1803.
Shall I go to war with my American brethren? A discourse addressed to all concerned in determining that important question. First published at London, 1769. To which are now added, a preface and appendix. By John Erskine, D. D. one of the ministers of Edinburgh.

Edinburgh: Printed in the year M DCC LXXVI. [1776]

Collation: 20 cm. (12mo): pi^4 (pi3+ A-B^6) chi^2 (pi4 missigned C1; pi1 and chi2 versos blank). vi, [1], 4-31, [1] p.

Notes: First published: London, 1769. Appendix. No. I. A letter first inserted in the Caledonian Mercury Oct. 4th 1775, under the signature of A True North Briton: p. 23-27. Number. II. A treasonable paper under the signature of A South Briton.: p. 28-31.

References: Sabin 22793; Adams, T. R. Brit. pamphlets, 69-15b.

Locations: CtY DLC ICN InU MH-AH MiU-C NN PHi RPJCB.

FLETCHER, ANDREW, 1655–1716.
Two discourses concerning the affairs of Scotland; written in the year 1698.

Edinburgh, 1698.

Collation: 17 cm. (8ᵛᵒ): A-F⁸ G⁴ (A1 verso blank). 50, 54 p.

Notes: Published anonymously. By Andrew Fletcher.

References: Wing (2nd ed.) F1298; Aldis, H. G. Scotland, 3810; Kress. Lib. 2081; Goldsmiths' Lib. cat., 3474.

JCB Library Copy: Acquired in 1994 with the assistance of the Harper Fund.

Locations: CtY CSmH DFo ICN ICU InU MiU-C MH-BA MnU NIC NNC PPrHi PU RPJCB.

FLETCHER, HENRY, d. 1803.
[Seven Year's War journal of the proceedings of the 35th Regiment of Foot, by a British officer, and illustrated by a military engineer]

[British North America, the Caribbean and England, August 1757-December 1765]

Collation: 21 cm. 76 leaves, incl. 25 ill., interleaved: [110 p.]: maps, views and plans (some folded).

Notes: Lieutenant-Colonel Fletcher was the field commander of this regiment during the period described in the notebook. In a notebook mainly of single quarter-sheets, sewn before writing. On paper, watermarked; with grey-blue blotting paper interleaving. The illustrations in ink and water colors.

JCB Library Copy: Acquired in 1966, with the assistance of the Metcalf Fund.

Locations: RPJCB.

GILLIES, JOHN, 1712–1796.
Memoirs of the life of the Reverend George Whitefield, M. A. late chaplain to the Right Honourable the Countess of Huntingdon: in which every circumstance worthy of notice, both in his private and public character, is recorded. Faithfully selected from his original papers, journals, and letters. Illustrated by a variety of interesting and entertaining anecdotes, from the best authorities. To which are added, a particular account of his death and funeral; and extracts from the sermons, which were preached on that occasion. Compiled by the Rev. John Gillies, D. D.

New-York: Printed by Hodge and Shober, at the newest printing-office, in Maiden-Lane. M.DCC.LXXIV. [1774]

Collation: 17 cm. (12ᵐᵒ): A-N¹² (A1 verso blank). xxiv, [25]–311, [1] p., [1] leaf of plates: port.

Notes: Engraved portrait by Elisha Gallaudet, sculpr. N. York, 1774. Bookseller's advertisements: p. [iv]-[v]. "List of subscribers.": p. [vi]–xviii.

References: Sabin 27415; Evans 13298; Stauffer, D. M. American engravers, 1025.

JCB Library Copy: Bound in contemporary calf. Provenance: Brown University Library: stamp. Acquired in 1907 from Brown University.

Locations: CtHT CtY DLC GU-De ICU MBAt MH MWA NjR NHi NN NSyU PPL PPrHi RPJCB.

GORDON, PETER, fl. 1734.
A view of Savanah as it stood the 29th of March, 1734.

[London, 1734].

Engraved view; 40.3 cm. X 56 cm.

Notes: "P. Gordon Inv."; "P. Fourdrinier Sculp." Dedicated by Peter Gordon to the Honble. the Trustees for establishing the Colony of Georgia in America. Two states noted: one with; the other without additional title in French: Vüe de Savanah dans la Georgie.

References: Stokes-Haskell. Amer. historical prints, B-62, Plate 13b. T. C. Bannister, "Oglethorpe's Sources for the Savannah Plan" in Journal of the Society of Architectural Historians, reprint, May, 1961, vol. 20, n. 2, p. 49. Cf. De Renne, W. J. Cat. of the Georgia Lib., III, p. 1279.

JCB Library Copy: This copy lacks the French title. Acquired in 1868.

HUME, DAVID, 1711–1776.
The life of David Hume, Esq; the philosopher and historian, written by himself. To which are added, The travels of a philosopher, containing observations on the manners and arts of various nations, in Africa and Asia. From the French of M. Le Poivre, late envoy to the King of Cochin-China, and now intendant of the isles of Bourbon and Mauritius.

Philadelphia: Printed and sold by Robert Bell, next door to St. Paul's Church, in Third-Street. M,DCC,LXXVIII. [1778]

Collation: 20 cm. (8ᵛᵒ): [A]⁴ B-H⁴ ([A]1, B3 and B4 versos blank). 62, [2] p.

Notes: Also issued as part of: Miscellanies for sentimentalists.... Philadelphia: Robert Bell, 1778 (Evans 15914). "Letter from Adam Smith,

LL. D. to William Strahan, Esq; giving some account of Mr. Hume, during his last sickness." —p. [9]–13. "Travels of a philosopher: containing, observations on the manners and arts of various nations, in Africa and Asia. From the French of M. Le Poivre…"—p. [15]–62, with separate title page. Bookseller's advertisements: p. [2] at the end.

References: Evans 15853; Hildeburn, C. R. Pennsylvania, 3716.

JCB Library Copy: Acquired in 1914.

Locations: CtY DLC MWA MiU-C NN NcD PHi PPL PPRF PU RPJCB.

HUTCHESON, FRANCIS, 1694–1746.
[Philosophiae moralis institutio compendiaria. English]

A short introduction to moral philosophy, in three books; containing the elements of ethicks, and the law of nature. By Francis Hutcheson, LLD. late professor of philosophy in the University of Glasgow. Translated from the Latin.

Fifth edition.

Philadelphia, Printed and sold by Joseph Crukshank, in Market Street, between Second and Third Streets., MDCCLXXXVIII. [1788]

Collation: 17 cm. (12mo): a-b⁶ B-2B⁶ 2C⁴ chi⁴ (-chi1). xxiii, [1], 292, [6] p.

Notes: First published: Glasgow, 1742. Cf. BM. Page 186 misnumbered 189. Bookseller's advertisement: p. [1]–[6] at the end.

References: Evans 21164; BM (compact ed.) 12:791.

JCB Library Copy: Provenance: John H. Cheyney: autograph; R. Frazer: autograph. Bound in contemporary pigskin. Acquired in 1911.

Locations: CU DLC LU MB MiU-C NjR NNUT PHi PU RPJCB.

A LETTER, GIVING A DESCRIPTION of the isthmus of Darian: (where the Scot's colonie is settled;) from a gentleman who lives there at present. With an account of the fertilness of the soil, the quality of the air, the manners of the inhabitants, and the nature of the plants, and animals. &c. And a particular mapp of the isthmus, and entrance to the river of Darian.

Edinburgh, Printed for John Mackie, in the Parliament-Closs, and James Wardlow on the north side of the Street a little below the Cross, at the sign of the Bible. M. DC. XC. IX. [1699]

Collation: 19 cm. (4to): A-C⁴ (A1 verso blank). 24 p., [1] folded leaf of plates: map.

References: Sabin 78222; Scott, J. Darien Company, 63; Wing (2nd ed.) L1549; Aldis, H. G. Scotland, 3865.

JCB Library Copy: Acquired in 1905.

Locations: DLC MB NN RPJCB.

LOCH, DAVID, d. 1780.
Essay on the trade, commerce, and manufactures of Scotland. By David Loch of Over Carnbie, merchant in Edinburgh.

Edinburgh: Printed for the author, and sold by all the booksellers in town and country. M, DCC, LXXV. [1775]

Collation: 21 cm. (8vo): pi² (superscript pi)A⁴ A-L⁴ M² (pi1 and (superscript pi)A4 versos blank). [4], vii, [1], 92 p.

References: Sabin 41716; Adams, T. R. Brit. pamphlets, 75–85; Kress Lib. 7136; Goldsmiths' Lib. cat., 11226.

JCB Library Copy: Acquired in 1980 with the assistance of the Harper Fund. Provenance: inscribed by the author to the Earl of Haddington.

Locations: CaOTU CSmH CtY DLC InU ICN MH MH-BA MdBJ MiU NN RPJCB.

MACPHERSON, JAMES, 1736–1796.
The rights of Great Britain asserted against the claims of America: being an answer to the declaration of the general congress.

London: Printed for T. Cadell, in the Strand. M DCC LXXVI. [1776, i.e. 1775]

Collation: 21 cm. (8vo): [A]² B-L⁴ M² N⁴. [4], 92 p., [1] folded leaf of plates.

Notes: Attributed to Macpherson by Adams. Frequently attributed to John Dalrymple and to Lord George Germain. Publication date from Adams. "A declaration by the representatives of the united colonies of North America… setting forth the causes and necessity of their taking up arms." —p. 85–92, dated July 6, 1775.

References: Sabin 18347; Adams, T. R. Amer. pamphlets, 220a; Adams, T. R. Brit. pamphlets, 75–95a.

JCB Library Copy: Imperfect: folding table wanting. Acquired in 1944.

Locations: DLC CtY ICN InU MB MH NIC NSyU PPL RPJCB.

MARCHANT, JOHN, 18TH CENT.
[Bloody tribunal]

A review of the bloody tribunal; or the horrid cruelties of the Inquisition, as practised in Spain, Portugal, Italy, and the East and West-Indies, on all those whom the Church of Rome brands with the name of hereticks. Containing a description of the most dreadful and exquisite tortures on the several persons who have unhappily fallen into the hands of those tyrants over mens consciences, the Jesuits and popish priests: by John Marchant, gentleman, and others, &c.

Perth: Printed and sold by G. Johnston, the publisher, where subscribers may call for their copies. 1770.

Collation: 19 cm. (4to): A-3B^4 (A1 verso blank). vii, [8]–384 p.

Notes: Originally published as: The bloody tribunal, or, An antidote against popery. London, 1756.

JCB Library Copy: Bound in contemporary calf. Acquired in 1960 with the assistance of the JCB Associates.

Locations: IaU MnU NN RPJCB.

A NEW PLAN of the Harbour, City, & Forts OF CARTAGENA; with the progress of the British fleet in their several stations & attacks from the 4th. of March 1741, till the 1st of April, when Captn. Lawsa came away. Sent over by Mr. Richardson from on board the Norfolk.

[Edinburgh, 1741]

Engraved map: 15.3 × 28.2 cm.

Notes: From the Scots Magazine, 1741, v. 3, p. 228. "Tho: Smith Sculp".

References: Kapp, K. S. Early Maps of Columbia, no. 68.

JCB Library Copy: 1957 gift of Thomas B. Card.

PAPERS RELATING TO AN AFFIDAVIT made by His Reverence James Blair, clerk, pretended president of William and Mary College, and supposed commissary to the bishop of London in Virginia, against Francis Nicholson, esq; governour of the said province. Wherein His Reverence's great respect to government, and obedience to the ninth commandment, Thou shalt not bear false witness, &c. will plainly appear; as will also his gratitude to the said governour, from whom he had received so many favours, and to whom he was himself so highly obliged, in several original letters under his own hand, some whereof are here published, and more (God willing) shall hereafter.

[London: s.n.], Printed in the year 1727.

Collation: 19 cm. (8vo): [A]^2 B-G^8 H^4 (A1 verso blank). [4], 104 p.

Notes: Place of imprint from Alden-Landis.

References: Alden-Landis. European Americana, 727/178.

JCB Library Copy: Acquired between 1871 and 1927.

Locations: MiU-C RPJCB.

PATERSON, WILLIAM, 1658–1719.

An essay concerning inland and foreign, publick and private trade; together with some overtures, shewing how a company or national trade, may be constituted in Scotland, with the advantages which will result therefrom.

[Edinburgh?: s.n., 1705]

Collation: 21 cm. (4to): A^4. 8 p.

Notes: Caption title. Signed at the end: T. W. Philiopatris. Saxe Bannister, in his 'Life and writings of William Paterson', 1858 dates this work to 1705 and attributes it to Paterson. A reply to the paper money scheme enunciated by John Law in 'Two overtures' and 'Money and trade', both published in Edinburgh, 1705. Place of imprint from Alden-Landis.

References: Alden-Landis. European Americana, 705/135; Scott, J. Darien Company, 152; Hanson 346; Kress Lib., 2422; Goldsmiths' Lib. cat., 4065.

JCB Library Copy: Bound in tooled calf decorated with gold leaf and signed McKelvie & Sons, Binders, Greenock. Acquired in 1906.

Locations: InU MH-BA MdBJ NNC RPJCB.

PENNECUIK, ALEXANDER, 1652–1722.
Caledonia Triumphans: a panegyrick to the King.

Edinburgh, Printed by the heirs and successors of Andrew Anderson, printer to the Kin[g's] most Excellent Majesty, 1699.

Collation: 42 × 34 cm. (1°). 1 sheet ([1] p.).

Notes: Coat of arms of the Darien Company at head of title. Verse. Signed at the end: By a Lover of Caledonia and the Muses. A copy in the Advocates Library (s.v. Pennecuik, Alex.) has in manuscript "D. Pennecook of Romana in Tweedeel." See Scott.

References: JCB Lib. cat., 1675–1700, 399; Scott, J. Darien Company, 84; Wing (2nd ed.) C285.

JCB Library Copy: Acquired in 1883.

Locations: RPJCB.

A PLAN of the City and Harbour of LOUISBURG, in which are pointed out the principal places mentioned in the Account of the Siege of that Fortress by the New Englanders in 1745.

[Edinburgh, 1762]

Engraved map: 17.6 × 23.9 cm.

Notes: Below title: "See Scots Mag. Vol. VIII. page 301–306." At lower right, "A Bell & Company. Sc." Inset, at left: A Map of the Island of Cape Breton.

References: Phillips, 364.

JCB Library Copy: Acquired in 1947.

The PRESENT STATE of the tobacco plantations in America.

[London(?), 1708?]

Collation: 31 × 20 cm. (fol.) 1 sheet ([2] p.)

Notes: With a docket title. Imprint information from Alden-Landis.

References: Brown, J.C. Cat., 1493–1800, III: 423; Alden-Landis. European Americana, 708/101; Hanson 942.

JCB Library Copy: Broadside folded and bound in marbelled boards (19 cm.). Acquired in 1851.

Locations: NN RPJCB.

PRINCE, THOMAS, 1687–1758.
A sermon delivered at the South Church in Boston, N. E. August 14. 1746. Being the day of general thanksgiving for the great deliverance of the British nations by the glorious and happy victory near Culloden. Obtained by His Royal Highness Prince William Duke of Cumberland April 16. last. Wherein the greatness of the publick danger and deliverance is in part set forth, to excite their most grateful praises to the God of their salvation. By Thomas Prince, M. A. and a pastor of said church.

Boston: Printed for D. Henchman in Cornhil, and S. Kneeland and T. Green in Queen-Street. 1746.

Collation: 21 cm. (4to): [A]^4 B-E^4 (E4 verso blank). 38, [2] p.

Notes: Half-title: Mr. Prince's thanksgiving sermon on the glorious victory near Culloden. Running title: A thanksgiving sermon for the victory near Culloden. Errata: p. 38 and p. [1] at the end.

References: Sabin 65612; Evans 5857.

JCB Library Copy: Acquired in 1936 from the American Antiquarian Society.

Locations: CtY CSt DLC ICN ICU MdBJ MdBP MB MBAt MH MHi MiU-C MoU MWA MWiW-C NcD NN NNC PPL RPJCB TxU.

PROPOSALS CONCERNING THE PROPAGATING of Christian knowledge, in the Highlands and Islands of Scotland and forraign [sic] parts of the world.

[Edinburgh? s.n., 1707?]

Collation: 31 cm. (fol.). 4 p.

Notes: According to G. P. Johnstone, James Kirkwood probably wrote this work. Cf. Publications of the Edinburgh Bibliographical Society. Vol. 6 (1906), pp. 1–18, esp. p. 4. Caption title. Imprint information from ESTC.

References: ESTC T197119.

JCB Library Copy: Acquired in 1964.

Locations: RPJCB.

RAMSAY, ALLAN, 1713–1784.
Letters on the present disturbances in Great Britain and her American provinces.

London [i.e. Rome] reprinted MDCCLXXVII. [1782]

Collation: 21 cm. (8vo): a-e^4 (a1 verso blank). 40 p.

Notes: Three letters reprinted from the London Public Advertiser of April 18, 1771 and January 25 and 26, 1775, the first signed Marcellus, the second and third signed Britannicus.

References: Sabin 67676; Adams, T. R. Brit. pamphlets, 77–77.

JCB Library Copy: Imprint replaced by Rome in manuscript.

Locations: CSmH HtY DLC ICN InU MB MH MiU-C NNC NsyU NjP PHi PPAmP RPJCB.

RAMSAY, JAMES, 1733–1789.
An essay on the treatment and conversion of African slaves in the British sugar colonies. By the Reverend James Ramsay, M. A. Vicar of Teston, in Kent.

London: Printed and sold by James Phillips, George-Yard, Lombard-Street. M.DCC.LXXXIV. [1784]

Collation: 22 cm. (8vo): a^8 b^2 chi1 A-S^8 T^4 U^2 (a1 and chi1 versos blank). xx, [2], 298, [2] p.

Notes: Errata: p. [1] (2nd count). Contents: Of the various ranks in social life—The advancement of slaves would augment their social importance—The advancement of slaves must accompany their religious importance—Natural capacity of African slaves vindicated—Plan for the improvement and conversion of African slaves.

References: Brown, J. C. Cat., 1493–1800, III: 3044; Sabin 67713.

JCB Library Copy: Imperfect: p. [1]–[2] at the end (advertisement leaf) wanting. Bound in contemporary calf. Acquired before 1874.

Locations: CaOHM CSmH CSt CtY DLC FTaSU ICN ICU LU MB MH-BA MH MHi MdBJ MiU MnU MoU NIC NN NNC NjP OClWHi PHi PPL RPJCB TxU.

ROBE, JAMES, 1688–1753.

A short narrative of the extraordinary work at Cambuslang; in a letter to a friend. With proper attestations. By ministers, preachers and others.

Boston: Re-printed and sold by S. Kneeland, and T. Green in Queen-Street. 1742.

Collation: 18 cm. (8vo): A-C^4. 24 p.

Notes: Taken from: Robe, James. Mr. Robe's first[-fourth] letter to… J. Fisher. Glasgow, 1742. Cf. the Dictionary of national biography. Attestations by William M'Culloch and nine others.

References: Sabin 80667; Evans 5047.

JCB Library Copy: Acquired in 1936 exchange with the American Antiquarian Society.

Locations: CtY MB MH MHi MWA PHi PPAmP RPJCB.

ROBERTSON, WILLIAM, 1721–1793.
[History of America. Books 1–8]

The history of America. By William Robertson…

London: Printed for W. Strahan; T. Cadell, in the Strand; and J. Balfour, at Edinburgh. MDCCLXXVII. [1777]

Collation: 31 cm. (4to): v. 1: pi^4 a-b^4 B-3Q^4 (pi1, pi2, b1, b4, I1, Z4, 2I3, and 3H2 versos blank); v. 2: pi^2 B-3I^4 3K^2 (-3K2) 3L-4A^4 4B^2 (pi1, pi2, U1, 2X4, 3L1, 3U4, and 3X4 versos blank). Leaf 3H3 of v. 1 and leaf 4A4 of v. 2 each signed as "*"; leaf I1 of v. 2 signed as "l". 2 v. (v. 1: xvii, [7], 488 p.; v. 2: [4], 433 p., p. 434/440, p. [441]-535, [21] p., [1] folded leaf of plates): ill.

Notes: First edition, in two volumes in quarto, first state (without the four maps that are present in the second state). Contains Books I–VIII, the history of the discovery of America and the conquest of Mexico and Peru. Includes bibliographical references and index, among them: "A catalogue of Spanish books and manuscripts." (v. 2: p. [523]–535). "Short account of what is contained in the letter sent to the Emperor, mentioned Preface, p. xi." (v. 2: p. [521]–522). Errata: v. 2: p. [21] at end.

References: Brown, J.C. Cat., 1493–1800, 3: 2418; Sabin 71973; Palau y Dulcet (2nd ed.) 270979; ESTC T078961.

JCB Library Copy: Half title leaf v. 1 wanting. Acquired before 1871.

Locations: CSmH CSt CU CaBVaU CaOHM CaOTU CtHT CtY DLC FU ICN IU InU MH MWA MiU-C MnU NIC NcU NjP NjR OCl RPJCB TxU ViU ViWC.

ROMANS, BERNARD, CA. 1720–CA. 1784.

A concise natural history of East and West Florida; containing an account of the natural produce of all the southern part of British America, in the three kingdoms of nature, particularly the animal and vegetable. Likewise, the artificial produce now raised, or possible to be raised, and manufactured there, with some commercial and political observations in that part of the world; and a chorographical account of the same. To which is added, by way of appendix, plain and easy directions to navigators over the bank of Bahama, the coast of the two Floridas, the north of Cuba, and the dangerous Gulph Passage. Noting also, the hitherto unknown watering places in that part of America, intended principally for the use of such vessels as may be so unfortunate as to be distressed by weather in that difficult part of the world. By Captain Bernard Romans. Illustrated with twelve copper plates, and two whole sheet maps. Vol. I.

New-York: Printed for the author,
M,DCC, LXXV. [1775]

Collation: 18 cm. (8vo): [a]^2 b^4 A-2T^4 2U^2 chi1 ^{2}A-^{2}K^4 ^{2}L^2 ^{2}M^2 ^{2}chi1 (^{2}chi1 verso blank). 4, viii, 1-175, 178-342, [2], lxxxix, [5] p., [12] leaves of plates (1 folded): ill., maps.

Notes: The second volume was not published. The "two whole sheet maps" of East and West Florida mentioned in the title were not issued with this work, but were eventually published separately in 1781. Cf. Library of Congress. Maps and charts of North America and the West Indies 1750–1789. Washington, 1981, p. 352. Horizontal chainlines from signature A to signature 2A; chi1-^{2}H and ^{2}K-^{2}M. "List of subscribers to this work": p. i–viii and p. [2] (5th count). Errata: p. lxxxix and p. [2]–[3] at the end.

References: Brown, J.C. Cat., 1493–1800, III: 2138; Sabin 72992; Evans 14440; Church, E. D. Discovery, 1124.

JCB Library Copy: Imperfect: 6 plates wanting; pages 123–124 torn with loss of text. Provenance: Peter L. Poole: autograph. Acquired before 1870.

Locations: CtY DLC FMU FTaSU InU ICN MBAt MH MiU-C MWiW-C NcD NHi NN PPAmP PPL RPJCB TxU ViU.

St. Andrew's Club, of the City of Charleston, in South-Carolina.
Rules of the St. Andrew's Club, at Charlestown in South-Carolina: established in the year MDCCXXX.

The second edition: with a list of the members.

Charlestown: Printed for the Society by Robert Wells. MDCCLXII. [1762]

Collation: 18 cm. (4to): A-C^4 D^2 (A1 verso blank). 28 p.

References: Gould & Morgan. South Carolina, 203.

JCB Libraray : Accompanied by a certificate of membership dated Nov. 30, 1768. Acquired in 1988 with the assistance of the Harper and Wroth Funds.

Locations: NcU RPJCB.

Scot, George, d. 1685.
The model of the government of the province of East-New-Jersey in America; and encouragements for such as designs to be concerned there. Published for information of such as are desirous to be interested in that place.

Edinburgh, Printed by John Reid, and sold be [sic] Alexander Ogston stationer in the Parliament Closs. Anno Dom. 1685.

Collation: 14 cm. (8vo): A^4 ²A^8 B-O^8 P-U^4 (A1 blank except for signature mark). [8], 272 p.

Notes: Dedicatory epistle signed (p. [7] (1st count): George Scot. "It was, says the author, the outcome of a visit to London in 1679, when he enjoyed 'the opportunity of frequent converse with several substantial and judicious gentlemen concerned in the American plantations'…The most valuable part of the work is a series of letters from the early settlers in New Jersey. 'The Model' was plagiarized by Samuel Smith in his 'History of New Jersey', 1721, and is quoted by Bancroft; but James Grahame, author of the 'Rise and progress of the United States' [1827] first attached due importance to it. … In some copies a passage (p.37) recommending religious freedom as an inducement to emigration is modified." —Dict. nat. biog. Pages 62 and 63 transposed. Two states noted: In one, the last paragraph on p. 37 begins: "I find removal likewise allowable in case of persecution," etc. In the other, this paragraph begins: "Where people find themselves straitned in the point of their opinions," etc.

References: Brown, J. C. Cat., 1482–1700, II: 1323; Sabin 78186; Church, E. D. Discovery, 697; Baer, E. 17th cent. Maryland, 120; Wing (2nd ed.) S2036.

JCB Library Copy: First state; imperfect: p. [1]–[2] (first count) wanting. Acquired in 1846.

Locations: CSmH DLC GU ICN MH MdBJ MdBP MiU-C N NHi NN NjP PHi PPL RPJCB ViU.

The Scotch Butchery, Boston. 1775.
[London]: Pub^d according to Act of Parl^{mt}… 1775.

Engraving: 23.6 cm. × 35.5 cm. (mounted on sheet 28.4 cm. × 45.5 cm.)

Notes: A symbolical representation of the situation in Massachusetts in 1775. Key figures: Lords Bute and Mansfield and numerous British and Scotch soldiers.

References: George, 5287.

JCB Library Copy: Acquired in 1952 from the collection of R. T. Haines Halsey.

Scotland.
[Act for a company trading to Africa and the Indies]

An act of Parliament, for encourageing the Scots Affrican and Indian Company. Edinburgh, June 26, 1695.

[Edinburgh? s.n., 1695]

Collation: 19 cm. (4to): A^4 (A^4 verso blank). [8] p.

Notes: Caption title.

References: Brown, J. C. Cat., 1482–1700, II: 1476; Sabin 78198; Scott, J. Darien Company, 2c; Wing (2nd ed.) S1127.

JCB Library Copy: Closely trimmed with some loss of text. Acquired in 1851.

Locations: RPJCB.

Scotland's Lament for their misfortunes.
[Edinburgh: s.n., 1700]

Collation: 32 × 20 cm. (fol.). 1 sheet ([1] p.).

Notes: Verse.

References: JCB Lib. cat., 1675–1700, 424; Scott, J. Darien Company, 130b; Wing (2nd ed.) S2016A.

JCB Library Copy: Acquired in 1883.

Locations: RPJCB.

Scotus Americanus.
Informations concerning the province of North Carolina, addressed to emigrants from the Highlands and Western Isles of Scotland. By an impartial hand.

Glasgow: Printed for James Knox, bookseller, Glasgow, and Charles Elliot, bookseller Parliament Close, Edinburgh. MDCCLXXIII. [1773]

Collation: 23 cm. (8vo): pi1 A-C^4 D^4(-D4) (A1 verso blank). 32 p.

Notes: Signed at the end: Scotus Americanus.

References: Brown, J. C. Cat., 1493–1800, III: 1873; Sabin 34708.

JCB Library Copy: Acquired in 1861.

Locations: FMU FU ICN MiU-C MoU NcD NcU NHi NN NNC RPJCB UU.

SMITH, ADAM, 1723–1790.

An inquiry into the nature and causes of the wealth of nations. By Adam Smith, LL. D. and F. R. S. formerly professor in the University of Glasgow. In two volumes.

London: Printed for W. Strahan; and T. Cadell, in the Strand. MDCCLXXVI. [1776]

Collation: 28 cm. (4to): v. 1: A⁴ a² B-M⁴ (±M3) N-Q⁴ (±Q1) R-U⁴ (±U3) X-2Z⁴ (±2Z3) 3A⁴ (±3A4) 3B-3O⁴ (±3O4) 3P-3T⁴ (-3T4; a2 verso, 2T3 verso, 3N1 verso blank); v. 2: [A]² B-D⁴ (±D1) E-3Z⁴ (±3Z4) 4A-4E⁴ 4F² ([A]1 verso, 2P1 verso blank). Leaf + 2Z3 in v. 1 signed as: "Z3" (cipher "2" added by hand in ink). 2 v. ([12], 510; [4], 587, [1] p.)

Notes: Volume 2: 288 misnumbered: "289"; v. 2: p. 556 misnumbered: "5 6". Errata (v. 2: p. [4] (1st count)). Published by the same author,..." (v. 1: p. [2] (1st count). —"Books printed for and sold by T. Cadell, in the Strand." (v. 2: p. [1] at end, verso of p. 587). Scattered references to America, especially in Book IV. Chap. VII. Of colonies (v. 2: p. 146–256).

References: Sabin 82302; Goldsmiths' Lib. cat. 11392; Kress Lib. 7261; Watt, R. Bib. Britannica 2: 862a; ESTC T096668.

JCB Library Copy: Acquired in 1909.

Locations: CtY CLU CSt CU DLC ICN ICU InU LU MB MH-BA MdBJ MiU MiU-C MnU MWiW-C NjP NIC NNC PPL PU RPJCB TxU UU ViU ViW.

SMITH, WILLIAM, 1727–1803.

A general idea of the College of Mirania; with a sketch of the method of teaching science and religion, in the several classes; and some account of its rise, establishment and buildings. Address'd more immediately to the consideration of the trustees nominated, by the Legislature, to receive proposals, &c. relating to the establishment of a college in the province of New York.

New-York: Printed and sold by J. Parker and W. Weyman, at the new printing-office in Beaver-Street, 1753.

Collation: 20 cm. (4to): [A]⁴ B-K⁴ L⁴ (-L4). 86 p.

Notes: Outlining "a purely fictitious institution" to show the kind of college William Smith thought suitable for a new country. The concept informed the founding of the University of Pennsylvania. Cf. Wood, G. B. Early hist. of the Univ. of Penn. (1896). Signed (p. 81): W. Smith. Errata: p. [3].

References: Brown, J. C. Cat., 1493–1800, III: 1006; Sabin 84614; Evans 7121.

JCB Library Copy: Provenance: Henry Remsen, 1736–1792: autograph. Acquired in 1859.

Locations: DLC MBAt MiU NN NIC PHi PPRF PU RPJCB.

SMITH, WILLIAM, 1728–1793.

Information to emigrants, being a copy of a letter from a gentleman in North-America: containing a full and particular account of the terms on which settlers may procure lands in North-America, particularly in the provinces of New-York and Pensilvania. As also, the encouragement labourers, mechanics, and tradesmen of every kind may find by going there to settle. To which is added, observations on the causes of emigration.

Glasgow: Printed for, and sold by Morrison and M'Allum at their shop in Gibson's land Saltmarket, and at J. Galbraith's Printing-office. [1773]

Collation: 17 cm. (12mo): A-B⁴ (A1 verso blank). 16 p.

Notes: "The following proposals, informations and directions drawn up, and signed by the Hon. Mr. Smith of New-York, June 11th 1773...": p. [3].

References: Sabin 84574.

JCB Library Copy: Acquired in 1909 from the Rhode Island Historical Society.

Locations: DLC NjP RPJCB.

STIRLING, WILLIAM ALEXANDER, EARL OF, 1567 or 8–1640.

An encouragement to colonies. By Sir William Alexander, knight.

London: Printed by William Stansby. 1624.

Collation: 18 cm. (4to): A-G⁴ (Leaves A2 and G4 versos blank). [8], 47, [1] p., [1] folded leaf of plates: map.

References: JCB Lib. cat., pre-1675, II: 182–3; Alden-Landis. European Americana, 624/156; STC (2nd ed.) 341; Church, E. D. Discovery, 400.

JCB Library Copy: Imperfect: p. [1]–[2] at the beginning (blank leaf?) wanting. Portrait of the author bound in before title page. Provenance: British Museum: stamp. Acquired in 1846.

Locations: CSmH MH NHi NN NNC RPJCB.

TAILFER, PATRICK.
A true and historical narrative of the colony of Georgia in America, from the first settlement thereof, until this present period; containing, the most authentick facts, matters and transactions therein. Together with His Majesty's Charter, representations of the people, letters, &c. and a dedication to His Excellency General Oglethorpe. By Pat. Tailfer, M. D. Hugh Anderson, M. A. Da. Douglas, and others, landholders in Georgia, at present in Charles-Town in South-Carolina.

[London?] Printed for P. Timothy, in Charles-Town, South-Carolina; and sold by J. Crokatt, in Fleet-Street, London. [1741?]

Collation: 21 cm. (8vo): [A]² (-[A]2) B-R⁴. [2], xvi, 112 p.

Notes: A criticism of the constitution of the colony and of Oglethorpe's administration. Place and date of publication suggested in the Catalogue of the Wymberly Jones De Renne Library, p. 96. The first edition (Evans 4816) was printed at Charleston by P. Timothy in 1741; the present edition and another edition (Evans 4817; xviii, 78, 87–118 p., dated M.DCC.XLI and bearing P. Timothy's imprint) were apparently printed in London in the same year.

References: Brown, J. C. Cat., 1493–1800, III: 696; Alden-Landis. European Americana, 741/224; De Renne, W. J. Cat. of the Georgia Lib., I, p. 96-97; Sabin 94217; Vail, R. W. G. Old frontier, 415.

JCB Library Copy: Provenance: Perceval, John, Earl: autograph. This copy is interleaved and contains numerous manuscript notes by John Perceval, Earl of Egmont, refuting Tailfer's arguments; bound in contemporary mottled calf. Acquired before 1870.

Locations: GU GU-De MH NN PHi PPL PU RPJCB ViU.

TOD, T. (THOMAS), fl. 1781.
Consolatory thoughts on American independence; shewing the great advantages that will arise from it to the manufactures, the agriculture, and commercial interest of Britain and Ireland. Published for the benefit of the Orphan Hospital at Edinburgh. By a merchant.

Edinburgh: Printed by James Donaldson, 1782.

Collation: 21 cm. (8vo): pi² A-H⁴ I². [4], 68 p.

Notes: Signed at end: T. True Briton. "Attributed to 'Tod of Kirtland' in the article on Thomas Somerville in the Dictionary of National Biography." —Sabin. Written in part in response to Thomas Somerville, Candid thoughts, London, 1781.

References: Brown, J. C. Cat., 1493–1800, III: 2756; Sabin 96076; Adams, T. R. Brit. pamphlets, 82–89; Goldsmiths' Lib. cat. 12258.

JCB Library Copy: Acquired before 1859.

Location: CaOTU CSmH CtY ICN ICU IU InU LNT MB MBAt MH-BA MH MHi MShM MWA MiU-C MnU NHi NIC NN NNC PHi PPAmP RPB RPJCB.

TWEED, MR.
Considerations and remarks on the present state of the trade to Africa; with some account of the British settlements in that country, and the intrigues of the natives since the peace; candidly stated and considered. In a letter addressed to the people in power more particularly, and the nation in general. By a gentleman, who resided upwards of fifteen years in that country.

Lonnon [i.e. London]: Printed for and sold by Mess. Robinson and Roberts, in Pater-noster Row. M DCC LXXI. [1771]

Collation: 22 cm. (8vo): pi² A-L⁴ (pi1 and pi2 versos blank). [4], 88 p.

Notes: Attributed to Mr. Tweed by Higgs. Half-title: Considerations on the present state of the trade to Africa. Some copies contain a map.

References: Brown, J. C. Cat., 1493–1800, III: 1781; Sabin 15942; Kress Lib. 6782; Goldsmiths' Lib. cat. 10757; Higgs, H. Bib. of Economics, 1751–1775, 5236.

JCB Library Copy: Imperfect: p. [1]–[2] at the beginning (half-title) wanting. Acquired before 1871.

Locations: CSmH MH-BA MdBJ NNC NN RPB RPJCB.

TYRTAEUS.
[Elegies. Latin & Greek]

Spartan lessons; or the praise of valour; in the verses of Tyrtaeus; an ancient Athenian poet, adopted by the republic of Lacedaemon, and employed to inspire their youth with warlike sentiments.

Glasgow: Printed by Robert and Andrew Foulis. M DCC LIX. [1759]

Collation: 19 cm. (4to): [a]² b-g² chi² A-E² chi1 F-G² H² (-H2). xxvii, [5], 20, [3], 22-30 p.: ill., ports.

Notes: Variant issue has p. 30 misnumbered p. 26. With a biographical introduction in English, the Greek text, notes on the text, and the Latin text taken from Stephens' edition of 1579. With half-titles to the Greek and Latin texts. "These remains of ancient panegyric on martial spirit and personal valour; of old, the daily lessons of the Spartan youth; are, with propriety, inscribed, to the young gentlemen; lately, bred at the University of Glasgow; at present, serving their country, as officers of the Highland battalions now in America." Dedication: p. [iii]. Errata: p. 20.

References: Gaskell, P. Foulis, 376.

JCB Library Copy: Acquired in 1909.

Locations: CtY CSmH MH MiU-C N NIC NN NNC RPJCB.

WILCOCKE, SAMUEL HULL, 1766?–1833.
A narrative of the occurrences in the Indian countries of North America, since the connexion of the Right Hon. the Earl of Selkirk with the Hudson's Bay Company, and his attempt to establish a colony on the Red River: with a detailed account of His Lordship's military expedition to, and subsequent proceedings at Fort William, in Upper Canada.

London: Printed by B. McMillan, Bow-Street, Covent-Garden, printer to His Royal Highness the Prince Regent. Sold by T. Egerton, Whitehall; Nornaville and Fell, New Bond-Street; and J. Richardson, Royal Exchange. 1817.

Collation: 23 cm. xiv, 152, [4], 87, [1] p.

Notes: Attributed to Samuel Hull Wilcocke—cf. Dict. of Canadian Biog. VI, 814–815. Also attributed to Simon McGillivray or to Edward Ellice, the elder—cf. NUC pre-56. Published also in French under title: Récit des événements qui ont eu lieu sur le territoire des sauvages dans l'Amérique septentrionale, depuis les liaisons du tres Hon. comte de Selkirk avec la Compagnie de la Baie d'Hudson, et la tentative faite par ce comte de fonder une colonie sur la rivière Rouge.

References: Sabin 20699; Goldsmiths' Lib. cat., 21786.

JCB Library Copy: Probably acquired before 1874.

Locations: CaOTU CtY DLC MB MH MdBP MnU NN OCl PPAmP RPJCB ViU.

WITHERSPOON, JOHN, 1723–1794.
Address to the inhabitants of Jamaica, and other West-India islands, in behalf of the College of New-Jersey.

Philadelphia: Printed by William and Thomas Bradford, at the London Coffee-House. M,DCC,LXXII. [1772]

Collation: 20 cm. (8vo): [A]⁴ B-C⁴ D² (A1, A2 and D2 versos blank). 27, [1] p.

Notes: Signed (p. 27): John Witherspoon. Half-title: Address in behalf of the College of New-Jersey.

References: Brown, J.C. Cat., 1493–1800, III: 1847; Sabin 104930; Evans 12627; Hildeburn, C.R. Pennsylvania, 2839; Trinterud, L.J. Amer. Presbyterianism, 467.

JCB Library Copy: Acquired before 1871.

Locations: MdBJ MBAt NjP NN NNUT PHi PPL PPPrHi RPJCB.

Selected Additional Resources Relating to Scotland and The Americas

AN ABSTRACT OF THE EVIDENCE delivered before a select committee of the House of Commons in the years 1790, and 1791; on the part of the petitioners for the abolition of the slave trade.

Edinburgh: Printed for J. Robertson, No 39 South Bridge-street. MDCCXCI. [1791]

[2], 128 p., [2] folded leaves of plates: ill., map.; 18 cm. (12mo)

Notes: "An alphabetical list of the names of witnesses examined by the Select Committee of the House of Commons, on the part of the petitioners of Great Britain, for the abolition of the slave trade": p. [7]–11.

References: Sabin 81746; Hogg, P. C. African Slave trade, 12; Handler, J. S. Barbadoes, p. 55; Ragatz, L. J. Brit. Caribbean Hist. p. 409.

AESOP IN SCOTLAND, exposed in ten select fables relating to the times. Viz. I. The young lyon and dogs. II. The mad lyon and woolf. III. The fox and eagle. IV. The man and his ass. V. The cat and the eagle VI. The merchant and soldiers. VII. The magpye and rook. VIII. Northern trumpeter IX. The bees and hornets X. The farmer and weasel.

London, Printed in the year 1704.

8 p.; 18 cm. (8vo)

Notes: Jacobite political satires in verse; fable 5: The merchants, and soldiers, refers to the Darien settlement.

References: Alden-Landis. European Americana, 704/3; Scott, J. Darien Company, 151; Foxon A115.

ALVES, ROBERT, 1745–1794.
Ode to Britannia. (For the year 1780.) Occasioned by our late successes. By Robert Alves…

Edinburgh: Printed for William Creech. M,DCC,LXXX. [1780]

12 p.; 22 cm. (4to)

Notes: Poem describing the siege of Savannah and the progress of Cornwallis's army in the South.

References: Sabin 985; Adams, T.R. Brit. pamphlets, 80-3.

ANDERSON, JAMES, 1739–1808.
Free thoughts on the American contest.

Edinburgh: Printed in the year M,DCC,LXXVI. [1776]

[2], 59, [1] p.; 21 cm. (8vo)

Notes: First published in the Edinburgh Weekly Magazine under the signature "Timoleon". Attributed to James Anderson by Sabin and Adams. Postscript (p. 57–59): a reply to Paine's Common Sense.

References: Sabin 1399; Adams, T. R. Brit. pamphlets, 76-6.

ASSOCIATE PRESBYTERY OF PENNSYLVANIA (1753–1782)

Act of the Associate Presbytery in Pennsylvania, for a public fast. At Philadelphia, the seventh day of November, one thousand seven hundred and seventy-four years.

[Glasgow]: Philadelphia printed, and Glasgow reprinted in the year, M,DCC,LXXV. [1775]

16 p.; 21 cm. (8vo)

Notes: First published: Philadelphia, 1774.

ASSOCIATE PRESBYTERY OF PENNSYLVANIA (1782–1801)

Declaration and testimony, for the doctrine and order of the Church of Christ, and against the errors of the present times. To which is prefixed, a narrative, concerning the maintenance of the reformation-testimony. By the Associate Presbytery of Pennsylvania.

The second edition.

[Edinburgh]: Printed at Philadelphia in the year 1784. Edinburgh: reprinted for A. Brown, Bridge-street, 1786.

135, [1] p.; 18 cm. (12mo)

AUCKLAND, WILLIAM EDEN, BARON, 1744–1814.
Four letters to the Earl of Carlisle, from William Eden, Esq. On certain perversions of political reasoning; and on the nature, progress, and effect of party-spirit and of parties. On the present circumstances of the war between Great Britain and the combined powers of France and Spain. On the public debts, on the public credit, and on the means of raising supplies. On the representations of Ireland respecting a free-trade.

Edinburgh: Printed in MDCCLXXIX. And sold for R. and G. Fleming, Old Fish-market Close. [1779]

86 p.; 21 cm. (8vo)

Notes: First published in London in the same year.

References: Sabin 21827; Adams, T. R. Brit. pamphlets, 79–6c; Kress Lib. B171.

BARCLAY, ROBERT, 1648–1690.
The anarchy of the ranters, and other libertines; the hierarchy of the Romanists, and other pretended churches, equally refused and refuted, in a two-fold apology for the church and people of God, called in derision, Quakers. Wherein they are vindicated from those that accuse them of disorder and confusion on the one hand, and from such as calumniate them with tyranny and imposition on the other; shewing, that as the true and pure principles of the Gospel are restored by their testimony; so is also the antient apostolick order of the church of Christ re-established among them, and settled upon its right basis and foundation. By Robert Barclay.

Philadelphia: Re-printed, and sold by B. Franklin, and D. Hall, 1757.

viii, 111, [1], 23, [1] p.; 18 cm. (8vo)

Notes: First published: [London?], 1676. "An epistle to the national meeting of Friends, in Dublin, concerning good order and discipline in the church. Written by Joseph Pike." 23, [1] p. at the end.

References: Sabin 3363; Smith, J. Friends' books, I, p. 179; Evans 7840; Evans 8008; Hildeburn, C. R. Pennsylvania, 1516; Hildeburn, C. R. Pennsylvania, 1552; Miller, C. W. Franklin, 655.

BARCLAY, ROBERT, 1648–1690.
A catechism and confession of faith, approved of, and agreed unto, by the general assembly of the patriarchs, prophets, and apostles, Christ himself chief speaker in and among them. Which containeth a true and faithful account of the principles and doctrines which are most surely believed by the churches of Christ in Great-Britain and Ireland, who are reproachfully called by the name of Quakers; yet are found in the one faith with the primitive church and saints; as is most clearly demonstrated by some plain Scripture-testimonies (without consequences or commentaries) which are here collected and inserted by way of answer to a few weighty, yet easy and familiar questions, fitted as well for the wisest and largest, as for the weakest and lowest capacities. To which is added, an expostulation with, and appeal to all other professors. By R.B. a servant of the church of Christ.

Newport: Printed by James Franklin, at the Town-School-house. 1752.

[8], 151, [9] p.; 16 cm. (8vo)

Notes: Preface signed by Robert Barclay. First published: London, 1673.

References: Evans 6812; Smith, J. Friends' books, I, p. 175–6; Alden, J. E. Rhode Island, 114.

BARCLAY, ROBERT, 1648–1690.
Truth triumphant through the spiritual warfare, Christian labours and writings of that able and faithful servant of Jesus Christ Robert Barclay. Who deceased at his own house at Urie, in the kingdom of Scotland, the 3 day of the 8 month 1690.

London, Printed for Thomas Northcote in George-Yard in Lombard-Street, MDCXCII. [1692]

[2], xxxviii, [16], 908, [16] p.; 30 cm. (fol.)

Notes: Each work has a separate t.p., with same imprint, dated 1691. "Introduction by William Penn"—Brit. Mus. Catalogue.

References: Sabin 3367; Wing (2nd ed.) B740; Smith, J. Friends' books, I, p. 187.

THE BATTLE OF BROOKLYN, a farce of two acts: as it was performed at Long-Island, on Tuesday the 27th of August, 1776, by the representatives of the tyrants of America, assembled at Philadelphia.

Edinburgh: [s.n.], Printed in the year M,DCC,LXXVII. [1777]

35, [1] p.; 17 cm. (12mo)

References: Cf. Sabin 8282; Adams, T. R. Brit. pamphlets, 76–12b; Hill, F. P. Amer. plays, 14.

BLAIR, HUGH, 1718–1800.
Lectures on rhetoric and belles lettres. By Hugh Blair, D. D. one of the ministers of the High Church, and professor of rhetoric and belles lettres in the University, of Edinburgh.

Philadelphia: Printed and sold by Robert Aitken, at Pope's Head in Market Street., MDCCLXXXIV. [1784]

viii, 454, [12] p.; 25 cm. (4to)

Notes: First published: London, 1783.

References: Evans 18369; Hildeburn, C. R. Pennsylvania, 4435.

BORLAND, FRANCIS, d. 1722.
Memoirs of Darien: giving a short description of that countrey, with an account of the attempts of the Company of Scotland, to settle a colonie in that place. With a relation of some of the

many tragical disasters, which did attend that design. With some practical reflections upon the whole. Written mostly in the year 1700. While the author was in the American regions.

Glasgow: Printed by Hugh Brown. M. DCC. XV. [1715]

102, [2] p.: map.; 19 cm. (8vo)

Notes: Attributed to Borland by Alden-Landis. First published: Glasgow, 1714.

References: Brown, J.C. Cat., 1493–1800, III: 202; Alden-Landis. European Americana, 715/27; Scott, J. Darien Company, 210.

BORLAND, FRANCIS, d. 1722.
[Memoirs of Darien]

The history of Darien. Giving a short description of that country, an account of the attempts of the Scotch nation to settle a colony in that place, a relation of the many tragical disasters, which attended that design; with some practical reflections upon the whole. By the Rev. Mr. Francis Borland, sometime minister of the Gospel at Glassford; and one of the ministers who went along with the last colony to Darien. Written mostly in the year 1700, while the author was in the American regions. To which is added, A letter to his parishoners [sic].

Glasgow: Printed by John Bryce; and sold at his shop opposite Gibson's-Wynd, Saltmarket. 1779.

iv, 5–100 p.; 21 cm. (8vo)

Notes: First published: Glasgow, 1714, under title: Memoirs of Darien. A letter written by the Reverend Mr. Francis Borland to his parishioners. Boston, New-England, 19th Nov. 1770 [i.e. 1700]: p. 98–100.

References: Brown, J.C. Cat., 1493–1800, III: 2529; Sabin 6428; Scott, J. Darien Company, 214.

BURT, EDWARD, D. 1755.
Letters from a gentleman in the north of Scotland to his friend in London; containing the description of a capital town in that northern country; with an account of some uncommon customs of the inhabitants: likewise an account of the Highlands, with the customs and manners of the Highlanders. To which is added, a letter relating to the military ways among the mountains, began in the year 1726. The whole interspers'd with facts and circumstances intirely new to the generality of people in England, and little known in the southern parts of Scotland. In two volumes.

London: Printed for S. Birt, in Ave-Maria Lane. MDCCLIV. [1754]

2 v. (Vol. 1: x, 344 p., [6] leaves of plates; v. 2: [2], 368 p., [3] leaves of plates.): ill., map.; 21 cm. (8vo)

Notes: "Letter from Donald Mc. Pherson a young Highland lad, who was sent to Virginia with Captain Toline...": v. 1, p. 250–255.

BYFIELD, NATHANAEL, 1653–1733.
An account of the late revolution in New-England. Together with the Declaration of the gentlemen, merchants, and inhabitants of Boston, and the countrey adjacent, April 18. 1689. Written by Mr. Nathanael Byfield, a merchant of Bristol in New England, to his friends in London.

Edinburgh, [s.n.], Re-printed in the year. 1689.

7, [1] p.; 18 cm. (4to)

Notes: Originally published: London, 1689. "The Declaration of the gentlemen, merchants, and inhabitants of Boston, and the countrey adjacent, April 18. 1689": p. 3–7, drawn up by Cotton Mather, first published Boston, 1689, as a broadside.

References: Brown, J.C. Cat., 1482–1700, II: 1373; Sabin 9708; Wing (2nd ed.) B6380; Church, E.D. Discovery, 709; Holmes, T.J. Cotton Mather, 85c.

CAMPBELL, CHARLES, b. 1793.
Memoirs of Charles Campbell, at present prisoner in the jail of Glasgow. Including his adventures as a seaman, and as an overseer in the West Indies. Written by himself. To which is appended, an account of his trial before the Circuit Court of Justiciary, at Glasgow, 27th April, 1826.

Glasgow: James Duncan & Co. 8, Wilson Street, J.T. Smith & Co., Hunter's Square, Edinburgh, and James Duncan, London. MDCCCXXVIII. [1828]

4, 43, [1] p.; 22 cm.

Notes: "The account of the trial is taken verbatim from the Glasgow Free Press newspaper of the 29th April, 1826." —p. 4. Trial of Charles Campbell, before the Circuit Court of Judiciary at Glasgow, 27th April, 1826: p. [31]–43.

References: Ragatz, L.J. Brit. Caribbean Hist., p. 220.

CAMPBELL, COLIN, d. 1782, defendant.
Proceedings of a general court martial, held at Fort Royal, in the island of Martinico, on the 6th, and continued by adjournments to the 14th of April, 1762, upon the tryal of Major Commandant Colin Campbell.

London: Printed by J. Towers in Piccadilly, 1762.

75, [1] p.; 19 cm. (8vo)

Notes: Trial for the murder of Capt. John McKaarg.

References: Sabin 96846.

CAMPBELL, JOHN, 1708–1775.
[Concise history of Spanish America]

The Spanish empire in America. Containing a succinct relation of the discovery and settlement of its several colonies; a view of their respective situations, extent, commodities, trade, &c. And a full account and clear account of the commerce with Old Spain by the galleons, flota, &c. Also of the contraband trade with the English, Dutch, French, Danes, and Portuguese. With an exact description of Paraguay. By an English merchant.

London: Printed for M. Cooper in Pater-noster Row. 1747.

viii, [4], 330, [2] p.; 21 cm. (8vo)

Notes: Another (third) issue; only title page different from original issue, published under title: A concise history of the Spanish America. London, 1741. Previous issue has title: A compleat history of Spanish America. London, 1742.

References: Alden-Landis. European Americana, 747/28; Sabin 10240; Halkett & Laing (2nd ed.) 1: p. 396; Howes, W. U.S.iana (2nd ed.), C93.

CHAUNCY, CHARLES, 1705–1787.
The counsel of two confederate kings to set the son of Tabeal on the throne, represented as evil, in it's [sic] natural tendency and moral aspect. A sermon occasion'd by the present rebellion in favour of the Pretender. Preach'd in Boston, at the Thursday-Lecture, February 6th. 1745,6. By Charles Chauncy, D. D. Pastor of the First Church of Christ in said town.

Boston: Printed for D. Gookin, over against the Old South Meeting House. 1746.

43, [1] p.; 22 cm. (4to)

References: Sabin 12331n; Evans 5752.

CHAUNCY, CHARLES, 1705–1787.
A letter from a gentleman in Boston, to Mr. George Wishart, one of the ministers of Edinburgh, concerning the state of religion in New-England.

Edinburgh: Printed in the year MDCCXLII. [1742]

24 p.; 22 cm. (8vo).

Notes: A discussion of the effects of George Whitefield's preaching in New England.

References: Brown, J.C. Cat., 1493–1800, III: 712; Alden-Landis, D.C. European Americana, 742/49.

COLMAN, BENJAMIN, 1673–1747.
A sermon preach'd at Boston in New-England on Thursday the 23d. of August. 1716. Being the day of publick thanksgiving, for the suppression of the late vile and traiterous rebellion in Great Britain. By Benjamin Colman, M.A. pastor of a church in Boston.

Boston: Printed by T. Fleet and T. Crump; sold by Samuel Gerrish on the North side of the Town-House. 1716.

28 p.; 16 cm. (8vo)

References: Sabin 14515; Evans 1805.

CUMBERLAND, RICHARD, 1732–1811.
The West Indian; a comedy. As it is acted at the Theatre Royal in Drury-Lane. By Richard Cumberland.

Perth: Printed by R. Morison junior, for R. Morison and Son, booksellers, Perth. M.DCC.XC. [1790]

[2], 79, [3] p.; 16 cm. (12mo)

Notes: Epilogue. Written by D. G. Esq. [=David Garrick]—Spoken by Mrs. Abington." (p. [1]–[2] (3rd count)).

References: NCBEL 2:814; ESTC T018511.

DALRYMPLE, JOHN, SIR, 1726–1810.
Reflections upon the military preparations which are making at present in Scotland.

Edinburgh: Printed in the year M,DCC,LXXVIII. [1778]

13, [3] p.; 20 cm. (8vo)

Notes: Concerned with the raising of Scottish regiments to aid England against the rebel Americans after the defeat of Burgoyne.

References: Sabin 68726; Adams, T.R. Brit. pamphlets, 78-26; Halkett & Laing (2nd ed.), IV, p. 48.

DUNBAR, JAMES, d. 1798.
Caledonia, a poem.

London: Printed for T. Cadell in the Strand. M,DCC,LXXVIII. [1778]

vi, [2], 63, [1] p.; 20 cm. (4to)

Notes: Contains references to the "Danger of… colonizing the boundless regions of the American continent." (cf. p. [1], 2nd count).

Edwards, Jonathan, 1703–1758.
A careful and strict inquiry into the modern prevailing notions of the freedom of will, which is supposed to be essential to moral agency, virtue and vice, reward and punishment, praise and blame. By Jonathan Edwards, A.M.

The third edition.

London: Printed for J. Johnson, no. 8, in Paternoster-Row, M.DCC.LXVIII. [1768]

xi, [5], 414, [8], 18 p.; 21 cm. (8vo)

Notes: Remarks on the Essays on the principles of morality and natural religion, in a letter to a minister of the Church of Scotland: by the Reverend Mr. Jonathan Edwards... (A criticism of Lord Kames' Essays...): p. [1]–18 at the end.

References: Sabin 21930; Johnson, T. H. Edwards, 186.

Edwards, Jonathan, 1703–1758.
A history of the work of redemption. Containing, the outlines of a body of divinity, in a method entirely new. By the late reverend Mr Jonathan Edwards, president of the College of New Jersey.

Edinburgh: Printed for W. Gray, Edinburgh, and J. Buckland and G. Keith, London. MDCCLXXIV. [1774]

xi, [1], 378, [2] p.; 21 cm. (8vo)

Notes: Originally a series of sermons preached in Northampton in 1739, edited after the author's death, from his manuscripts, by John Erskine. Preface signed: Jonathan Edwards [the younger]. Newhaven, Feb. 25, 1773.

References: Johnson, T. H. Edwards, 243.

Edwards, Jonathan, 1703–1758.
Some thoughts concerning the present revival of religion in New-England, and the way in which it ought to be acknowledged and promoted; humbly offer'd to the publick, in a treatise on that subject, in five parts.... By Jonathan Edwards, A.M. pastor of the Church of Christ at Northampton.

[Edinburgh]: Boston, printed: Edinburgh, reprinted by T. Lumisden and J. Robertson, and sold at their printing-house on the Fishmarket., M. DCC. XLIII. [1743]

iv, 124, 129-221, [1] p.; 18 cm. (8vo)

Notes: First published: Boston, 1742.

References: Brown, J. C. Cat., 1493–1800, III: 736; Alden-Landis. European Americana, 743/81; Johnson, T. H. Edwards, 84.

Elegy on the murnful banishment of James Campel of Burnbank to the West-Indies.

[Edinburgh: s.n., 1721 or 1722]

1 sheet ([1] p.); 32 X 19 cm. (1/2°)

Notes: Verses beginning: Now let salt-tears run down our cheeks..., consisting of 23 stanzas and an epitaph of 4 stanzas. Another version, containing 19 stanzas, issued apparently in the same year, with title: Elegy on the mournful banishment of James Campbell. Cf. Foxon E76.

References: Foxon E77.

An encomium on the Indian and African company's undertaking, as it is faithfully translated out of the Amstelodam-Laydon Gazette, May 13. 1700. N. S.

[London?: s.n., 1700?]

1 sheet ([1] p.); 31 X 19 cm. (fol.)

References: Scott, J. Darien Company, 126b; Wing (2nd ed.) E722A.

Everard, Giles.
De herba panacea, quam alii tabacum, alii petum, aut nicotianam vocant, brevis comentariolus. Quo admirandae ac prorsus diviné huius Peruanae stirpis facultates & usus explicantur. Auctore Aegidio Everarto, Antverpiano.

Vltrajecti, Pro Davide ab Hoogenhuysen, Anno MDCXLIV. [1644]

305, [7] p.; 13 cm. (12mo)

Notes: De Herba panacea / Giles Everard (p. 5–58) 1st published Antwerp, 1583 with five additional pieces, different from the ones in this collection—Iohannes Neandri Bremani Tabacologia (p. [59]–144). —Epistolae et iudicia clarissimorum aliquot medicorum. De tabaco (p. [145]–197 [i.e., 195])—Misocapnus, siue De abusu tobacci / James I, King of Gt. Brit. (p. [197]–223). —Hymnus Tabaci, / Autore Raphaele Thorio (p. [225]–305).

References: Alden-Landis. European Americana, 644/62.

Fletcher, Andrew, 1655–1716.
The political works of Andrew Fletcher, esq:...

London: Printed by James Bettenham, for A. Bettesworth and C. Hitch, and C. Davis in Pater-noster-row. MDCCXXXVII. [1737]

[18], 448 p.; 21 cm. (8vo)

Notes: Contents: (from t.p.): I. A discourse of government with relation to militia's. II,III. Discourses concerning the affairs of Scotland; written in the year 1698. IV. Discorso delle cose di Spagna scritto nel mese di Luglio 1698. V. A speech upon the state of the nation; in April 1701. VI. Speeches by a member of the Parliament, which began at Edinburgh the 6th of May 1703. VII. An account of a conversation concerning a right regulation of governments for the common good of mankind: in a letter to the Marquis of Montrose, the Earls of Rothes, Roxburg and Haddington, from London the 1st of December, 1703.

References: Alden-Landis. European Americana, 737/91.

FOXCROFT, THOMAS, 1697–1769.
The ruling & ordaining power of Congregational bishops, or presbyters, defended. Being remarks on some part of Mr. P. Barclay's Persuasive, lately distributed in New-England. By an impartial hand. In a letter to a friend.

Boston Printed for Samuel Gerrish and sold at his shop near the Brick Meeting-House in Cornhill, 1724.

[2], 45, [1] p.; 17 cm. (8vo)

Notes: A reply to: A persuasive to the people of Scotland...by P[eter] Barclay..., London: Printed for Jonah Bowyer: and sold by the booksellers in Edinburgh, Dublin, and Boston in New-England, 1723. Intended as an appendix to: Sober remarks...[By Edward Wigglesworth], Boston: Printed for Samuel Gerrish..., 1724. See Foxcroft's statement, p. 2–3.

References: Sabin 25402; Evans 2531.

GERARD, ALEXANDER, 1728–1795.
Liberty the cloke of maliciousness, both in the American rebellion, and in the manners of the times. A sermon preached at Old Aberdeen, February 26. 1778, being the fast-day appointed by proclamation, on account of the rebellion in America. By Alexander Gerard, D. D. professor of divinity in King's College.

Aberdeen: Printed by J. Chalmers & Co. sold by Alexander Thomson, bookseller, Aberdeen; T. Cadell, London; and W. Creech, Edinburgh. MDCCLXXVIII. [1778]

24 p.; 22 cm. (8vo)

References: Adams, T. R. Brit. pamphlets, 78-39.

GLAS, JOHN, 1695–1773.
Christian songs; written by Mr. John Glas, and others.

The seventh edition.

[Providence]: Perth (Scotland) printed: Providence (Rhode-Island): re-printed by Bennett Wheeler, at his office in Westminster-Street, MDCCLXXXVII. [1787]

129, [3] p.; 18 cm. (12mo)

Notes: The Dictionary of national biography entry for John Glas credits his son Alexander with writing "some of the best of the 'Christian songs'." "Elegies." —p. [121]–129. "Index." —p. [1]–[2] at the end.

References: Evans 20391; Alden, J. E. Rhode Island, 1075.

GLEN, JAMES, 1701–1777.
A description of South Carolina; containing, many curious and interesting particulars relating to the civil, natural and commercial history of that colony, viz. the succession of European settlers there; grants of English charters; boundaries; constitution of the government; taxes; number of inhabitants, and of the neighbouring Indian nations, &c. The nature of the climate; tabular accounts of the altitudes of the barometer monthly for four years, of the depths of rain monthly for eleven years, and of the winds direction daily for one year, &c. The culture and produce of rice, indian corn, and indigo; the process of extracting tar and turpentine; the state of their maritime trade in the years 1710, 1723, 1740 and 1748, with the number or tonnage of shipping employed, and the species, quantities and values of their produce exported in one year, &c. To which is added, a very particular account of their rice-trade for twenty years, with their exports of raw silk and imports of British silk manufactures for twenty-five years.

London: Printed for R. and J. Dodsley in Pall-Mall. MDCCLXI. [1761]

viii, 110, [2] p.; 21 cm. (8vo)

Notes: Evidently based on a manuscript entitled: Answers from James Glen, esq. govr. of South Carolina, to the queries from the right honourable the lords commissioners for trade and plantations (first published in P. C. J. Weston's Documents connected with the history of South Carolina, London, 1856, p. [61]–99).

References: Brown, J. C. Cat., 1493–1800, III: 1306; Sabin 27572; Church, E. D. Discovery, 1039

GORDON, JAMES, 1640?–1714.
The character of a generous prince drawn from the great lines of heroick fortitude. From which by the rule of contraries, may be delineated the effigies of a prodigious tyrant. The vertues of the former, and the vices of the latter, being fully represented; by a pleasant variety of examples, from ancient and modern history. By a hearty well-wisher of Her Majesty's government, and the Church of England.

London, Printed for Edw. Evets, at the Green-Dragon in St. Paul's-Church-yard. 1703.

[16], 439, [1] p.; 20 cm. (8vo)

Notes: Includes references to the Scots' Darien Colony. "...a short view of a French Plantation in Florida," p. 318–323.

References: Alden-Landis. European Americana, 703/65; Scott, J. Darien company, additions, 147b.

GORDON, WILLIAM, Rector of St. James's, Barbadoes.
A representation of the miserable state of Barbadoes, under the arbitrary and corrupt administration of his Excellency, Robert Lowther, Esq; the present governor. Humbly offer'd to the consideration of his most sacred Majesty, and the right honourable the lords of his Majesty's most honourable privy-council. With a preface, containing remarks on an address, printed in the Postman, and in the Whitehall Evening-Post of May 14. 1719.

London: Printed for Bernard Lintot, between the Temple-Gates. [1719]

[4], xii, 13–44 p.; 19 cm. (8vo)

References: Brown, J. C. Cat., 1493–1800, III: 241; Sabin 3285; Handler, J. S. Barbados, p. 22–23; Hanson 2526.

GRAY, MR.
The memoirs life and character of the Great Mr. Law and his brother at Paris. Down to this present year 1721, with an accurate and particular account of the establishment of the Missisippi [sic] Company in France, the rise and fall of it's stock, and all the subtle artifices used to support the national credit of that Kingdom, by the pernicious project of paper-credit. Written by a Scots gentleman.

London: Printed for Sam Briscoe, at the Bell-Savage on Ludgate-hill, 1721.

[16], 44 p.; 19 cm. (8vo)

References: Alden-Landis. European Americana, 721/79; Goldsmiths' Lib. cat. 5995; Kress S2998.

HALKETT, JOHN, 1768–1852.
Statement respecting the Earl of Selkirk's settlement upon the Red river, in North America; its destruction in the years 1815 and 1816; and the massacre of Governor Semple and his party. With observations upon a recent publication, entitled "A narrative of occurrences in the Indian countries," &c.

London: John Murray, Albemarle Street. 1817.

viii, 194, [2], c p., [1] folded leaf of plates: map; 23 cm. (4to)

Notes: Enlarged edition of the author's "Statement respecting the Earl of Selkirk's settlement of Kildonan," London, 1817.

References: Sabin 20704; Toronto Public Library. Canadiana, 1093.

HAMILTON, GEORGE, 1757–1832.
Epistle from the Marquis de La Fayette to General Washington.

Edinburgh: Printed by Mundell & son, Royal Bank Close; for Mundell & Son Edinburgh; and Longman & Rees, and J. Wright, London., 1800.

[4], 32 p.; 20 cm. (12mo)

References: Sabin 38570.

HELVETIUS, JEROME.
Paul-Jones, ou Prophéties sur l'Amérique, l'Angleterre, la France l'Espagne, la Hollande, &c. par Paul-Jones corsaire, prophète & sorcier comme il n'en fût jamais. Y joint Le rêve d'un Suisse sur la révolution de l'Amérique, dédié à Son Excellence Mgneur l'ambassadeur Franklin, & à Leurs Nobles & Hautes Puissance Messeigneurs du Congrès.

[Basle : s.n.], de l'ere de l'independence de l'Amérique, L'an V. [1781]

120 p.; 20 cm. (8vo)

Notes: "Le rêve d'un suisse.," p. [105]–120, has separate title page. Imprint reads: A Basle en Suisse., MDCCLXXXI. [1781].

References: Sabin 36567; Dippel, H. Americana Germanica, 251; Knuttel 19494.

THE HISTORY OF THE VOYAGES OF CHRISTOPHER COLUMBUS, in order to discover America and the West-Indies.

Glasgow, Printed for Robert Urie., MDCCLXI. [1761]

[2], 141, [1] p.; 18 cm. (12mo)

References: Sabin 14656; Palau y Dulcet (2nd ed.) 115413.

HOULDBROOKE.
A short address to the people of Scotland, on the subject of the slave trade, with a summary view of the evidence delivered before a committee of the House of Commons, on the part of the petitioners, for its abolition.

Edinburgh: Printed by J. Robertson, No. 39, South Bridge; at the expense of the society instituted for the abolition of the African Slave Trade. MDCCXCII. [1792]

30, [2] p.; 21 cm. (8vo)

References: Sabin 80593; Ragatz, L. J. British Caribbean, 456; Hogg, P. C. African Slave Trade, 2145; Kress Lib. B.2344.

JOHNSTONE, GEORGE, 1730–1787.
Governor Johnstone's speech, in the House of Commons, at the opening of the session, on Thursday, November 26, 1778.

[London: s.n., 1778]

8 p.; 23 cm. (4to)

Notes: A reply to a number of Parliamentary speeches concerning the conduct of the American commissioners.

References: Adams, T. R. Brit. pamphlets, 78–52.

JOHNSTONE, GEORGE, 1730–1787.
Gov. Johnstone's speech, on the question of recommitting the address declaring the colony of Massachusets in rebellion: to which is added the two most masterly letters of Junius, to the people of England in favour of the Americans.

London: Printed for G. Allen, no. 59, Pater-Noster-Row. [1775]

32 p.; 22 cm. (8vo)

References: Brown, J. C. Cat., 1493–1800, III: 2258; Adams, T. R. Brit. pamphlets, 75–70; Sabin 36398.

JOHNSTONE, GEORGE, 1730–1787.
Gov. Johnston's [sic] speech on American affairs, on the Address in answer to the King's speech.

Edinburgh: Printed for, and sold by, John Wood, Luckenbooths. M,DCC,LXXVI. [1776]

[2], 16 p.; 19 cm. (12mo)

Notes: Delivered in the House of Commons, 26 October 1776, in response to a speech by Sir Adam Ferguson.

References: Brown, J. C. Cat., 1493–1800, III : 2259; Adams, T. R. Brit. pamphlets, 76–72; Sabin 36399.

KAMES, HENRY HOME, LORD, 1696–1782.
Elements of criticism. With the author's last corrections and additions.

First American from the seventh London edition.

Boston: From the press of Samuel Etheridge, for J. White, Thomas & Andrews, W. Spotswood, D. West, W. P. Blake, E. Larkin, & J. West. MDCCXCVI. [1796]

2 v. (v. 1: viii, [9]–408 p.; v. 2: 440 p.); 22 cm. (8vo)

Notes: Attributed to Lord Kames in the Dictionary of national biography. Originally published: Edinburgh, 1762. Includes index.

References: Evans 30578.

KAMES, HENRY HOME, LORD, 1696–1782.
Sketches of the history of man. Considerably enlarged by the last additions and corrections of the author. In four volumes.

Edinburgh: Printed for A. Strahan and T. Cadell, London; and for William Creech, Edinburgh. M,DCC,LXXXVIII. [1788]

4 v. (v. 1: xii, 501, [3] p.; v.2: [8], 467, [1] p.; v. 3: [8], 432 p.; v. 4: [6], ii, 492 p.); 22 cm. (8vo)

Notes: First published: London, 1774.

KEITH, GEORGE, 1639?–1716.
The standard of the Quakers examined or An answer to the Apology of Robert Barclay. By George Keith, A. M.

London, Printed for B. Aylmer, at the Three Pidgeons in Cornhill, and C. Brome at the Gun, at the West-End of St. Paul's, and George Strahan, at the Golden Ball over against the Royal Exchange. 1702.

[16], 512 p. 18 cm. (8vo)

References: Alden-Landis. European Americana, 702/112; Smith, J. Friends' books, II, p.40.

LEE, ARTHUR, 1740–1792.
Dissertatio medica inauguralis, de cortice peruviano: quam, annuente summo numine, ex auctoritate reverendi admodum viri, Gulielmi Robertson, S. S. T. P. Academiae Edinburgenae praefecti; nec non amplissimi Senatus Academici consensu, et nobilissimae facultatis medicae decreto; pro gradu doctoratus, summisque in medicina honoribus et privilegiis rite ac legitime consequendis, eruditorum examini subjicit, Arthur Lee, Virginiensis. Ad diem Septembris, hora locaque solitis.

Edinburgi: In aedibus A. Donaldson et J. Reid., MDCCLXIV. [1764]

[4], 47, [1] p.; 20 cm. (8vo)

Notes: Thesis (doctoral)—University of Edinburgh, 1764.

References: Waring, E. J. Bib. therapeutica, 344.

LOVER OF TRUTH.
An address to the Rev. Dr. Alison, the Rev. Mr. Ewing, and others, trustees of the Corporation for the Relief of Presbyterian ministers, their Widows and Children being a vindication of the Quakers from the aspersions of the said trustees in their letter published in the London Chronicle, no. 1223. To which is prefixed, the said letter. By a lover of truth.

[Philadelphia]: Printed [by William Dunlap], in the year 1765.

[4], iii, [1], 47, [1] p.; 19 cm. (8vo)

Notes: Possibly written by Joseph Galloway.

References: Sabin 42384; Sabin 66908; Evans 9892; Hildeburn, C. R. Pennsylvania, 2098.

McAlpine, J. (John)
Genuine narratives, and concise memoirs of some of the most interesting exploits & singular adventures, of J. McAlpine a native Highlander, from the time of his emigration from Scotland, to America 1773; during the long period of his faithfull attattchment [sic] to, and hazardous attendance on the British Army's [sic] under the command of the generals Carelton [sic] and Burgoyne, in their several operations that he was concerned in; till December 1779 to complain of his neglected services; and humbly to request government for reparation of his losses in the Royal cause. Every circumstance related faithfully, and with all delicacy, containing nothing but indisputable facts that can be well vouched, and are mostly known to many gentleman of good character, in both the private and military lines of life; carefully arranged, and published for the use of the public at large.

Greenock. Printed and sold by W. McAlpine, bookseller at his shop Cathcart Street, 1780.

vi, 7–63, [1] p.; 17 cm. (8vo)

References: Sabin 42932; Adams, T. R. Brit. pamphlets, 80–52.

McKenney, Thomas Loraine, 1785–1859.
History of the Indian tribes of North America, with biographical sketches and anecdotes of the principal chiefs. Embellished with one hundred and twenty portraits, from the Indian gallery in the Department of War, at Washington. By Thomas L. M'Kenney, late of the Indian Department, Washington, and James Hall, Esq. of Cincinnati.

Philadelphia: Published by Edward C. Biddle, 23 Minor Street. 1836–1844.

3 v.: col. ill., facsims., map, col. ports.; 52 cm. (fol.)

Notes: "History of the Indian tribes of North America": v. 3, p. [1]–44. "An essay on the history of the North American Indians. By James Hall": v. 3, p. [45]–196.

References: Sabin 43410a; Howes, W. U.S.iana (2nd ed.), M–129.

Macpherson, Charles.
Memoirs of the life and travels of the late Charles Macpherson, Esq. in Asia, Africa, and America. illustrative of manners, customs, and character; with a particular investigation of the nature, treatment, and possible improvement, of the negro in the British and French West India Islands. Written by himself chiefly between the years 1773 and 1790.

Edinburgh: Printed for Arch. Constable, and sold in London by Vernor and Hood. 1800.

xv, [1], 258 p.; 19 cm. (4to)

Notes: Sometimes attributed to Hector Macneill—cf. DNB.

References: Sabin 43625.

Macpherson, James, 1736–1796.
The poems of Ossian, the son of Fingal. Translated by James Macpherson, Esq.

A new edition, carefully corrected, and greatly improved.

Philadelphia: Printed by Thomas Lang, no 21, Church-Alley.

M DCC XC. [1790]

[2], vii, [6], 12–502, [2] p.; 22 cm. (8vo)

Notes: "A critical dissertation on the poems of Ossian, the son of Fingal. By Hugh Blair, D. D...." —p. [415]–502.

References: Evans 22633.

Macpherson, James, 1736–1796.
A short history of the opposition during the last session of Parliament.

London: Printed for T. Cadell, in the Strand. MDCCLXXIX [1779]

vi, 58 p.; 21 cm. (8vo)

Notes: Also attributed to Edward Gibbon.

References: Sabin 43633; Adams, T. R. Brit. pamphlets, 79–69a.

Macsparran, James, 1693–1757.
The sacred dignity of the Christian priesthood, vindicated in a discourse on Heb. v.4. Delivered at St. Paul's in Narraganset, on Sunday the 4th day of August, A. D. 1751. By the Rev. Dr. Macsparran.

Newport: Printed by J. Franklin. M,DCC,LII. [1752]

46, [2] p.; 17 cm. (8vo)

References: Evans 6870; Alden, J. E. Rhode Island, 18.

Marjoribanks, J. (John), d. 1797?.
Slavery: an essay in verse. By Captain Marjoribanks, of a late independent company; formerly lieutenant in His Majesty's 19th Regiment of Foot. Humbly inscribed to planters, merchants, and others concerned in the management or sale of negro slaves.

Edinburgh: Printed by J. Robertson, No. 39, South Bridge-Street., MDCCXCII. [1792]

31, [1] p.; 23 cm. (4to)

Notes: Title vignette: Am I not a man and a brother? "Letter sent with the following essay…to Mr. Haliburton, secretary of the Edinburgh Society for Promoting the Abolition of the African Slave Trade": p. [3]–6. "Stanzas on the execution of a Negro, at Spanish-town, Jamaica, August 1785": p. [29]–31.

References: Sabin 44610; Ragatz, L.J. British Caribbean, 523; Hogg, P. C. African Slave Trade, 4228.

MATHER, INCREASE, 1639–1723.
A sermon shewing that the present dispensations of providence declare that wonderful revolutions in the world are near at hand; with an appendix, shewing some scripture ground to hope, that within a few years, glorious prophecies and promises will be fulfilled. By the very reverend Mr. Increase Mather…

Edinburgh, Printed by the heirs and successors of Andrew Anderson, printer to the Queen's most excellent majesty, Anno Dom 1710.

32 p.; 21 cm. (4to)

Notes: First published in: A dissertation, wherein the strange doctrine…. Boston, 1708, p. 91–135.

References: Brown, J.C. Cat., 1493–1800, III: 139. Alden-Landis. European Americana, 710/95. Holmes, T. J. Increase Mather, 116A.

MÉMOIRES DE PAUL JONES, où il expose ses principaux services, et rappelle ce qui lui est arrivé de plus remarquable pendant le cours de la révolution américaine, particulièrement en Europe, écrits par lui-même en anglais, et traduits sous ses yeux le citoyen André.

A Paris, Chez Louis, libraire, rue Saint-Severin, no. 110., An VI. 1798.

[4], xix, [1], 244 p., [1] leaf of plates: ill., port.; 16 cm. (12mo)

Notes: "May be based on his conversation; in any case they have no value, and are certainly not his work." —Dictionary of National Biography, v. X, p. 1029.

References: Brown, J.C. Cat., 1493–1800, III : 3973; Sabin 36559.

MENZIES, ARCHIBALD, fl. 1763.
Proposal for peopling His Majesty's southern colonies on the continent of America.

[Edinburgh?: s.n., 1763]

4 p.; 33 cm. (fol.).

Notes: Signed (p. 4): Archibald Menzies. Megerny Castle, Perthshire, 23 October 1763. The author urges the settling of Greeks and Armenians in the newly acquired colonies of Florida.

MONTGOMERY, ROBERT, SIR, 1680–1731.
A discourse concerning the design'd establishment of a new colony to the south of Carolina, in the most delightful country of the universe. By Sir Robert Mountgomery, baronet.

London: [s.n.], Printed in the year. 1717.

[2], 30, 3, [1] p., [1] folded leaf of plates: plan; 20 cm. (8vo)

Notes: An account of a colony called Azilia, proposed to be established between the Savannah and Altamaha rivers. "Appendix to a discourse lately publish'd, concerning the establishment of a new colony in Azilia.": p. [1]–3 (3rd count).

References: Alden-Landis. European Americana, 717/113; De Renne, W. J. Cat. of the Georgia Lib., I, p. 6; Church, E. D. Discovery, 866; Hanson 2298.

MORGAN, JOHN, 1735–1789.
A discourse upon the institution of medical schools in America; delivered at a public anniversary commencement, held in the College of Philadelphia May 30 and 31, 1765. With a preface containing, amongst other things, the author's apology for attempting to introduce the regular mode of practising physic in Philadelphia: by John Morgan…

Philadelphia: Printed and sold by William Bradford, at the corner of Market and Front-Streets, MDCC,LXV. [1765]

vii, [1], xxvi, [2], 63, [1] p.; 19 cm. (8vo)

References: Sabin 50650; Evans 10082; Hildeburn, C. R. Pennsylvania, 2147; Austin, R. B. Early Amer. medical imprints, 1335; Guerra, F. Amer. medical bib., a367.

MURRAY, JAMES, 1732–1782.
An impartial history of the present war in America; containing an account of its rise and progress, the political springs thereof, with its various successes and disappointments, on both sides. By the Rev. James Murray, of Newcastle.

London: Printed for R. Baldwin, no. 47, Paternoster-Row; N. Frobisher, York: T. Robson, Side, Newcastle upon Tyne; Bayne and Mennons, Edinburgh; and Dunlop and Wilson, Glasgow. [1778–1779]

2 v. (v. 1: 573 [i.e. 575], [1] p. (p. 151–152 duplicated); v. 2: 576 p.): maps, plan, ports.; 21 cm. (8vo)

Notes: Issued in parts. Another issue has a Newcastle upon Tyne imprint. A third volume, which ends abruptly at p. 332, was issued in 1781 with a Newcastle upon Tyne imprint. Like no less than six other contemporary histories of the revolution, this work was chiefly plagiarized from "The Annual register", London. cf. Some pseudo histories of the American revolution. By O. G. Libby (Wisconsin Academy of Sciences, Arts and Letters. Madison, 1900. v. 13, pt. I, p. 419–425). Issued with 28 plates containing oval portraits, 2 maps and 1 plan. For a list, see Adams.

References: Cf. Sabin 51505–51506; Adams, T. R. Brit. pamphlets 78–73a; Adams, T. R. Brit. pamphlets 78–73d.

A NEW SONG.
[Edinburgh: s.n. ; 1755?]

1 sheet ([1] p.): ill.; 32 × 12 cm. (1/4to)

Notes: Verses beginning: Lord Loudon sent to our gracious King. Woodcut at head of title. Concerns recruiting of Scots troops for French and Indian War.

PAUL JONES: or the Fife coast garland. A heroi-comical poem. In four parts. In which is contained the oyster wives of Newhaven's letter to Lord Sandwich.

Edinburgh: [s.n.] Printed in the year M,DCC,LXXIX. [1779]

[2], 37, [1] p.; 28 cm. (4to)

Notes: Poem describing Scottish reaction to a threatened raid by John Paul Jones in 1779.

References: Sabin 36566; Adams, T. R. Brit. pamphlets, 79–87.

PRINCE, THOMAS, 1687–1758.
Extraordinary events the doings of God, and marvellous in pious eyes. Illustrated in a sermon at the South Church in Boston, N. E. on the general thanksgiving, Thursday, July 18. 1745. Occasion'd by taking the city of Louisbourg on the Isle of Cape-Breton, by New-England soldiers, assisted by a British squadron. By Thomas Prince, M. A. and one of the pastors of said church.

Edinburgh: Printed by R. Fleming and Company. 1746.

[2], 38 p.; 19 cm. (8vo)

Notes: First published: Boston, 1745.

References: Sabin 65596; Alden-Landis. European Americana, 746/166.

PRINCE, THOMAS, 1687–1758.
The salvations of God in 1746. In part set forth in a sermon at the South Church in Boston, Nov. 27, 1746. Being the day of the anniversary thanksgiving in the province of the Massachusetts Bay in New-England. Wherein the most remarkable salvations of the year past, both in Europe and North America, as far as they are come to our knowledge, are briefly considered. By Thomas Prince, M. A. and a pastor of the said church.

[London] Boston Printed: London Reprinted, and sold by T. Longman and T. Shewell, in Pater-Noster-Row. 1747.

36 p.; 20 cm. (8vo)

Notes: First published: Boston, 1746.

References: Brown, J. C. Cat., 1493–1800, III: 857; Alden-Landis. European Americana, 747/133.

PRINCE, THOMAS, 1687–1758.
A sermon deliver'd at the South-Church in Boston, New-England, August 14, 1746. Being the day of general thanksgiving for the great deliverance of the British nations, by the glorious and happy victory near Culloden. Obtained by His Royal Highness Prince William Duke of Cumberland, April 16, in the same year. Wherein the greatness of the publick danger and deliverance is in part set forth, to excite their most grateful praises to the God of their salvation. By Thomas Prince, M. A. and a pastor of said church.

Boston, Printed: Edinburgh, Re-printed by R. Fleming. 1747.

[2], 33, [1] p.; 19 cm. (8vo)

References: Cf. Sabin 65612; Alden-Landis. European Americana, 747/135.

RAMSAY, ALLAN, 1713–1784.
A succinct review of the American contest, addressed to those whom it may concern. First published in February, 1778, while the bills called Conciliatory were under the consideration of the House of Commons. By Zero.

London: Printed for R. Faulder, New Bond Street; R. Blaimire, Strand; and B. Law, Avemary Lane., [1782]

viii, 35, [1] p.; 22 cm. (4to)

References: Sabin 67678; Adams, T. R. Brit. pamphlets, 82–77.

RAMSAY, DAVID, OF EDINBURGH.
Military memoirs of Great Britain: or, A history of the war, 1755–1763. With elegant copperplates. By David Ramsay.

Edinburgh: Printed for the author, and sold by the principal booksellers in Great Britain, 1779.

[4], xii, [7]–473, [1] p., [12] leaves of plates: ports.; 19 cm. (8vo)

References: Brown, J. C. Cat., 1493–1800, III: 2591; Sabin 67680.

RAYNAL, ABBÉ (GUILLAUME-THOMAS-FRANÇOIS), 1713–1796.

[Révolution de l'Amérique. English]

The revolution of America by the Abbe Raynal .... A new edition.

Edinburgh: [s.n.], Printed in the year M,DCC, LXXXIII. [1783]

vi, [2], 191, [1] p.; 18 cm. (12mo)

References: Adams, T. R. Brit. pamphlets, 81-59s; Sabin 68104n.

ROBERTSON, WILLIAM, 1721–1793. [History of America. Books 1–8]

The history of America. By William Robertson...

London: Printed for W. Strahan; T. Cadell, in the Strand; and J. Balfour, at Edinburgh., MDCCLXXVII. [1777]

2 v. (v. 1: xvii, [7], 488 p. ; v. 2: [4], 433 p., p. 434/440, p. [441]–535, [21] p., [1] folded leaf of plates). ill.; 31 cm. (4to)

Notes: First edition, in two volumes in quarto, first state (without the four maps that are present in the second state). Contains Books I–VIII, the history of the discovery of America and the conquest of Mexico and Peru. For the importance of this work, see Humphreys, R. A.: William Robertson and his History of America. London; Oxford, 1954 (The Canning House annual lecture). "A catalogue of Spanish books and manuscripts." (v. 2: p. [523]–535.)

References: Brown, J. C. Cat., 1493–1800, III: 2418; Sabin 71973; Palau y Dulcet (2nd ed.) 270979; ESTC T078961.

SALMON, THOMAS, 1679–1767.

A new geographical and historical grammar: wherein the geographical part is truly modern; and the present state of the several kingdoms of the world is so interspersed, as to render the study of geography both entertaining and instructive.... Together with an account of the air, soil, produce, traffic, curiosities, arms, religion, language, universities, bishoprics, manners, customs, habits, and coins, in use in the several kingdoms and states described. By Mr. Salmon. Illustrated with a new set of maps of the countries described, and other copper-plates, ten whereof were not in any former edition.

A new edition, with large additions, which bring the history down to the present time.

Edinburgh: Printed by Sands, Murray, and Cochran, for James Meuros, bookseller in Kilmarnock. MDCCLXVII. [1767]

xii, [2], 7–601, [15] p., [33] leaves of plates (some folded): ill., maps, ports.; 22 cm. (8vo)

References: Cf. Sabin 75828.

SANDEMAN, ROBERT, 1718–1771.

Some thoughts on Christianity. In a letter to a friend. By Mr. Sandeman, author of the Letters on Theron and Aspasio. To which is annexed by way of illustration, The conversion of Jonathan the Jew, as related by himself.

Boston N. E. Printed and sold, by W. M'Alpine, and J. Fleeming, in Morlborough [sic] street, M,DCC,LXIV. [1764]

54, [2] p.; 19 cm. (12mo)

Notes: First published: Newcastle upon Tyne, 1750.

References: Sabin 76340; Evans 9824.

SCOTT, JONATHAN, 1744–1819.

A brief view of the religious tenets and sentiments, lately published and spread in the province of Nova-Scotia; which are contained in a book, entitled "Two mites, on some of the most important and much disputed points of divinity, &c." and "in a sermon preached at Liverpool, November 19, 1782;" and in a pamphlet, entitled "The antitraditionist:" all being publications of Mr. Henry Alline. With some brief reflections and observations: also, a view of the ordination of the author of these books: together with a discourse on external order. By Jonathan Scott, pastor of a church in Yarmouth.

Halifax [N.S]: Printed by John Howe, in Barrington-Street. MDCCLXXIV. [1784]

viii, 334, [2] p.; 21 cm. (8vo)

References: Sabin 78322; Tremaine 442.

TAILFER, PATRICK.

A true and historical narrative of the colony of Georgia, in America, from the first settlement thereof until this present period: containing, the most authentick facts, matters and transactions therein. Together with His Majesty's Charter representations of the people, letters, &c. and a dedication to His Excellency General Oglethorpe. By Pat. Tailfer, M. D. Hugh Anderson, M.A. Da. Douglas, and others, land-holders in Georgia, at present in Charles-Town in South Carolina.

Charles-Town, South-Carolina: Printed for P. Timothy, for the authors, 1741.

[2], xxiv, 176 p.; 21 cm. (8vo)

Notes: A criticism of the constitution of the colony and of Oglethorpe's administration. The first edition. A subsequent edition (Evans 4817; xviiii, 78, 87–118 p.), dated M.DCC.XLI and bearing P. Timothy's imprint, was probably printed in London.

References: Cf. De Renne, W.J. Cat. of the Georgia Lib., I, p. 95–97; Sabin 94215; Evans 4816; Vail, R. W. G. Old frontier, 413; Gould & Morgan. South Carolina, 79.

TAILFER, PATRICK.
A true and historical narrative of the colony of Georgia in America, from the first settlement thereof until this present period: containing the most authentick facts, matters and transactions therein; together with His Majesty's Charter, representations of the people, letters, &c. and a dedication to His Excellency General Oglethorpe. By Pat. Tailfer, M. D. Hugh Anderson, M. A. Da. Douglas, and others, land-holders in Georgia, at present in Charles-Town in South-Carolina.

Charles-Town, South-Carolina [i.e., London?]: Printed by T. Timothy, for the authors, M.DCC. XLI. [1741]

xviii, 78, 87–118 p.; 22 cm (8vo)

Notes: "This edition seems to have been really printed in London, preceded by the genuine Charleston edition having 1 preliminary leaf, xxiv, 176 p." —Catalogue of the Wymberly Jones De Renne Georgia Library, p. 96.

References: Sabin 94216; Evans 4817; Vail, R. W. G. Old frontier, 414; Church, E. D. Discovery, 940; De Renne, W. J. Cat. of the Georgia Lib., I, p. 95–96.

THOMPSON, EDWARD, 1738?–1786.
Sailor's letters. Written to his select friends in England, during his voyages and travels in Europe, Asia, Africa, and America. From the year 1754 to 1759. By Edward Thompson, lieutenant of the navy. In two volumes.

Dublin: Printed by J. Hoey, sen. Skinner-row, and J. Potts, at Swift's-Head in Dame-street. MDCCLXX. [1770]

2 v.; 17 cm. (12mo)

References: Cf. Sabin 95488.

THOMSON, WILLIAM, 1746–1817.
Memoirs of the life and gallant exploits of the old Highlander, Serjeant Donald Macleod, : whom having returned, wounded, with the corpse of General Wolfe, from Quebec, was admitted an out-pensioner of Chelsea Hospital, in 1759; and is now in the CIII.d year of his age.

London: From Peterborouh[sic]-House Press, by D. and D. Stuart. Sold by J. Forbes, Covent-Garden; J. Debrett, Piccadilly; and J. Sewell, Cornhill., MDCCXCI. [1791]

[4], 90, [2] p.; 21 cm. (8vo)

References: Brown, J.C. Cat., 1493–1800, III: 3469; Sabin 95606.

TOD, T. (THOMAS), fl. 1781.
Observations on American independency.

[Edinburgh? : s.n., 1779?]

16 p.; 20 cm. (8vo)

Notes: Signed (p. 16): Sept. 1779 T. True Briton.

References: Brown, J. C. Cat., 1493–1800, III: 2587; Sabin 56492; Sabin 96077; Adams, T. R. Brit. pamphlets, 79–108a.

TWEEDIE, ALEXANDER.
The naval achievements of Admiral George Lord Brydges Rodney. To which is added, Thoughts on the conduct of the late minority, now the present ministry of Great Britain. With a poem inscribed to Satan. By A. Tweedie...

Edinburgh: Printed by W. Darling, Advocates' Close. MCCLXXXII. [1782]

[2], 139 [i.e. 149], [3] p., [1] folded leaf of plates: ill.; 23 cm. (8vo)

Notes: Frontispiece is a large, hand-colored engraving of Rodney's ship the Formidable showing Charles James Fox and another man (Rockingham?) being keel-hauled.

References: Sabin 97531; Adams, T. R. Brit. pamphlets, 82–94.

VAUGHAN, WILLIAM, 1577–1641.
The golden fleece divided into three parts, under which are discouered the errours of religion, the vices and decayes of the kingdome, and lastly the wayes to get wealth, and to restore trading so much complayned of. Transported from Cambrioll Colchos, out of the southermost part of the iland, commonly called the Newfoundland, by Orpheus Iunior, for the generall and perpetuall good of Great Britaine.

London, Printed for Francis Williams, and are to bee sold at his shop at the sign of the globe, ouer against the Royall Exchange, 1626.

[28], 149, [3], 105, [3], 96 p., [1] folded leaf of plates: map.; 19 cm. (4to)

Notes: An allegory with many interesting references to Vaughan's colony in Newfoundland, and an early map of the island. The map has title: Insula olim vocata Nova Terra. This island called of olde Newfound Land described by Captaine John Mason an industrious gent. who spent seven yeares in the country.

References: JCB Lib. cat., pre-1675, 2:204; Alden-Landis. European Americana, 626/143;

STC (2nd ed.) 24609; Church, E. D. Discovery, 409; Baer, E. 17th-Century Maryland, 12.

WALKER, FOWLER, 1731 or 2–1804.
The case of Mr. John Gordon, with respect to the title to certain lands in East Florida, purchased of His Catholick Majesty's subjects by him and Mr. Jesse Fish, for themselves and others his Britannick Majesty's subjects: in conformity to the twentieth article of the last definitive treaty of peace. With an appendix.

London: Printed in the year M.DCC.LXXII. [1772]

32, [42] p., [1] folded leaf of plates: map.; 25 cm. (4to)

Notes: Signed (p. 32): Fowler Walker. "Appendix. J. M. J. St. Augustine, in the year 1763. Acts and records relative to the property of a landed estate called Palica, belonging to Francisco Chrisostomo, a native and inhabitant of this town.": p. [1]–[42] (2nd count).

References: Brown, J. C. Cat., 1493–1800, III: 1825; Sabin 27981; Sabin 101042; Vail, R. W. G. Old frontier, 616A.

WASHINGTON, GEORGE, 1732–1799.
[Farewell address]

General Washington's farewel [sic] address to the people of the United States, on his resignation of the presidency of the executive government of America.

Glasgow: Printed for and sold by Cameron & Murdoch, booksellers and stationers, Irongate. [1796]

16 p.; 21 cm. (8vo)

Notes: Originally published as: The President's address to the people. Philadelphia, 1796. Dated on p. 16: "United States, September 17, 1796".

References: Sabin 101565.

WHITEFIELD, GEORGE, 1714–1770.
Britain's mercies, and Britain's duty, represented in a sermon preach'd at the new-building in Philadelphia, on Sunday August 24, 1746. Occasion'd by the suppression of the late unnatural rebellion. By George Whitefield, A. B. late of Pembroke College, Oxon.

Philadelphia: Printed and sold by W. Bradford, at the Bible in Second-Street, MDCCXLVI. [1746]

27, [1] p.; 20 cm. (4to)

References: Sabin 103503; Evans 5883.

WHITEFIELD, GEORGE, 1714–1770.
The Lord our righteousness. A sermon preached on Fryday [sic] forenoon, September 11th 1741. In the High-Church-Yard of Glasgow, upon Jer. xxxiii. 16. By the Reverend Mr. George Whitefield. Taken from his own mouth, and published at the earnest desire of many of the hearers. And since revised and corrected. Note. The substance of the following sermon was delivered at the Old S. Church in Boston, Octob. 1740.

Boston: Printed & sold by S. Kneeland and T. Green, in Queenstreet over against the prison. 1742.

28 p.; 17 cm. (12mo)

Notes: First published: Glasgow, 1741.

References: Sabin 103567; Evans 5090.

WILLISON, JOHN, 1680–1750.
[Looking unto Jesus]

Looking to Jesus. Being an earnest exhortation and most excellent perswasive to fly to the Lord Jesus Christ by faith, in order to obtain eternal life through him. By Mr. John Willison, minister of the Gospel at Dundee.

Boston: Printed for B. Gray in Milk-Street. 1743.

[2], 24 p.; 16 cm. (12mo)

Notes: First published: Boston, 1731, with title: Looking unto Jesus. "Looking unto Jesus. By another hand." —p. [33]–34.

References: Bristol B1228; Shipton & Mooney 40322.

WILSON, JAMES, 1742–1798.
Considerations on the nature and the extent of the legislative authority of the British Parliament.

Philadelphia: Printed and sold, by William and Thomas Bradford, at the London Coffee-House. M.DCC.LXXIV. [1774]

iv, 35, [1] p.; 20 cm. (8vo)

Notes: Sometimes attributed to John Witherspoon.

References: Brown, J. C. Cat., 1493–1800, III: 1910; Sabin 104629; Evans 13775; Adams, T. R. Amer. pamphlets, 149; Hildeburn, C. R. Pennsylvania, 3137.

YOUNG, JOHN, minister of the Gospel at Hawick, in Scotland.

Essays on the following interesting subjects: viz. I. Government. II. Revolutions. III. The British constitution. IV. Kingly government. V.

Parliamentary representation & reform. VI. Liberty & equality. VII. Taxation. And, VIII. The present war, & the stagnation of credit as connected with it. By John Young, D. D, minister of the Gospel at Hawick.

Fourth edition.

Glasgow: Printed and sold by David Niven, bookseller, Trongate; also by W. Creech, and Bell & Bradfute, booksellers, Edinburgh, and Vernor and Hood, booksellers, London. M,DCC,XCIV. [1794]

[4], 160 p.; 22 cm. (8vo)

Notes: First published: Edinburgh, 1794.

References: Cf. Sabin 106079; Kress Lib. B2874.

This catalogue was designed by Gilbert Design Associates, Providence, and printed at Meridian Printing in East Greenwich. The photographs are by Richard Hurley.

The design on the cover is an adaptation of the printer's headband on p. iii of Thomas More, *Utopia: or the Happy Republic*, trans. Gilbert Burnet (Glasgow: Robert Foulis, 1743).

The typeface is Scotch Roman. It is the Scottish variant of the nineteenth-century modern style developed as Bodoni in Italy and Didot in France. The Monotype version used in this catalogue is based on the early nineteenth-century work of William Miller's type foundry in Edinburgh.

The paper is Consort Royal Silk Tint, manufactured by the Donside Paper Company, Aberdeen, Scotland.

1250 softcover and 250 casebound copies for the John Carter Brown Library on the occasion of the opening of the exhibition at the Forbes Magazine Galleries, September 1995.